LAW, PRIVACY
AND SURVEILLANCE IN CANADA
IN THE POST-SNOWDEN ERA

LAW, PRIVACY AND SURVEILLANCE IN CANADA IN THE POST-SNOWDEN ERA

EDITED BY

Michael Geist

University of Ottawa Press

2015

u Ottawa

The University of Ottawa Press gratefully acknowledges the support extended to its publishing list by Canadian Heritage through the Canada Book Fund, by the Canada Council for the Arts, by the Federation for the Humanities and Social Sciences through the Awards to Scholarly Publications Program and by the University of Ottawa.

Copy editing: Joanne Muzak
Proofreading: Susan James
Typesetting: Édiscript enr.
Cover design: Llama Communications and Édiscript enr.

Library and Archives Canada Cataloguing in Publication

Law, privacy, and surveillance in Canada in the post-Snowden era / edited by Michael Geist.

(Law, technology and media)
Includes bibliographical references.
Issued in print and electronic formats.
ISBN 978-0-7766-2207-1 (paperback).
ISBN 978-0-7766-2183-8 (pdf).
ISBN 978-0-7766-2182-1 (epub)

1. Electronic surveillance — Law and legislation — Canada. 2. Privacy, Right of — Canada. 3. Technology and law — Canada. I. Geist, Michael, 1968-, author, editor II. Series: Law, technology and media

KE9328.L34 2015   345.71′052   C2015-903727-1
KF9670.L34 2015   C2015-903728-X

Printed in Canada

Table of Contents

Acknowledgements

Publishing a peer-reviewed book with numerous contributors on a rapidly evolving, high-profile issue requires a special group of contributors, publishers, editors, and reviewers. Thanks are due first and foremost to the contributors. Each was presented with challenging timelines to complete their submissions and often asked to submit revised versions based on reviewer comments within days. Each contributor embraced this project with enthusiasm and professionalism.

Many thanks go to Wesley Wark, who contributed enormously to the vision behind the book and to the recruitment of contributors.

Once the initial articles were delivered, many additional contributors emerged. Thanks to a terrific group of student editors, including Emily Murray, Jennifer Shamie, Chelsea Sauve, Kavi Sivasothy, Mila Falkenstein, and Karina Pogosyan, who provided citation and fact checking reviews.

Thanks also to Elizabeth Schwaiger, who oversaw the production of the book from copy-editing through proofreading, layout, and printing.

Thanks to the University of Ottawa Press, particularly Lara Mainville and Dominike Thomas, who offered tremendous support for this book project.

Thanks as well to the Social Sciences and Humanities Research Council of Canada and the Canada Research Chair program, as this book benefited from their financial support.

Thanks also to my colleagues and family for their support throughout this project. It is a great honour to work with such an exceptional, supportive group of colleagues at the University of Ottawa.

My wife, Allison, remains the foundation of our family and a remarkable source of love and support. Jordan, Ethan, and Gabrielle are more than just fantastic children, who make their parents proud each and every day. They are true digital citizens, engaged with issues related to surveillance and privacy, as they are part of a generation that does not know a world without the Internet, nor, it would appear, without network surveillance.

March 2015
Ottawa, Ontario

Introduction

Edward Snowden burst into the public consciousness in June 2013 with a series of astonishing revelations about US surveillance activities. The Snowden leaks, which have continued for more than eighteen months, have confirmed that fears of all-encompassing network surveillance and data capture that were envisioned as worst-case scenarios more than a decade ago have become reality. With scant debate or public awareness, surveillance agencies around the world have become remarkably adept at capturing network communications at the very time that billions of people have come to rely on the Internet as their primary tool for communication, social connection, and information gathering. As a result, the "open Internet" is a far cry from what millions of users might have otherwise expected or believed, with openness more aptly referencing their openly accessible private communications.

Snowden's primary focus has been centred on the United States. However, the steady stream of documents have laid bare the notable role of allied surveillance agencies, including the Communications Security Establishment (CSE), Canada's signals intelligence agency. The Canadian-related leaks — including disclosures regarding surveillance over millions of Internet downloads, airport wireless networks, spying on the Brazilian government, and the facilitation of spying at the G8 and G20 meetings hosted in Toronto in 2010 — have unsurprisingly inspired some domestic discussion and increased media coverage of privacy and surveillance issues.

Yet, despite increased public and media attention, the Snowden leaks have thus far failed to generate sustained political debate in Canada. Privacy issues, particularly lawful access and warrantless disclosure of Internet and telecom subscriber information, emerged as important issues in 2014 and forced the government to respond to mounting concerns over the privacy protections afforded to Canadians' personal information. Moreover, the Supreme Court of Canada issued the landmark *R. v. Spencer* decision in June 2014, which removed any lingering doubt that Canadians have a reasonable expectation of privacy in subscriber information.

While that decision may have led to changes in law enforcement practices, and revelations about subscriber information requests resulted in some uncomfortable questions in the House of Commons, neither had any discernable impact on the broader legislative agenda. Bill C-13, the government's lawful access bill, received royal assent months after the *Spencer* decision, with no significant amendments or reforms incorporated into the bill in response to the decision. In fact, the shocking attack on Parliament Hill in the fall of 2014, in which a single gunman killed a Canadian soldier and then penetrated deep into the Parliament buildings, only stiffened government resolve for increased surveillance and police powers. By January 2015, the government moved swiftly to introduce Bill C-51, the anti-terrorism bill, which greatly expands information sharing between CSE, the Canadian Security Intelligence Service (CSIS), and fifteen other government departments and agencies.[1]

Notwithstanding the somewhat muted initial political response to the Snowden leaks in Canada, the issue of privacy and surveillance seems certain to remain very much in the public eye. As politicians, policy makers, and the broader public grapple with the long-term implications of surveillance activities, this book aims to enhance the public debate by providing a Canadian perspective on the legal issues.

The nine contributions in the book are grouped into three parts: understanding surveillance in Canada, legal issues, and prospects for reform and accountability. Each contribution is briefly introduced below, but two themes run throughout the book.

The first theme is secrecy. That secrecy is linked to surveillance may seem unsurprising. However, secrecy now extends far beyond the specific surveillance programs or activities undertaken by Canada's surveillance agencies. For example, Canada's network architecture remains largely shrouded in secrecy, with the lack of domestic Internet exchange points creating a network framework that diverts considerable domestic traffic through the United States. Moreover, Canada's legal framework is often hidden behind ministerial authorizations that are not public, judicial decisions that are secret or heavily redacted, and government legal opinions that are privileged and confidential.

The second theme points to serious cracks in the Canadian surveillance law framework. Contributors point to a myriad of problems with a legal framework that appears ill-equipped to address modern-day communications networks and privacy expectations. Several contributors raise concerns related to global networks, cross-border information sharing, the legal treatment of metadata, and the efficacy of current oversight mechanisms. As the fault lines become larger, a robust public and political debate is needed. While there is no shortage of potential changes — most authors offer their own recommendations — successfully transitioning toward a reform agenda represents an enormous challenge for all concerned with privacy and surveillance in Canada.

I am honoured to have served as editor (and to have contributed my own work on why oversight alone will not address the privacy problems associated with Canadian surveillance), but it should be noted that contributors were granted total freedom to address any aspect of the issue as they saw fit. There was no editorial attempt to prescribe a particular outcome or perspective. Indeed, the contributors differ in their views of Canadian surveillance and the need (if any) for reform. Moreover, while the contributions fit neatly within three sections, each contribution stands on its own and can be read independent of the others.

Part I: Understanding Surveillance

The book opens with two contributions that help unpack the realities of modern Canadian surveillance technologies and programs. Andrew Clement and Jonathan Obar place the spotlight on Canada's Internet infrastructure, coining the term "boomerang routing" to call attention to the fact that a significant portion of Canadian Internet traffic transits through the United States, even when the sender and recipient are both located within Canada. The surveillance implication of boomerang routing is that Canadian data is more easily accessed by US surveillance agencies.

For example, an examination of thousands of data routes originating in Canada revealed that nearly one-quarter transited through the United States on their way to Canadian destinations. In every instance, the US transit point was a city with a known National Security Agency splitter that would allow for potential capture of the Canadian transmission. In fact, Clement and Obar note that accessing Canadian government websites, as well as major banks and other financial institutions, often involves an exchange in the United States.

The Clement and Obar contribution persuasively argues that the boomerang routing effect has major implications for privacy and network sovereignty. The authors suggest that the solution does not lie in legal reforms, but rather in the creation of a Canadian network architecture that is more likely to retain domestic Internet traffic within the country. They note that this will require the development of new Canadian Internet exchange points, which will decrease the costs of network exchange and make Canadian-based exchanges more likely.

While Clement and Obar reveal the intricacies of Canada's Internet infrastructure and its implications for network surveillance, Steve Hewitt focuses on the limits of network-based surveillance by discussing the role of covert human intelligence sources in Canada. Hewitt starts by arguing that surveillance does not affect all people equally. Rather, "certain groups and individuals have long been subjected to more intrusive surveillance and dramatic consequences because of their ideology or race and ethnicity, or gender or sexuality or religion or nationality or some combination of these factors."

Hewitt notes that technology is often involved in increased intrusive targeted surveillance, yet it would be a mistake to overlook the role that human intelligence continues to play in such activities. Hewitt's concern stems from the likelihood that this form of surveillance will be largely overlooked as politicians and the public grapple with the post-Snowden environment and the urge to focus attention on network-based surveillance.

Hewitt's contribution offers an intriguing look back at the role of human intelligence sources in Canada, which dates to the very founding of the country. Even as technological surveillance emerged as an increasingly important source of information, there remained a critical role for human intelligence sources. For example, Hewitt notes the limitations of the effectiveness of technological surveillance, as e-mails may be encrypted or coded messages used within network communications. Indeed, he points to a 1996 US congressional report that explicitly addressed the limitations of such surveillance:

> They [technological surveillance] do not, however, provide sufficient access to targets such as terrorists or drug dealers who undertake their activities in secret or to the plans and intentions of foreign governments that are deliberately concealed from the outside world. Recruiting human sources — as difficult, imperfect, and risky as it is — often provides the only means of such access.[2]

While technology has evolved since 1996, Hewitt's contribution emphasizes the need for a more holistic perspective on surveillance that broadly incorporates reforms such as warrant-based oversight.

Part II: Legal Issues

Three contributors provide a legal lens on the Canadian privacy and surveillance issues in a post-Snowden environment. Tamir Israel's contribution focuses on the foreign intelligence issues raised by a networked environment that necessarily cuts across national borders. Israel provides helpful context behind the legal frameworks that support signals intelligence activities, noting that the mandates extend far beyond imminent and serious threats. Moreover, the current frameworks offer limited oversight, with most legal interpretations remaining secret.

Israel is critical of the broad powers granted to CSE, maintaining that the agency is rarely forced to justify its decisions before the courts. The scope of its powers juxtaposed with the lack of public review is stunning: few judicial decisions, legally privileged Department of Justice opinions, and ministerial authorizations that only see the light of day in response to access to information requests. Given the secrecy, Israel argues that assessing CSE's conduct is exceptionally challenging.

Israel also links the legal challenges with CSE's relationship with foreign intelligence agencies, most notably the "Five Eyes" consortium of Canada, the United States, the United Kingdom, Australia, and New Zealand. He notes that "while CSE cannot obligate its Five Eyes partners to adopt *Charter*-compliant information gathering activities, it *can* more effectively constrain its own intelligence gathering and tasking of FVEY [Five Eyes] resources to reflect the privacy of affected targets."

Lisa Austin's contribution builds on this analysis by focusing on what she describes as "lawful illegality." Her key insight is that discussion of the legality of surveillance requires a careful analysis of the systemic features of surveillance that place a strain on the rule of law.

Austin provides three examples of how the legal surveillance framework itself raises serious concerns. First, she identifies the emphasis on secrecy, particularly in a national security context. Echoing Israel's concern with the lack of transparency associated with CSE review, Austin notes that the secrecy of the legal framework invariably leads to unilateral, rather than objective (and public), interpretations of the law.

Austin also points to the legal concerns that arise through the blurring of law enforcement, border control, and terrorism investigations. By creating legal reforms that apply in all contexts, it becomes exceptionally difficult for the participants in the reform process to effectively account for the implications of legislative proposals or court decisions. The obvious example in this regard is the Canadian government's lawful access legislation, which is also the focus of Christopher Parsons's contribution in Part III.

While the complexity of domestic reforms hampers the legislative process, Austin also cites the international challenge posed by surveillance activity that effortlessly cuts across national borders. Her work builds on the Clement and Obar contribution by layering the legal implications on top of the cross-border network architecture that is the focal point of their analysis.

If Austin's legal analysis raises troubling questions about the broader implications of the legal surveillance framework, Craig Forcese narrows the discussion by highlighting the issues arising from CSE's metadata program. Previously confined largely to technical experts, the Snowden revelations brought the collection and use of metadata into the popular lexicon. The US metadata program has attracted the lion's share of debate, yet Forcese expertly chronicles how Canada has also long maintained a metadata collection program that raises similar legal concerns.

Forcese's contribution helpfully describes the growth of CSE's metadata program, drawing on documents obtained under the *Access to Information Act* by *Globe and Mail* journalist Colin Freeze. Forcese explores the program with a comprehensive legal review that draws on statutory definitions, case law, and government documents.

His analysis makes it clear that there remains considerable legal uncertainty regarding metadata collection, both with respect to the CSE's governing statute and under the *Charter of Rights and Freedoms*. He concludes that changes to current practices are needed, including increased use of ministerial authorizations and legislative reform that provides judges with an oversight role over those authorizations.

Part III: Reforms and Accountability

Having assessed the surveillance framework and the resulting legal issues that arise in Canada, Part III turns to potential reforms and developing more effective accountability mechanisms.

Kent Roach's contribution points to gaps in accountability for surveillance activities and discusses several potential remedies. Drawing on his experience with the Arar and Air India Commissions, he notes, "accountability is impossible to achieve if the information is kept secret from those demanding accountability."

Roach also highlights the shortcomings associated with legislative and judicial accountability. In the aftermath of the Snowden leaks, many commentators (including members of Parliament) have emphasized the benefits of strengthened parliamentary review. Yet Roach cautions that parliamentary reviews are often hamstrung by limited access to secret information, while specialized courts run the risk of being seen as too close to the government. As a result, those reviews may do little to enhance public confidence.

While Roach does not reject parliamentary and judicial accountability mechanisms, he argues that the most effective mechanism lies with the executive. In Canada, these mechanisms include the role of retired judges as commissioners for the CSE who are granted substantial public inquiry powers. Moreover, Roach cites the benefits of whistle-blowing, which, though controversial, has repeatedly succeeded in placing surveillance issues on the public agenda.

Reg Whitaker provides an alternate perspective on accountability, drawing on the importance of Snowden and other whistle-blowers to make the case that their work is better understood as "guerilla accountability" that arises in the absence of official forms of accountability.

Whitaker emphasizes that the international dimension of the surveillance activities hamstrings domestic review efforts, which are typically limited in scope. The inability to effectively assess activities that involve multiple agencies in numerous countries renders guerilla accountability increasingly important. Indeed, he concludes with a statement that will strike some as obvious and others as controversial:

> unless [there are] truly radical revisions in how official accountability is allowed to operate, most importantly including the expansion of its scope to the international dimension, it is certain that if the powerful spy agencies are to be held to account and to operate under the rule of law, guerilla accountability will remain a necessary part of the process.

My own contribution argues that while the instinctive response to the Snowden leaks may be to focus on improved oversight and accountability mechanisms, the bigger challenge will be to address the substantive shortcomings of the current Canadian legal framework. Indeed, improved oversight without addressing the limitations within current law threatens to leave many of the core problems in place. In short, watching the watchers is not enough.

Some of the areas of concern with the legal framework are canvassed in detail in other chapters: the legal implications of metadata (Forcese), the jurisdictional blurring of surveillance activities (Austin), and the routing of domestic data through the United States (Clement and Obar). My contribution discusses those issues and identifies several additional concerns, including the weakness of the Canadian privacy law framework, the lack of legal protection found in cross-border data transfer agreements, and the limited protections afforded to Canadians once data is collected by US agencies.

I conclude that as Canadians learn more about the current state of surveillance activities and technologies, there is a budding recognition that current surveillance and privacy laws were crafted for a much different world. The recent call for improved oversight and accountability of Canada's surveillance agencies is both understandable and long overdue. However, the bigger challenge will be to address the substantive shortcomings of the current Canadian legal framework, as well as the limitations found in foreign frameworks that have a direct impact on the privacy of Canadians.

Christopher Parsons illustrates the enormity of the reform challenge by providing a case study of the legislative battles over lawful access, a closely related issue. The Canadian policy debate over lawful access extended over a decade, with many of the same stakeholders, and security and privacy concerns that arise within the surveillance discussion.

Parsons's contribution traces back to the initial debates over lawful access in 2001, highlighting the "meandering" policy environment that saw the legislation and its justifications repeatedly change over time. Parsons identifies several factors that are crucial in influencing legislative outcomes, including government responsiveness (namely, minority governments), media coverage, and public engagement.

The lawful access experience provides important lessons for the debate over Canadian surveillance that lies ahead. The Snowden revelations have succeeded in placing Canadian participation in global surveillance activities on the public radar screen. As the contributions in this book demonstrate, Canada's active participation raises critical questions about the sovereignty of the Canadian Internet, the adequacy of the surveillance legal framework, and a myriad of possible reforms to address both legal and accountability shortcomings. If the lawful access debate is any indication, addressing these issues will take many years, as Canadians grapple with how best to strike the balance between privacy and security in a post-Snowden environment.

Notes

1. See http://antiterrorlaw.ca/, a website written by Professors Forcese and Roach that provides an exhaustive analysis of the far-reaching implications of Bill C-51.
2. "Preparing for the 21st Century," http://www.gpoaccess.gov/int/report.html, as quoted in Mark D. Villaverde, "Structuring the Prosecutor's Duty to Search the Intelligence Community for Brady Material," *Cornell Law Review* 88: 5 (2003): 1521.

PART I

UNDERSTANDING SURVEILLANCE

Canadian Internet "Boomerang" Traffic and Mass NSA Surveillance: Responding to Privacy and Network Sovereignty Challenges[1]

Andrew Clement and Jonathan A. Obar

Introduction

The 2013 revelations of US National Security Agency (NSA) surveillance programs that whistle-blower Edward Snowden's release of hitherto secret internal documents brought to public attention have sparked a storm of controversy.[2] Their breathtaking scope, scale, and questionable legality have led many countries to urgently assess the risks of NSA surveillance and to consider various actions to better protect the privacy of their citizens as well as their national sovereignty.

Given the large proportion of international Internet communications routed through the United States[3] where foreigners' data receives scant legal protection, a major focus of controversy is the NSA's mass (near total) Internet traffic interception capability.[4] Besides the extraordinary technical prowess the United States is able to deploy in the service of its perceived surveillance and security needs, it also enjoys a strategic advantage in that a disproportionate share of international data communications passes through it. This is an advantage the NSA is well aware of, as noted in a presentation deck for the top-secret PRISM program: "Much the world's communications flow through the U.S. ...Your target's communications could easily be flowing into and through the U.S." See Figure 1.[5]

Figure 1: U.S. as World's Telecommunications Backbone

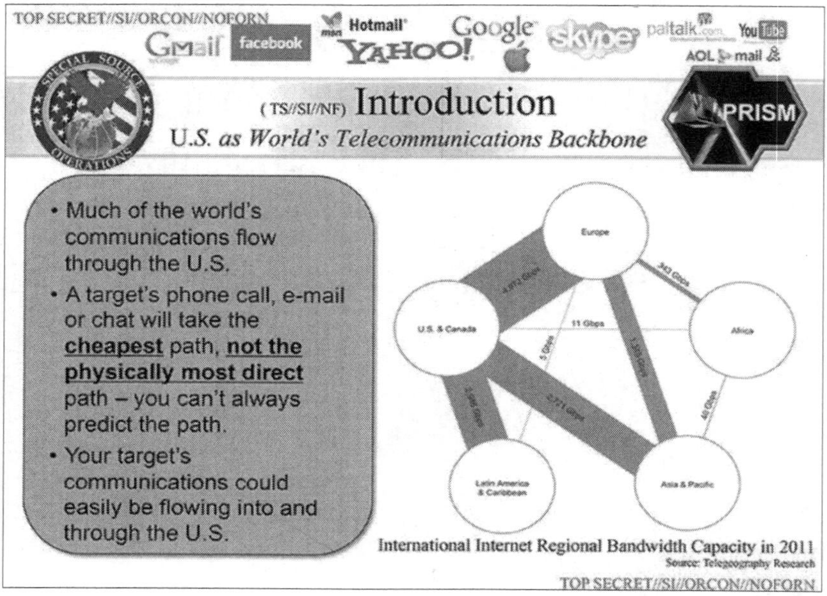
TOP SECRET//SI//ORCON//NOFORN
Hotmail
Google
Gmail
facebook
YAHOO!
skype
paltalk.com
YouTube
AOL mail
(TS//SI//NF) Introduction
U.S. as World's Telecommunications Backbone
SPECIAL SOURCE OPERATIONS
PRISM
• Much of the world's communications flow through the U.S.
• A target's phone call, e-mail or chat will take the cheapest path, not the physically most direct path – you can't always predict the path.
• Your target's communications could easily be flowing into and through the U.S.
Europe
U.S. & Canada
Africa
Latin America & Caribbean
Asia & Pacific
343 Gbps
11 Gbps
5 Gbps
International Internet Regional Bandwidth Capacity in 2011
Source: Telegeography Research
TOP SECRET//SI//ORCON//NOFORN

Source: Washington Post

Well-founded suspicions about this surveillance potential have been reported for years, but the Snowden revelations now strongly reinforce the serious allegations of clandestine spying that author James Bamford, retired AT&T technician Mark Klein and others have raised.[6] Given Canada's proximity to the United States and the structure of the North American Internet, it isn't just Canada's international traffic that is subject to suspicionless, dragnet NSA surveillance. Due to a phenomenon we term "boomerang routing"[7] — when Internet traffic originating and terminating in the same country transits another — a great deal of Canadian domestic Internet communications boomerang through the United States and are subject to NSA surveillance.[8]

This chapter examines the phenomenon of Canada-to-US-to-Canada boomerang traffic, focusing specifically on the privacy and related risks associated with NSA surveillance as well as the policy implications and remedial responses. As public understanding of how the Internet operates is generally inadequate for discussing the policy dimensions of Internet backbone surveillance, we begin with a brief overview of the technical aspects of Internet routing and then show how surveillance capabilities can be built into relatively few "choke points" yet capture the great bulk of Internet traffic. In contradistinction to the common metaphor of the Internet as a spaceless, featureless "cloud," we demonstrate that, with interception points in under twenty major cities, the NSA is capable of intercepting a large proportion of US Internet traffic. We turn then to Canadian Internet routing patterns, showing that boomerang routing is commonplace, that such routing exposes Canadians' data to NSA surveillance, and that Internet users across Canada conducting a wide range of everyday communications are subject to it. Even communications between public institutions across the street from each other can be routinely exposed to NSA interception. Both to collect data about these Internet routing patterns and reveal its physical, geographic characteristics, we draw on a research-based Internet analysis and visualization tool known as IXmaps, developed to map Internet exchange points and the traffic routed through them. The software tool found at IXmaps.ca[9] aggregates crowd-sourced Internet users' "traceroutes" and shows them where their personal traffic is likely to have been intercepted by the NSA.

The next section considers the policy implications of Canadian boomerang traffic, especially from the point of view of its privacy risks. We also consider the economic inefficiencies and point to the broader issue of the impairment of Canada's network sovereignty. The final major section offers possible remedies for the various negative aspects of boomerang routing. To reduce boomerang traffic, we propose several ways for keeping domestic data within Canadian networks and legal jurisdiction. Building public Internet exchange points in Canada would contribute to keeping domestic traffic inside national boundaries while promoting more efficient routing. To mitigate the privacy and democratic governance risks in particular, we advance ideas for greater transparency and accountability on the part of telecommunications carriers and government agencies. While recognizing the need to address the risks from mass surveillance by Canadian state agencies as well as to develop stronger international regimes for protecting privacy, freedom of expression, and civil liberties online, we close by calling for a greater assertion of Canadian network sovereignty within the norms of a free and democratic society.

NSA Interception of Canadian Internet Traffic

The almost weekly revelations from the Snowden trove of yet more NSA surveillance programs contributes to the strong and accurate impression that the NSA has largely succeeded in Director Keith Alexander's reported mission to "collect it all,"[10] and developed a global, ubiquitous spying infrastructure capable of capturing the details of nearly everyone's electronic transactions. However, it is hard for all but the most dedicated and technically sophisticated observer to keep track of the various programs and their particular characteristics. The details matter in terms of who is targeted, the types of information collected, the relevant legal jurisdictions, the parties implicated and the possible remedies. The PRISM program in which the NSA has partnered with nine major Internet companies, such as Google, Facebook, Twitter, Microsoft, and Apple, to obtain "direct" access to stored personal data, is among the best known.[11] However, the NSA programs that intercept Internet communications in transit, while less well reported, are arguably the most significant in terms of their potential impact because they can capture data from all Internet users across a wide range of on-line activities. It is these programs for capturing data "on the fly" that we examine in this chapter. To understand them and their implications, it is helpful to understand how Internet data is routed.

The Internet Is Not a Cloud: Routing Basics

Unlike the telephone system, which relies on establishing a continuous dedicated circuit between the two ends of the communication path, all Internet communication is based on packet switching. Every e-mail message, voice conversation, video, image, web page, etc., is broken into in a series of small data packets. Each packet consists of two parts: a header, containing among other items, source and destination IP addresses, much like the return and to addresses on a conventional piece of mail; and a payload, containing the content. Each packet "hops" from the originator through a succession of routers, with each router examining the packet header to determine the destination and then passing the packet to the next router in the intended direction, again much like the conventional postal service routes mail. At the destination, the packets are reassembled into the original message. The response, whether it is a web page, video, file transfer, etc., consists of another set of data packets, that individually hop their way through a succession of routers back to the originator. These routers and the links between them constitute the Internet backbone.

It is commonplace to refer to the Internet as a "cloud," as a seemingly boundaryless ethereal space in which physical location of wires and equipment is largely irrelevant. While this metaphor may be helpful in marketing Internet services, it does not well serve understanding how the Internet actually works, especially in matters of public policy around state surveillance. In fact, Internet traffic switching is mainly done by massive banks of routers crammed into large anonymous buildings located in the downtown core of major cities. These switching centres are linked by bundles of fibre optic cables each capable of transmitting tens of billions of bits per second[12] Mainly large telecommunication companies own these cables and routers, and the policies they adopt for who can connect to their networks and on what terms fundamentally determines how the Internet operates. And gaining access to the routers and cables to intercept the data packets streaming through them for surveillance purposes typically requires obtaining the cooperation of these often giant telecommunications enterprises.

NSA Internet Backbone Surveillance

The New York Times first reported the interception of US domestic communications by the NSA in late 2005.[13] But it wasn't until Mark Klein, a recently retired AT&T technician, revealed the existence of a secret "splitter" operation at 611 Folsom St. in San Francisco that the scope and technical details of NSA surveillance came to public light. Klein reported that AT&T had spliced fiber optic splitters into sixteen "peering links" that connected its network with other major carriers and Internet exchange points, directing an exact copy of all the traffic passing through these links into a "secret room" on the sixth floor, Room 641A. Here a deep packet inspection device, the Narus STA 6400, analyzed all the packets passing by, providing "complete visibility for all Internet applications," according to its vendor.[14] In other words, this operation enables the NSA to monitor not only who is communicating with whom, but potentially the entire contents of these communications as well.

Klein's revelations provoked strong reaction by civil liberties organizations, resulting in over forty court cases against US telecom carriers and the federal government. These cases allege that the carriers illegally complied with multiple surveillance requests from the NSA during the Bush administration to provide without warrants specific information about US citizens.[15]

The secrecy that pervades this topic makes it difficult to determine whether the NSA surveillance program is continuing or not, but the recent reports strongly suggest that not only is it ongoing, but is expanding during the Obama administration. James Bamford's article in the March 2012 issue of *Wired* details the construction of an enormous data centre in Bluffdale, Utah, capable of storing and analyzing the complete record of interpersonal Internet traffic.[16] In July 2012, three whistle-blowers, William E. Binney, Thomas A. Drake, and J. Kirk Wiebe, all former NSA employees, gave evidence in the Electronic Frontier Foundation's (EFF's) (2012) lawsuit against the government's mass surveillance program, *Jewel v. NSA* in support of the surveillance allegations. In particular, Binney, a former NSA technical director, claims the then current program, known as Stellar Wind, was capable of intercepting virtually all e-mail in the United States and much else.[17] The more recent revelations by whistle-blower Edward Snowden further confirm the earlier claims and identify this form of interception as part of the "Upstream" suite of surveillance programs.

Given that the NSA's Internet surveillance is ongoing but its details still a closely guarded secret, how can we determine where it is being conducted, and whose traffic is capable of being intercepted? These are the central questions we now examine. We will focus our investigation on AT&T, and the splitter installation at 611 Folsom Street, as this is the best documented case and provides a model for the interception of Internet traffic at other major Internet exchange points in the United States and presumably by other major carriers.

Where Are the NSA Splitter Sites?

While we know of the NSA splitter site at 611 Folsom Street, what about additional suspected sites? Based on his conversations and meetings with other AT&T technical staff, Klein reported that similar installations were installed in five other locations — Seattle, San Jose, Los Angeles, San Diego, and Atlanta.[18] However, these six sites would not be sufficient to comprehensively intercept US Internet traffic, as there are other, more important routing centres that would be much more attractive for interception purposes. Scott Marcus, a former Federal Communications Commission expert, estimated that

AT&T had fifteen to twenty splitter sites.[19] However, he wasn't able to identify any sites in particular without further specific evidence. Presuming that the NSA's goal was to be able to intercept the largest proportion of US Internet traffic with the fewest possible sites (a hypothesis well confirmed by the subsequent Snowden revelations), we developed a rough schema for scoring cities based on how much Internet traffic was likely to pass through them. Using only our personal estimates of three determinants of Internet prominence, with crude relative weightings — telecom infrastructure (10); city size (population) (5); and geographic location in relation to other major population centres and telecommunications traffic patterns (4) — we developed an ordered ranking of the US cities most likely to host an NSA splitter installation.[20]

To test our hypothesis, and more generally provide a means for Internet users to see where their data travelled and was possibly subject to surveillance, we developed the IXmaps software system. Using a crowd-sourced approach, we invite geographically scattered users to install a customized version of the common traceroute program that populates our database.[21] We add location data for the routers encountered using a variety of standard geolocation techniques and from this users can then selectively map their own or others' traceroutes via a Google Maps mash-up. In early 2015, the database contained over 36,000 traceroutes contributed by more than 300 submitters from over 340 originating addresses (mainly in North America) to in excess of 2,800 destination URLs. We examined all the US-only routes in the IXmaps database, which numbered 4,200. Of these, 4,068 passed through at least one of the 18 cities we identified as the most likely sites for NSA splitter operations. In other words, installing splitters in the major Internet exchange points in just these cities would be sufficient for the NSA to intercept 97 percent of our US only traceroutes! These are shown in Figure 2.

While this result does not prove that these cities actually have NSA splitter operations, nor that the NSA has access to all the Internet exchange points in them, it is powerful confirmation that if the NSA installs splitters in relatively few strategic Internet choke points, it would be technically feasible for it to intercept a very large proportion of US Internet traffic. This high percentage helps justify our claim that these cities are strongly suspected of hosting NSA warrantless surveillance facilities. It also vividly challenges the popular image of the Internet as a "cloud."

Figure 2: 18 US Cities most likely to Host NSA Splitters[22]

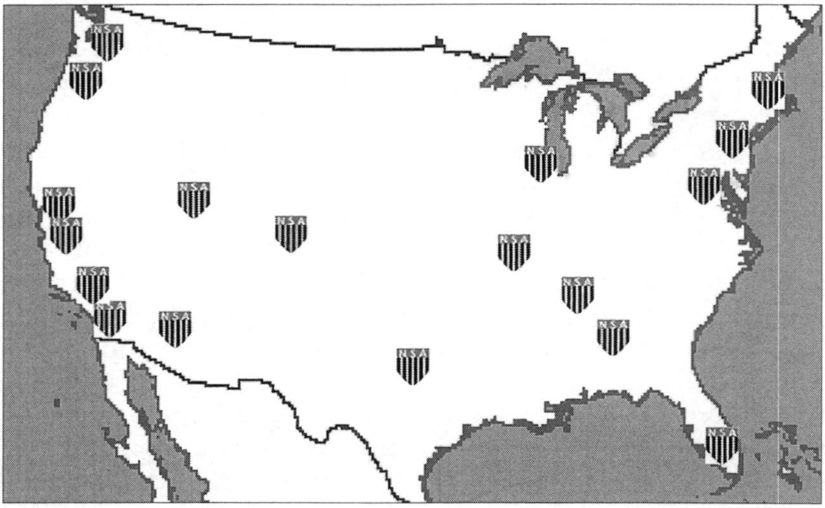

Source: IXmaps

Canadian Boomerang Routing

So far we have concentrated on showing how and where the NSA can intercept Internet traffic within US borders, but how does this relate to Canadian domestic traffic? One of our discoveries in the IXmaps project is that a relatively large number of the traceroutes in our database that originate in Canada and terminate in Canada pass through the United States along the way. We refer to these as boomerang routes because the transmissions often travel considerable distances away from the sender before arriving at a receiver who is not nearly as far from the sender as the transmission path would suggest. While this phenomenon is familiar to those in the Canadian Internet routing business, its scale, causes, and implications are not well known more widely.

For example, a particularly revealing example of boomerang routing is depicted in Figure 3, showing a route that begins and ends in Toronto, between the University of Toronto and the Ontario government nearby, but passes through New York and Chicago. (The shield icons indicate cities with suspected NSA splitter operations.)

In early 2015, the IXmaps database contained 9,233 traceroutes that originated and terminated in Canada, and, of those, 2,049, or 22 percent, boomeranged through the United States. Nearly all of these boomerang routes passed through at least one of the cities

Figure 3: A Canadian Boomerang Route Based in Toronto: UofT <> OSAP

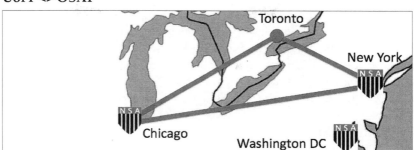

Source: IXmaps.ca/explore TR6896

we identified as containing NSA splitter operations. This pattern of high likelihood of NSA interception of Canadian boomerang traffic has been consistent over the several years we have tracked this phenomenon.[23] Given their size and proximity to the Canadian border, unsurprisingly the main US cities for boomerang routings are New York, Chicago, and Seattle, but we also found boomerang routes through many other US cities, including San Francisco, Los Angeles, and even as far south as Miami.

In attempting to account for patterns of boomerang routing, one might expect that it is largely a matter of geography. Given that Internet backbone capacity is much greater south of the border, it makes some sense to find routes between the West and East Coasts or between Vancouver and Toronto that boomerang.

However, geography clearly does not account for the frequent occurrence of routes that start and end in the same city but nevertheless transit the United States, such as the example above. In that case, the endpoints are across the street (Queen's Park Circle) from each other, and pass through switching facilities at 151 Front Street both to and from the United States. To help explain this curious phenomenon we need to take account of the particular carriers involved. In brief, carriers are selective about who they exchange traffic with directly: the larger ones typically are reluctant to exchange traffic with their smaller competitors and have an incentive to make it difficult for them to reach destinations outside their immediate networks. As Internet expert William Norton describes in *The Internet Peering Playbook*, dominant Internet carriers adopt this oligopolistic strategy.[24] One of the most visible illustrations of this is the fact that while many smaller Canadian ISPs offer the chance to peer openly at public Internet exchange points, such as the Toronto Internet Exchange (TorIX) housed in 151 Front Street, none of the major ISPs (e.g., Bell, Rogers, Telus) do so.[25]

One effect of these business practices is to force a considerable amount of Canadian Internet traffic onto the networks of large US carriers such as Cogent, Hurricane Electric, Level 3, as well as Tata (Indian) and TeliaSonera (Swedish). These foreign carriers typically, but not exclusively, meet the large Canadian carriers for data hand-offs in the United States.[26]

IXmaps Boomerang Findings

The close correlation between boomerang routing and contractual arrangements between ISPs around intercarrier routing means that it touches all Canadian Internet users, regardless of where they are located and which ISP they directly subscribe to. For the same reason, it is also a factor in nearly every type of web-based transaction across the full range of service organizations that Canadians rely on in their everyday affairs. To illustrate this we draw on IXmaps examples of cit-izens interacting online with their federal and provincial governments as well as online banking and other everyday Internet transactions.

A citizen's ability to communicate freely with government and fellow citizens is central to the concept of democracy. This is one reason that Canada's *Telecommunications Act* of 1993 affirms that Canadian telecommunications services play "an essential role in the maintenance of Canada's identity and sovereignty."[27]

We have documented numerous cases where those accessing the websites of federal departments or agencies from within Canada would have their personal data routed via the United States. Even accessing the main Government of Canada site (canada.gc.ca) will involve boomerang routing for significant numbers of Canadians. Table 1 shows a sample of other examples, selected from the IXmaps database. Figure 4 shows a map produced by IXmaps, displaying the routes between users located in Canada and various federal govern-ment sites. One can easily imagine scenarios in which a Canadian would regard the information communicated to any one of these sites, or even the fact of a visit when viewed in the light of other online activities, highly sensitive and feel uncomfortable with this being available to the NSA or any other national security agency. As we will discuss more fully in the next section, unavoidable boomerang routing to government sites also calls into question the government's ability to protect the integrity of its communications with citizens and undermines trust in vital governmental institutions.

Table 1: Selected Examples of Canadian Federal Department/ Agency/Office Websites Subject to Boomerang Routing

Federal Department/Agency/Office	Website
Canadian Air Transport Security Authority (CATSA)	www.catsa.gc.ca
Canadian Human Rights Tribunal	www.chrt-tcdp.gc.ca
Canadian Judicial Council	www.cjc-ccm.gc.ca
Citizenship and Immigration Canada	cic.gc.ca
Health Canada	www.hc-sc.gc.ca
Office of the Communications Security Establishment Commissioner	www.ocsec-bccst.gc.ca
Office of the Information Commissioner of Canada	www.oic-ci.gc.ca
Office of the Prime Minister	www.pm.gc.ca
Office of the Privacy Commissioner of Canada	www.priv.gc.ca
Parliament of Canada	www.parl.gc.ca
Privy Council Office	www.pco-bcp.gc.ca

Figure 4: A Selection of Canadian Boomerang Routes that Target Federal Government Sites

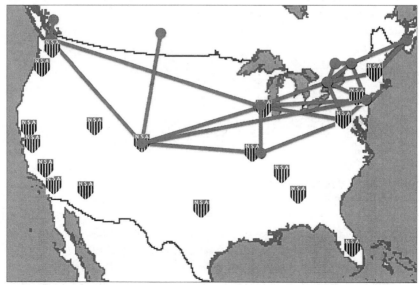

We've documented similar patterns of boomerang routing with provincial governments across the country. As the example depicted in Figure 3 illustrates, showing the route traffic follows between the University of Toronto and the Ontario Government, this boomerang pattern can even apply to Internet traffic between government institutions in the same province.

Table 2: Selected Examples of Commercial and other Websites Subject to Boomerang Routing

Banks	Website
Bank of Montreal	bmo.com
CIBC	cibc.com
Royal Bank	rbcroyalbank.com
Scotiabank	scotiabank.com
Toronto-Dominion	td.com
Universities	**Website**
Athabasca University	athabasca.ca
Dalhousie University	dal.ca
University of New Brunswick	unb.ca
University of Windsor	uwindsor.ca
York University	yorku.ca
Other Organizations	**Website**
Action Re-Buts	actionrebuts.org
Bell Canada	bell.ca
CPP Investment Board	cppib.com
Centre for Women in Business	centreforwomeninbusiness.ca
Dr. Tax	drtax.ca
Montreal Planetarium	espacepourlavie.ca
National Ballet of Canada	national.ballet.ca
Ottawa Public Library	biblioottawalibrary.ca
Royal Astronomical Society of Canada	rasc.ca
The Toronto Sun	torontosun.com
Vancouver Economic Commission	vancouvereconomic.com

Commercial transactions over the Internet with Canadian businesses will also be subject to boomerang routing depending on the particular combination of ISPs at the customer and business ends of the communication. Banking, for instance, which is rightly treated to especially strong security measures, for many Canadians is routinely subject to boomerang routing and the attendant dragnet NSA surveillance. We have documented that for every one of the Big Five banks, which dominate Canadian banking — BMO, CIBC, RBC, Scotiabank, and TD — there will be some customers whose interactions from home with their bank's website may be subject to foreign surveillance. Similarly, the IXmaps database contains traceroutes originating in Canada and destined for a wide variety of Canadian universities and colleges showing a similar pattern of US routing. Communication with the sites of non-governmental organizations, commercial organizations, libraries, media outlets, and cultural organizations have all shown evidence of boomerang routing. As Table 2 suggests, accessing any website, no matter the content or the context, could result in a boomerang route. A bank transaction, university research discussion, donation to a cultural organization, non-profit or advocacy campaign, tax software purchase, video view on a media outlet's site, and even library book check-out are all online activities that could involve a boomerang transmission path and consequent NSA surveillance.

Third Country Boomerang Routing

It is also worth noting that much of Canadian international Internet communications with countries other than the United States show similar boomerang characteristics, in the sense that the traffic passes through the United States, usually via a city where the NSA has splitter interception facilities. In this case, an obvious explanation is the location of transoceanic fibre optic cables and their landing points. As shown in the Telegeography's Authoritative Submarine Cable Map,[28] there are only two transatlantic fibre optic cables landing on Canada's East Coast (Hibernia Atlantic), compared with twelve landing in the United States. There are no trans-Pacific fibre optic cables landing on Canada's West Coast, whereas thirteen land in the United States.[29]

So far we have argued that the highly concentrated character of Internet interconnection has enabled the NSA to intercept nearly all traffic within and passing through the United States. Due to geographic factors, but also to the business relations among Canadian ISPs, a significant portion of Canadian domestic as well as third country international Internet communication boomerangs through the United States, and therefore is subject to mass NSA surveillance. We turn now to consider the policy implications of these routing and surveillance practices.

Policy Issues with Boomerang Routing

The controversies over the NSA's surveillance activities provoked by the Snowden revelations have focused on several recurring issues, both within the United States and internationally. The threats to personal privacy as well as other civil liberties and the challenges to national sovereignty are the two we address most directly here. Our emphasis on boomerang routing leads us also to consider the policy issues around the economic implications for Canada, which, while not immediately linked to state surveillance practices, promise to be a crucial factor in the remedial responses we'll discuss in the following section.

Privacy

Personal privacy is the issue that springs immediately to mind when discussing surveillance of any kind. However, we need to be cautious about the often unquestioned assumption that all surveillance represents an unavoidable threat to privacy, freedom of expression, and other important civil liberties.

This chapter, drawing on surveillance studies perspectives,[30] views NSA interception not as an isolated occurrence, but as reflecting a wider societal phenomenon, in which surveillance, "monitoring people in order to regulate or govern their behaviour,"[31] is a central organizing principle. Surveillance is often benign, even essential, but is becoming so pervasive and inextricably connected to everyday activities that we can characterize our contemporary Western life as a surveillance society. At the same time, it is important to recognize that notwithstanding its burgeoning extent and intensity, surveillance and its effects are not uniform, affecting everybody, everywhere in the similar ways.

Surveillance becomes a malign threat to civil liberties when it is conducted in a way that violates the democratic norms that govern potentially intrusive measures by the state. In Canada, the Supreme Court articulated these norms in 1986 when it developed the now widely recognized Oakes Test, based on *R. v. Oakes*.[32] Federal and provincial privacy commissioners have adapted and repeatedly applied this case in privacy contexts, assessing four key criteria: Necessity, Effectiveness, Minimality, and Proportionality. Suspicionless mass interception of personal communications would appear to fail this constitutional test on every count.

What makes the NSA surveillance especially problematic from a Canadian perspective is that foreigners' data under US jurisdiction is protected only through the definition of "foreign intelligence information," which is notoriously elastic. Notwithstanding Canada/US data sharing agreements and opinions of the federal and Ontario privacy commissioners prior to the Snowden revelations, there are strong legal arguments for the view that the level of privacy protection of Canadians' personal information in the United States is not equivalent to that at home. Once the data flows beyond the border, it no longer enjoys Canadian constitutional and other legal safeguards.[33] This means the NSA or other US agencies can legally intercept and analyze it without warrants or other judicial oversight. Furthermore, Canadians have no legal basis to challenge or remedy any abuses.

Network Sovereignty

When foreign governments or private actors play such central roles in a nation's critical communication infrastructure that they can conduct with impunity mass surveillance of domestic Internet traffic, as the NSA has the capability to do, it is not just privacy and other civil liberties that are threatened — national sovereignty is also at stake. It is useful in this context to employ the concept of "network sovereignty," which refers to an authoritative quality or process whereby an entity or set of entities distinguishes the boundaries of a network and then exercises a sovereign will or control within and at those boundaries. The sovereign can control any number of the components specific to the network, including its structural design, its evolution, development, and operation, and the extent to which the network operates, in whole or in part, and at what speed and capacity. Sovereignty can also be measured in terms of the relative level of control over the flow of content made possible by the network.

Though a new term, network sovereignty is far from a new concept. Any controlling entity, from a feudal monarch to an elected government, exercises a form of network sovereignty when it constructs any number of network systems ranging from transportation (e.g., roads, railroads, highways), utilities (e.g., water, electric) to communication (e.g., mail routes, telecommunication). As sovereigns, they can decide where these networks go, who or what can travel on them, and at what price.

The Canadian government exercises network sovereignty to serve national purposes in a variety of contexts. The dozens of laws administered by Transport Canada[34] represent one example of the government's attempt to control Canadian transportation networks. For many years, network sovereignty has also been a focus of the Canadian media and telecommunications industry. Even before the Massey Commission of 1948 — which labelled the American media system an imminent threat to the maintenance of Canadian nationalism[35] — the notion that Canadian communication companies should remain in the hands of Canadians, and that those companies should be devoted to the maintenance of a national culture, were set as the primary goals of the Canadian communication system.[36] In the 1920s, when US-based radio stations were sending their signals well beyond the border, Canadian radio entrepreneur Graham Spry visited the US National Broadcasting Company for the purpose of studying their methods. While in New York, he learned of NBC's plan to "cover" Canada as "part of the North American radio orbit."[37] Speaking about the future of the Canadian broadcasting industry, he remarked famously, "It is a choice between the State and the United States."[38] Indeed, the concern that the United States could "cover" Canada in a grid of surveillance suggests that perhaps Spry's words are just as relevant now as they were almost one hundred years ago.

Following the long history of protectionist communication policy, the Canadian *Telecommunications Act* of 1993, still in effect to this day, already mandates Canadian Internet network sovereignty. The connection between the national telecommunications system, national sovereignty, and individual privacy is clear. The act states, "telecommunications performs an essential role in the maintenance of Canada's identity and sovereignty."[39] Among the various objectives of the Canadian telecommunication system, the act stipulates that the system is "to facilitate the orderly development throughout Canada of a telecommunications system that serves to safeguard, enrich and strengthen the social and economic fabric of Canada and its regions."[40] Furthermore, the system has as a primary objective "to contribute to the protection of the privacy of persons."[41]

The boomerang routing identified by the IXmaps project, and the resulting threat of NSA surveillance, suggests that many of the ISPs operating in Canada are at odds with the law by jeopardizing both the sovereignty and privacy of Canadians mandated by the *Telecommunications Act*.

Technical and Economic Inefficiency

The widespread boomerang routing we have discussed here raises serious policy issues not only for those concerned for Canadians' privacy and sovereignty, but also for those seeking primarily to advance the vitality of Canada's Internet industry and infrastructure more generally. In particular, the Canadian Internet Registration Authority (CIRA), whose mission is to "foster the development of .CA as a key public resource for all Canadians by providing stable, secure and trusted domain name services, and by taking a leadership role in shaping Canada's Internet for the benefit of .CA domain holders,"[42] is concerned that dependence on US routing of Canadian Internet traffic is inefficient and impairs the ability of Canadian Internet users to enjoy high quality Internet services. Well before the Snowden revelations, the CIRA commissioned an expert study of the Canadian Internet infrastructure, which compared all-Canadian routings with those that transited the United States and found significant inefficiencies with the latter. See Figure 5.

Figure 5: Boomerang Routing from an Efficiency Perspective

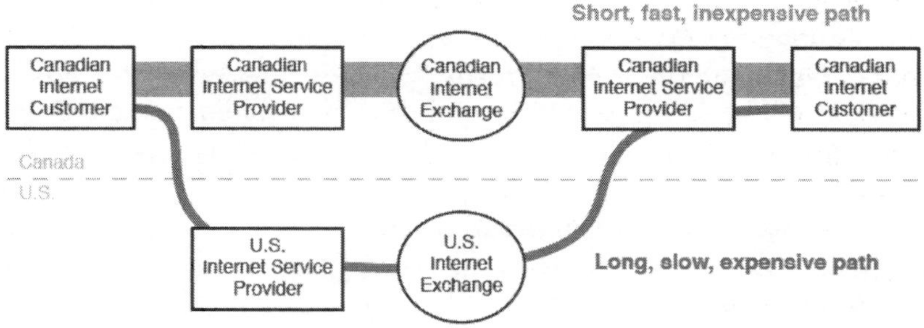

Source: Woodcock & Edelman, 2012

The CIRA's report concluded that

> Canadian Internet access is heavily and unnecessarily dependent upon foreign infrastructure, especially U.S. infrastructure. This dependence imposes significant burdens on Canadian Internet users:
> — Service prices are higher...[and] network speed is slower than would be the case if Canadian networks more densely interconnected domestically

— When data en route from one Canadian network to another passes through other countries, the data is subject to examinations by companies and government authorities in those companies. Canadian data-protection laws are understood not to protect data as it passes through other countries.[43]

Explicitly linking economic and civil liberties concerns over boomerang routing in this way opens up important possibilities for the policy responses that we turn to next.

Policy Responses: Keeping Canadian Data within Canada

The most obvious way to keep Canadian data away from NSA interception is by routing domestic Internet traffic through Canada. While fully achieving this would be impractical, and clearly wouldn't address the problems of Canada's own mass state surveillance (e.g. Pugliese, 12 Oct 2009), much can be accomplished by taking the first, relatively easy steps in this direction. This would involve a combination of interrelated, infrastructural, administrative and legal developments. We consider each of these policy measures in turn, concluding with broader calls for a strong international regime of protection for Internet freedom which includes changes in best practices that encourage greater transparency by telecom carriers about their routing policies and practices that present surveillance risks.

Invest in Canadian Internet Infrastructure

Keeping Canadian domestic Internet communication within Canadian jurisdiction, and subject to its constitutional and data protection regimes will require the development of greater technical capacity to route traffic efficiently through domestic facilities. These include, most notably, public Internet exchange points, where all carriers can freely hand traffic off to each other, as well as the high capacity fibre optic trunk lines that connect them. The former are vital, as they enable the various local networks, such as retail ISPs and institutional networks, to reach communicants on other networks without having to depend on buying transit services from foreign carriers.

The CIRA has taken the lead in this approach by acting as a catalyst for the development of more Internet Exchange Points (IXPs) across Canada. As noted above, it is pursuing this strategy to address

economic and privacy issues. More specifically, CIRA's report sum-
marizes the key benefits of this approach, including "reduc[ing]
networks operational costs,…increasing the amount of bandwidth
available to Canadian users,…reducing the risk of Canadian data
becoming subject to foreign laws and practices,…improving the
reliability of Internet access in Canada and its resilience to disaster
and attack.[44]

CIRA observes that Canada is far behind other countries in
developing IXPs, and that "IXPs typically cost less than $100,000 to
establish, and return on investment can be seen in as little as a few
days."[45] In 2012, the United States had eighty-five, whereas Canada
had just two — OttIX in Ottawa and TorIX in Toronto. CIRA subsequently mounted a program to promote Canadian public IXPs and,
by March 2015, had helped open three more — Montreal, Halifax, and
Calgary.[46] A further five are identified as high-priority and fifteen
as medium-priority.

Opening up access to trans-Canadian Internet backbone capacity, especially for linking these public IXPs, would also help avoid
boomerang routing. The topic of Internet capacity and congestion is
controversial and hampered by a lack of accurate public reporting
on infrastructural capabilities and performance, in part because this
information is treated as propriety competitive information.[47] In contrast to the need for financial investment and physical construction
in the case of developing more IXPs, expanding effective long-haul
backbone capacity for avoiding US routing may be more a matter of
obtaining access rights to existing dark fibre than it is in laying more
of it.[48] Should public funds be required, these appear to be available
if there was a change in priorities. In sharp contrast to the many
hundreds of millions of dollars the federal government has, appropriately, invested in extending Internet services to rural and remote
areas over the past decade,[49] no comparable financial commitments
have been made to ensuring that Canada's shared Internet backbone
well serves the public interest.

Another form of investment that would help protect privacy is
to enhance the security features of network infrastructure and operations to make mass suspicionless surveillance much more difficult.
Most prominent in cybersecurity discussions, especially following
the Snowden revelations, is to make end-to-end encryption a standard feature of Internet transmission. A substantive discussion of the
pros and cons of encryption as a remedy for surveillance is beyond

the scope of this chapter, but a few observations are pertinent. As the Snowden documents reveal, as well as the demonstrated ability of Snowden himself to have escaped notice by the NSA when communicating with journalists, there are encryption tools, notably TAILS and ToR, that when used properly do provide effective protection against government spying. However, these techniques currently demand a level of technical sophistication and discipline that are well beyond the abilities of most people to use reliably and safely. It would take years of concerted development work to ensure the wide availability of a privacy protective communication infrastructure secured through encryption.

While the development of reliable and easy to use encryption techniques is highly valuable and even necessary, they alone would not be sufficient to adequately address the threat of unfettered surveillance by security agencies. The NSA and its Five Eyes partners have proven to be adept in finding a variety of ways of defeating security based on encryption — from gaining the cooperation of large Internet service providers (e.g., Microsoft) simply to hand over encryption keys, to breaking into the networks of reluctant vendors to steal them in bulk (e.g., Gemalto), to weakening the encryption standards themselves so messages can be cracked more easily. A vivid example of this is the NSA's BULLRUN program, a $250-million-per-year effort that sought to "insert vulnerabilities into commercial encryption systems."[50] In light of the inadequacies of encryption as an effective security measure for population-wide communication, at least in the foreseeable future, keeping data away from the major sites of Internet interception would be a significant and worthwhile achievement.

Public Procurement Policies to Give Greater Priority to All-Canadian Routing and Privacy Protection

While developing additional Canadian Internet exchange points and opening access to long-haul transmission capacity will make it cheaper and easier for ISPs to keep Canadian data at home, these measures alone will not guarantee that result, especially given the oligopolistic character of Internet transit practices. The purchasing power of public institutions, when deployed to further public interest goals, offers another legitimate and potentially powerful means to encourage domestic routing when contracting for Internet services. Government procurement policies are already well-established and include various strictures designed to advance societal interests. In particular, the federal government's policy on contracting states the intention to "support long-term industrial and regional development and other appropriate national objectives."[51] An example of this in relation to the local storage of data can be seen in the Canadian government's current development of a cloud computing strategy. One of the proposed contract clauses, terms and conditions states that "The Services Provider (the Contractor) must not store any non-public, personal or sensitive data and information outside of Canada. This includes backup data and disaster recovery locations" (p. 27). It further considers the requirement "that all domestic data traffic be routed exclusively through Canada." (p. 8)[52] In a similar vein, a general procurement requirement that contractors providing Internet routing services peer openly at Canadian Internet points would "re-patriate" a significant portion of traffic that currently travels via the United States. For example, if the Ontario government adopted this procurement requirement, and insisted that its Toronto ISPs peered openly at TorIX, we would not see the peculiar New York/Chicago boomerang shown in Figure 3, just to cross Queen's Park Circle. If Canadian governments all peered openly at IXPs, it would provide a potent example and incentive for others to follow suit. It would also likely save money for the public purse, as well as for those interacting with government over the Internet.

The policy measures considered so far, of pro-IXP infrastructural development and procurement requirements, promise a variety of financial and other benefits, thereby helping align a diverse array of actors potentially supportive of intra-Canadian domestic Internet routing. To target more directly the privacy risks of boomerang routing, we turn to Canadian data protection law.

Insist on Comparable Levels of Privacy Protection for Canadian Data Routed through Other Jurisdictions

Under existing Canada privacy laws, notably the *Personal Information Protection and Electronic Documents Act* (PIPEDA), as well as various public sector laws, there is already a requirement that when a data custodian passes personal information to a third party, the custodian must ensure that the data enjoys comparable or higher levels of protection. The weaker legal protection Canadian data enjoys in the United States, and the overwhelming evidence that the NSA has largely unfettered access to foreigners' data passing through the

United States, strongly suggests that Canadian carriers that route domestic Internet traffic via the United States or even simply hand data over to US companies inside Canada for domestic delivery, are not on the face of it in compliance with Canadian law. However, this is not a well-recognized fact. Part of the difficulty is that, prior to the Snowden revelations, some commissioners have ruled that notwithstanding the broad and intrusive powers of the *Patriot Act*, the fact of data falling under US jurisdiction, especially when considered in light of Canada/US data-sharing agreements, does not in itself constitute a violation of the "comparability" standard, as the service contracts might contain adequate protective provisions.[53] While it is highly unlikely that such contracts are strong enough to withstand the formidable powers of US security agencies, an in-depth assessment would require examining the contractual provisions of the third-party access in each case. This is effectively stymied by the unwillingness of service providers to divulge these contracts, which are typically covered by non-disclosure agreements.

This situation draws attention to the need for two important privacy policy initiatives: revisiting the issue of "comparable" protection in light of the Snowden revelations, and requiring more proactive disclosure by Internet service providers of the terms of data agreements between contracting parties.[54]

Partly in response to ambiguities about the threats posed to personal information in the wake of 9/11 and the *Patriot Act*, two provinces, Nova Scotia and British Columbia, updated their privacy laws to explicitly require that public bodies ensure that the personal information they hold is stored and accessed only in Canada.[55] While these laws help clarify the need for Canadians' data to remain under Canadian jurisdiction for protection, they appear premised on the conventional database model of information handling, with its emphasis on storage and access, and do not address the need for protection while in transit. This may be because at the time of enactment, the possibility of interception on-the-fly and the NSA's surveillance operations using splitters at Internet gateways were not part of the discussion. This suggests the need to include consideration of routing paths, along with storage location, when assessing privacy risks and possible legal protections.

It is important to note that while the focus of this chapter is on surveillance of Internet boomerang routing, reducing NSA interception only addresses one of several layers of the current surveillance challenge facing Canadians. It is now well-documented that Canada's own signals intelligence agency, Communication Security Establishment (CSE) is involved in a variety of domestic surveillance activities.[56] This includes the potential interception of millions of Canadian Internet transmissions daily either via direct capture of the transmissions themselves, or through relationships developed with Internet carriers.[57] The Canadian government has also been attempting for years to expand the surveillance capabilities of federal agencies, and has recently been succeeding in the face of strong public opposition.[58] This domestic surveillance raises a host of privacy and other civil liberties concerns that are addressed in other parts of this book. Among them is the possibility that Canada/US data-sharing agreements may allow the NSA to circumvent the cross-border data routing debate entirely. But formidable as the challenges are to achieving surveillance reform within Canada, it remains the case that Canadians' data enjoy much better legal protection at home, with the prospects of protection from surveillance abroad much more remote. Advancing Canadian network sovereignty within a democratic framework will contribute to a broader movement to protect the privacy of Canadians from surveillance (foreign and domestic) in all its forms.

Conclusion

This chapter has examined the threats to Canadians' privacy, civil liberties, and national sovereignty posed by mass NSA surveillance of Canadian domestic Internet traffic. Drawing on IXmaps research project findings, we have demonstrated that a significant portion of this domestic Internet traffic transits the United States through prominent "choke point" sites of Internet backbone routing and NSA interception.

To address these threats, we propose an integrated set of policy responses involving infrastructural development, public procurement requirements, and stronger regulatory enforcement aimed principally at keeping Canadian data home. In pursuit of this goal, we propose

1. developing and promoting the use of Canadian public Internet exchange points (IXPs), in keeping with CIRA's initiative already underway;

2. opening access to Canada's long-haul Internet backbone, especially to facilitate traffic between public IXPs;
3. requiring Internet service providers in contracts with public bodies to include open peering at public Internet exchange points where these are available;
4. re-examining, in light of the Snowden revelations, the issue of comparable privacy protection for Canadians, personal data when exposed to US jurisdiction;
5. requiring greater transparency and accountability on the part of Canadian telecom carriers in terms of their internetwork routing practices, long-haul carriage capacity and utilization, and data-protection provisions in the contractual arrangements with transit providers.

Pursuing these measures implicates a range of public policy actors: Canadian Internet Registration Authority (1), Canadian Radio-television and Telecommunications Commission (1, 2, 4, 5), Industry Canada (1, 2), Privacy Commissioners (4, 5), and Treasury Board (3).

These measures are consistent with Canada's history of nation building through exercising and advancing network sovereignty in the face of the longstanding challenge of living peacefully but independently alongside the world's only remaining super power. We further argue that these measures are feasible and effective, even necessary in significantly reducing the flows of Canada's domestic Internet traffic that transits the United States and is hence exposed to NSA surveillance.

Of course these policy measures, even if adopted in full, are far from sufficient in addressing the many other challenges of mass state surveillance that Snowden has revealed. To begin with, they do not tackle the NSA's surveillance programs, such as PRISM, that through partnerships with major online service providers popular with Canadians, notably Google, Facebook, Microsoft, Yahoo, Twitter, and Apple, enable relatively direct access to troves of stored personal data. Furthermore, by concentrating more domestic traffic within Canada, they make more urgent the necessity of resolving the thorny issues around Canada's own suspicionless mass surveillance program that others in this volume discuss in more detail.[59] To secure Canadian domestic Internet communications from unaccountable state security agency intrusion, we need progress on both fronts, so in this sense efforts would complement each other.

Finally, whatever success is achieved in better protecting domestic communications, there will remain a vital public interest in ensuring safe, free, open and global Internet communication. This will require developing a robust international regime for protecting online privacy, free expression, and the other civil liberties that are the hallmark of democratic societies. Any efforts directed at better securing such public interests on a national scale should not interfere, but rather facilitate, achieving this transcendent goal. The policy responses outlined above are designed to accomplish this. Asserting national network sovereignty transparently and accountably in the pursuit of democratic ideals arguably provides one of the best bases for achieving similar ideals at a global scale. Pursuing the policy measures here can provide a valuable impetus in the global Internet governance enterprise by raising awareness of the issues at stake with boomerang routing, helping people understand better the hitherto murky but vital routing activities at the core of the Internet, and demonstrating that effective action can be taken to mitigate the menace of mass Internet surveillance.

Acknowledgements

The data reported in this chapter was generated through the IXmaps research project. We particularly appreciate the contributions of Antonio Gamba and Colin McCann. The project has been supported since 2009 by the Social Sciences and Humanities Research Council, the Office of the Privacy Commissioner of Canada and the Canadian Internet Registration Authority (CIRA). For more details, see IXmaps.ca

Notes

1. This chapter is a substantially revised and updated version of two previously published conference papers: Andrew Clement, "NSA Surveillance: Exploring the Geographies of Internet Interception," in *Proceedings on the iConference2014*, Berlin, 4–7 March 2014, and Andrew Clement, "IXmaps: Tracking Your Personal Data through the NSA's Warrantless Wiretapping Sites," 2013 *IEEE International Symposium on Technology and Society (ISTAS)*, Toronto, 27–29 June 2013, at 216, *IEEE-Explore Digital Library*, doi:10.1109/ISTAS.2013.6613122.

2. For a comprehensive, searchable collection of the documents Edward Snowden leaked and subsequently published by new media, see the Snowden Archive at <https://snowdenarchive.cjfe.org>.

3. James Bamford, *The Shadow Factory: The Ultra Secret NSA from 9/11 to the Eavesdropping on America.* (New York: Doubleday, 2008).

4. Andrew Clement, "NSA Surveillance: Exploring the Geographies of Internet Interception," in *Proceedings on the iConference2014*, Berlin, 4–7 March 2014.

5. *Washington Post*, "NSA Slides Explain the PRISM Data-Collection Program," 6 June 2013, updated 10 July 2013, <http://www.washington-post.com/wp-srv/special/politics/prism-collection-documents/>.

6. James Bamford, *The Puzzle Palace: A Report on America's Most Secret Agency.* (Boston: Houghton Mifflin, 1982); Bamford supra note 2; Mark Klein, *Wiring up the Big Brother Machine... and Fighting It* (Charleston, SC: BookSurge, 2009); Susan Landau, *Surveillance or Security? The Risks Posed by New Wiretapping Technologies* (Cambridge, MA: MIT Press, 2011).

7. Also referred to as "tromboning."

8. Jonathan A. Obar & Andrew Clement, "Internet Surveillance and Boomerang Routing: A Call for Canadian Network Sovereignty," in TEM 2013: *Proceedings of the Technology & Emerging Media Track – Annual conference of the Canadian Communication Association*, eds. P. Ross & J. Shtern (Victoria, 5–7 June, 2012), <http://papers.ssrn.com/sol3/papers.cfm?abstract_id=2311792>.

9. IXmaps research project, see <http://ixmaps.ca>.

10. Ellen Nakashima & Joby Warrick, "For NSA Chief, Terrorist Threat Drives Passion to 'Collect It All,' Observers Say," *Washington Post*, 14 July 2013, <http://www.washingtonpost.com/world/national-security/for-nsa-chief-terrorist-threat-drives-passion-to-collect-it-all/2013/07/14/3d26ef8 0-ea49-11e2-a301-ea5a8116d211_story.html>.

11. Barton Gellman & Laura Poitras, "U.S., British Intelligence Mining Data from Nine U.S. Internet Companies in Broad Secret Program," *Washington Post*, 6 June 2013, <http://www.washingtonpost.com/investi-gations/us-intelligence-mining-data-from-nine-us-internet-companies-in-broad-secret-program/2013/06/06/3a0c0da8-cebf-11e2-8845-d970ccb04497_story.html>.

12. Andrew Blum, *Tubes: A Journey to the Center of the Internet.* (New York, Ecco, 2012).

13. J. Risen & E. Lichtblau, "Bush Lets U.S. Spy on Callers without Courts," *New York Times*, 16 December 2005, <http://www.nytimes.com/2005/12/16/politics/16program.html?ex=1145419200&en=87817a067833b164&ei=5070>.

14. Klein, *supra* note 5.

15. While the Bush administration initially denied the role of telecom-munications carriers, it subsequently confirmed this in general terms.

Eric Lichtblau, "Role of Telecom Firms in Wiretaps Is Confirmed," *New York Times*, 24 August 2007, <http://www.nytimes.com/2007/08/24/washington/24nsa.html?ex=1345608000&en=4e8428cf3d46306c&ei=5090&partner=rssuserland&emc=rss>.

16. James Bamford, "The NSA Is Building the Country's Biggest Spy Center (Watch What You Say)," *Wired*, 15 March 2012, <http://www.wired.com/threatlevel/2012/03/ff_nsadatacenter/all/1>.

17. P. Harris, "US Data Whistleblower: 'It's a Violation of Everybody's Constitutional Rights,'" *The Guardian*, 15 September 2013, <http://www.guardian.co.uk/technology/2012/sep/15/data-whistleblower-constitutional-rights>.

18. Klein, *supra* note 5.

19. PBS Frontline, "Spying on the Home Front," 15 May 2007, <http://www.pbs.org/wgbh/pages/frontline/homefront/view/>.

20. For details of ratings and calculations see: <https://docs.google.com/spreadsheets/d/1x6aYnGmbQKzZGLUkWC4mX5eSRlDWpVKls_DjI_gV69A/edit?hl=en_US&authkey=CMeo8ZkG#gid=0>, accessed 5 May 2015.

21. See *Wikipedia*, s.v. "Traceroute," accessed 5 May 2015, <http://en.wikipedia.org/wiki/Traceroute>.

22. Biases in the sample of traceroutes contributed by users to the database mean that this particular list of cities and the relative amount of domestic US traffic that could by intercepted by NSA splitters installed in them needs to be treated with caution. The chronic difficulties, widely recognized in the Internet routing research community, in accurately geolocating routers based on hostnames, IP addresses, and latencies, further complicate the picture. Nevertheless, we believe the overall conclusions about a relatively small number cities being sufficient to capture a very large proportion of US traffic remains valid. For more on these issues and the IXmaps project generally, see A. Clement, "IXmaps – Tracking Your Personal Data through the NSA's Warrantless Wiretapping Sites," *2013 IEEE International Symposium on Technology and Society (ISTAS)*, Toronto, 27–29 June 2013, <https://www.dropbox.com/s/9y4xtavova2qtj4/ISTAS13%20paper%2026%20IXmaps%20%E2%80%93%20Tracking%20May%2022.pdf>.

23. Andrew Clement, "IXmaps: Tracking Your Personal Data through the NSA's Warrantless Wiretapping Sites," 2013 *IEEE International Symposium on Technology and Society (ISTAS)*, Toronto, 27–29 June 2013, at 216, *IEEE-Explore Digital Library*, doi:10.1109/ISTAS.2013.6613122.

24. William B. Norton, *The Internet Peering Playbook: Connecting to the Core of the Internet* (N.p.: DrPeering Press, 2012).

25. See the Peers list at http://www.torix.ca/peers.php. As of 21 April 2014, Bell and Telus are not mentioned, and Rogers and Allstream peer only conditionally, but smaller ISPs such as Teksavvy and Distributel peer

openly (i.e., accept traffic for delivery without charge while expecting the same for delivery of their own traffic).

26. Some of the US network operators, such as Hurricane Electric, carry Canadian domestic traffic entirely within Canada, but nevertheless as mentioned later are still covered by US legal jurisdiction.

27. *Telecommunications Act*, S.C. 1993, c. 38, s. 7.

28. PriMetria, TeleGeography, last updated on 27 April 2015. (Washington, D.C.) <http://www.submarinecablemap.com/>, accessed 5 May 2015.

29. Data collected by IXmaps supports this pattern, in that there are currently ten times as many international traceroutes destined for a third country that are routed through the United States (130) as do not show US routing. However, these figures are not reliable, since we have so far made no systematic attempts to collect, geolocate, and analyze non–North American routes. It is also worth noting that even those international traceroutes that don't show a US-located router may be subject to NSA surveillance when passing through US-based gateways, or more clandestinely via submarine or landing point interception.

30. David Lyon, *Surveillance Studies: An Overview* (Cambridge, UK: Polity Press, 2007).

31. J. Gilliom & T. Monahan, *SuperVision: An Introduction to the Surveillance Society* (Chicago: University of Chicago Press, 2013), at 2.

32. *R. v. Oakes*, [1986] 1 S.C.R. 103, <http://www.canlii.org/en/ca/scc/doc/1986/1986canlii46/1986canlii46.html>.

33. Austin, Chapter IV, this volume; Lisa Austin et al, "Our Data, Our Laws," *National Post*, 12 December 2013, <http://fullcomment.nationalpost.com/2013/12/12/our-data-our-laws/>. Similar principles apply even when data is handled in Canada by a US entity, such as the transit carriers mentioned above (e.g., Cogent, Level 3, Hurricane Electric), which are subject to US jurisdiction, notably to the *Patriot Act* (s. 215) and the *FISA Amendments Act* (s. 702).

34. Government of Canada, Transport Canada, *Acts and Regulations*, <http://www.tc.gc.ca/eng/acts-regulations/menu.htm>.

35. Mary Vipond, *The Mass Media in Canada*, 3rd ed. (Toronto: James Lorimer & Company), 2000.

36. Marc Raboy, *Missed Opportunities: The Story of Canada's Broadcasting Policy* (Montreal and Kingston: McGill-Queen's University Press, 1990); Standing Committee on Canadian Heritage, *Our Cultural Sovereignty: The Second Century of Canadian Broadcasting* (Ottawa: Parliament of Canada, June 2003), <http://cmte.parl.gc.ca/Content/HOC/committee/372/heri/reports/rp1032284/herirp02/herirp02--e.pdf>.

37. Cited in Raboy, *supra* note 34 at 23.

38. Raboy, *supra* note 34 at 40; Robert W. McChesney, *The 1997 Spry Memorial Lecture: The Mythology of Commercial Broadcasting and the Contemporary*

Crisis of Public Broadcasting (Montreal: 2 December 1997; Vancouver: 4 December 1997), <www.ratical.com/co-globalize/RMmythCB.pdf>.

39. *Ibid.* note 26, at 4.

40. *Ibid.*

41. *Ibid.*

42. Canadian Internet Registration Authority (CIRA), Mission Statement, <http://CIRA.ca>, accessed 2 March, 2015.

43. Bill Woodcock & Benjamin Edelman, *Toward Efficiencies in Canadian Internet Traffic Exchange, Canadian Internet Registration Authority* (September 2012), <http://cira.ca/sites/default/files/attachments/publications/toward-efficiencies-in-canadian-internet-traffic-exchange.pdff> at 1.

44. *Ibid.*

45. *Ibid.* at 2.

46. See CIRA Member News, "CIRA to Add Three More IXPs within Canada by 2015," 28 January 2013, <http://www.cira.ca/membership/enewsletters/vol-2-issue4/>.

47. Jesse Kline, "Why Canada Has 'Third World Access to the Internet,'" 24 September 2013, *National Post*, <http://fullcomment.nationalpost.com/2013/09/24/jesse-kline-why-canada-has-third-world-access-to-the-internet/>.

48. However, building greater trans-oceanic Internet backbone capacity for reaching other continents more directly and avoiding US transit, as Brazil is proposing, would involve considerable financial investment.

49. The federal government announced $305 million for rural high-speed Internet in its recent Canada 150 Digital Strategy. Canadian Press, "Ottawa's digital strategy targets privacy, rural internet: Long awaited 'Digital Canada 150' strategy unveiled by Industry Minister James Moore," *CBC News*, 4 April 2014, <http://www.cbc.ca/news/technology/ottawa-s-digital-strategy-targets-privacy-rural-Internet-1.2598097>.

50. James Ball, Julian Borger & Glenn Greenwald, "Revealed: How US and UK Spy Agencies Defeat Internet Privacy and Security," *The Guardian*, 6 September 2013, <http://www.theguardian.com/world/2013/sep/05/nsa-gchq-encryption-codes-security>.

51. Treasury Board of Canada Secretariat, "Contracting Policy," Policy statement, last modified on 9 October 2013, <http://www.tbs-sct.gc.ca/pol/doc-eng.aspx?section=text&id=14494>.

52. Government of Canada, Canada's Cloud Consultation, Request for Information, Cloud Computing Solutions, EN578-151297/B, 2 December 2014 <https://buyandsell.gc.ca/cds/public/2014/12/02/272bfba752891ec35226f730cca2847e/ABES.PROD.PW_EEM.B033.E28243.EBSU000.PDF>, reported in Michael Geist, "Government's Cloud Computing Strategy Focused on Keeping Data in Canada," 30 January

2015, michaelgeist.ca (blog), <http://www.michaelgeist.ca/2015/01/governments-cloud-computing-strategy-focused-keeping-data-canada/>.

53. Ontario Information and Privacy Commissioner, *Reviewing the Licensing Automation System of the Ministry of Natural Resources, A Special Investigative Report*, [PC12-39], June 2012, <http://www.ipc.on.ca/english/Decisions-and-Resolutions/Decisions-and-Resolutions-Summary/?id=8933>.

54. Andrew Clement & Jonathan Obar, *Keeping Users in the Know or in the Dark: Data Privacy Transparency of Canadian Internet Service Providers*, IXmaps Research Report, 27 March 2014, <http://ixmaps.ca/transparency.php> also available at: http://papers.ssrn.com/sol3/papers.cfm?abstract_id=2491847>; Andrew Clement & Jonathan Obar, Keeping Users in the Know or in the Dark: 2014 *Report on Data Privacy Transparency of Canadian Internet Carriers*, IXmaps Research Report, 12 March 2015, <http://ixmaps.ca/transparency-2014.php>.

55. In the case of Nova Scotia, a new law was enacted — the Personal Information International Disclosure Protection Act SNS 2006, c.3., <http://nslegislature.ca/legc/statutes/persinfo.htm>.

56. See Ryan Gallagher & Glenn Greenwald, "Canada Casts Global Surveillance Dragnet over File Downloads," *The Intercept*, 28 January 2015, <https://firstlook.org/theintercept/2015/01/28/canada-cse-levitation-mass-surveillance/>.

57. Alex Boutilier, "Government Agencies Seek Telecom User Data at 'Jaw-Dropping' Rates," *Toronto Star*, 29 April 2014, <http://www.thestar.com/news/canada/2014/04/29/telecoms_refuse_say_how_often_they_hand_over_customers_data.html>; Amber Hildebrandt, Michael Pereira, & Dave Seglins, "CSE Tracks Millions of Downloads Daily: Snowden Documents," *CBC News*, 28 January 2015, <http://www.cbc.ca/news/canada/cse-tracks-millions-of-downloads-daily-snowden-documents-1.2930120>.

58. For instance, "lawful access" legislation, Bill C-13, *Protecting Canadians from Online Crime Act*, passed into law 20 October 2014. Other federal bills include: S-4, Digital Privacy Act, 2014; C-44, *Protection of Canada from Terrorists Act*, 2014, passed 2 February 2015; and C-51, *Anti-Terrorism Act*, 2015, passed the Commons 6 May 2015, after an unprecedented popular opposition campaign. See <https://stopc51.ca/>, accessed 6 May 2015.

59. See Austin, Chapter IV, and Parsons, Chapter IX.

References

Austin, Lisa M., Heather Black, Michael Geist, Avner Levin and Ian Kerr. (Dec. 12, 2013). "Our data, our laws," Opinion piece, *National Post*, http://fullcomment.nationalpost.com/2013/12/12/our-data-our-laws/.

Bamford, James. (1982). *The Puzzle Palace: A Report on America's Most Secret Agency*. Houghton Mifflin.

Bamford, James. (2008). *The Shadow Factory: The UltraSecret NSA from 9/11 to the Eavesdropping on America*. New York: Doubleday.

Bamford, James. (Mar. 15, 2012). "The NSA Is Building the Country's Biggest Spy Center (Watch What You Say)." *Wired*. http://www.wired.com/threatlevel/2012/03/ff_nsadatacenter/all/1.

Boutilier, Alex. (Apr. 29, 2014). Government agencies seek telecom user data at 'jaw-dropping' rates, *Toronto Star*. http://www.thestar.com/news/canada/2014/04/29/telecoms_refuse_say_how_often_they_hand_over_customers_data.html.

Clement, Andrew (2014). "NSA Surveillance: Exploring the geographies of Internet interception." *Proceedings on the iConference2014*, Berlin, March 4-7, 2014.

Clement, Andrew (2013). "IXmaps – Tracking your personal data through the NSA's warrantless wiretapping sites," *2013 IEEE International Symposium on Technology and Society (ISTAS)*, Toronto, June 27-29, 2013. 216 - 223. published in IEEE-Explore DOI: 10.1109/ISTAS.2013.6613122.

Clement, Andrew and Jonathan Obar (2014, March 27) *Keeping Users in the Know or in the Dark: Data privacy transparency of Canadian Internet service providers*, IXmaps research report. http://ixmaps.ca/transparency.php.

Clement, Andrew, and Obar, Jonathan (Mar. 12, 2015). Keeping Users in the Know or in the Dark: 2014 Report on Data privacy transparency of Canadian Internet carriers, IXmaps research report. http://ixmaps.ca/transparency-2014.php.

Dodge, M. and R. Kitchen (2002). "New Cartographies to Chart Cyberspace," *Geoinformatics* (April/May):1.

Electronic Frontier Foundation. (July 2, 2012). "Three NSA Whistleblowers Back EFF's Lawsuit Over Government's Massive Spying Program." https://www.eff.org/press/releases/three-nsa-whistleblowers-back-effs-lawsuit-over-governments-massive-spying-program.

Gallagher, Ryan and Glenn Greenwald. (Jan. 28, 2015). Canada casts global surveillance dragnet over file downloads. *The Intercept*. https://firstlook.org/theintercept/2015/01/28/canada-cse-levitation-mass-surveillance/.

Gilliom, J., and T. Monahan. (2013). *SuperVision: An Introduction to the Surveillance Society*. Chicago: University of Chicago Press.

Hildebrandt, Amber, Michael Pereira and Dave Seglins. (Jan. 28, 2015). CSE tracks millions of downloads daily: Snowden documents. *CBC News*. http://www.cbc.ca/news/canada/cse-tracks-millions-of-downloads-daily-snowden-documents-1.2930120

Katz-Bassett, E., J. John, A. Krishnamurthy, D. Wetherall, T. Anderson, and Y. Chawathe. (2006, October). "Towards IP Geolocation Using Delay and Topology Measurements," in *ACM IMC '06*.

Klein, Mark. (2009). *Wiring up the Big Brother Machine... and fighting it*. Charleston, SC: BookSurge.

Landau, Susan. (2011). *Surveillance or Security? The Risks Posed by New Wiretapping Technologies*. Cambridge MA: MIT Press.

Lyon, David. (2007). *Surveillance Studies: An Overview*. Cambridge, UK: Polity Press.

McChesney, Robert W. (1997). *The 1997 Spry Memorial Lecture: The mythology of commercial broadcasting and the contemporary crisis of public broadcasting*. (Dec. 2, 1997). www.ratical.com/co--globalize/RMmythCB.pdf

Norton, William B. (2012). The Internet Peering Playbook: Connecting to the Core of the Internet. (N.p.: DrPeering Press, http://drpeering.net/core/bookOutline.html.

Obar, Jonathan A. and Andrew Clement. (2013). "Internet surveillance and boomerang routing: A call for Canadian network sovereignty." In P. Ross & J. Shtern (eds.), *TEM 2013: Proceedings of the Technology & Emerging Media Track — Annual conference of the Canadian Communication Association*.

PBS Frontline. (May 15, 2007). "Spying on the Home Front." <http://www.pbs.org/wgbh/pages/frontline/homefront/view/>.

Pugliese, David. (Oct. 12, 2009). Canadian spies' 'Camelot': defence hoping to attract world-class talent with $880M intelligence complex. *National Post*. Retrieved July 26, 2013 from http://news.nationalpost.com/2012/10/08/canadian-spies-camelot-defence-hoping-to-attract-world-class-talent-with-88om-intelligence-complex/.

Raboy, Marc. (1990). *Missed opportunities: The story of Canada's broadcasting policy*. Montreal, QC: McGill–Queen's University Press.

The Standing Committee on Canadian Heritage. (2003). *Our cultural sovereignty: The second century of Canadian broadcasting*. Retrieved from http://cmte.parl.gc.ca/Content/HOC/committee/372/heri/reports/rp1032284/herirpo2/herirpo2--e.pdf.

Vipond, Mary. (2000). *The mass media in Canada* (3rd ed.). Toronto, ON: James Lorimer & Company.

Woodcock, Bill and Benjamin Edelman. (Sept. 2012) *Toward Efficiencies in Canadian Internet Traffic Exchange, Canadian Internet Registration Authority*, http://www.cira.ca/assets/Uploads/Toward-Efficiencies-in-Canadian-Internet-Traffic-Exchange2.pdf.

CHAPTER II

Forgotten Surveillance: Covert Human Intelligence Sources in Canada in a Post-9/11 World

Steve Hewitt

Introduction

Surveillance does not affect everyone equally. Since Edward Snowden made his initial flight to Hong Kong with a treasure trove of documents digitally stuffed in his computer, stories about the surveillance reach of the modern technological state have abounded and continue to appear on a regular basis. Some accounts focus on generalized surveillance on a global scale; others are of particular interest to certain nations, as in the case of Canada and the Communications Security Establishment (CSE) trial, which involved the interception of Wi-Fi transmissions at a Canadian airport, or, in the United Kingdom, the warrantless interception of the communications of British citizens by Government Communications Headquarters (GCHQ).[1] There is a clear fascination in the media with the technology and the scale of the surveillance and the notion that the risk is equivalent for all of us.

This discourse, however, obscures important points. First, the notion of equality in the face of Big Brother's perpetual gaze in a "panoptic society" is, in several respects, ridiculous. While it is certainly true that all may see their communications intercepted, the key point frequently forgotten in the frenzy of discussion is what happens to the material collected. At this stage, the idea of equality breaks down as notions of threat and deviance emerge.[2] A version of what sociologist David Lyon refers to as "social sorting" comes into play.[3] Specifically, Lyon argues that

> the key practice here is that of producing coded categories
> through which persons and groups of persons may be sorted
> (Cayhan 2005; Lyon 2003b). If personal data can be extracted,
> combined, and extrapolated in order to create profiles of poten-
> tial consumers for targeted marketing purposes, then, by a
> similar logic, such data can be similarly processed in order to
> identify and isolate groups and persons that may be thought of
> as potential perpetrators of "terrorist" acts. Such "social sort-
> ing" has become a standard way of discriminating between
> different persons and groups for the purposes of providing
> differential treatment (whether this is encouraging certain
> classes of consumer to believe that they are eligible for certain
> exclusive benefits, for example, through club registration and
> membership, or facilitating or restricting traffic flow though
> airports by reference to watch lists and PNR [passenger name
> record] data).[4]

To put it in more real-world terms, I as a white, Euro-Canadian, middle-class male with slightly left-of-centre political views and agnostic religious beliefs have, through privilege, little to fear from blanket surveillance. Conversely, a change to one or several of those characteristics, such as religious belief, and suddenly a convergence can occur with the characteristics of a marginalized category that has been mapped onto the notion of a "threat" by structures of power. As a result, this shift can lead to far more intrusive surveil-lance and direct consequences as opposed to simply the collection of data. Accordingly, certain groups and individuals have long been subjected to more intrusive surveillance, and dramatic consequences as a result of that attention, because of their ideology, race, ethnicity, gender, sexuality, religion, nationality, social class, or some combi-nation of these variables.[5] The phenomenon of such targeting is not new, although arguably the scale is.

And although intrusive targeted surveillance can often involve technology, it can also feature a technique that predates the type of observation that is garnering the masses of media coverage in the twenty-first century. It is what Jean-Paul Brodeur referred to as "undercover policing," in that it involves "policing operations which are covert and involve deception."[6] It is human surveillance carried out by "covert human intelligence sources" or CHIS. A CHIS could be an undercover police officer or intelligence agent, or an informant working on behalf of a state agency.[7] The United Kingdom government offers the following official definition of a CHIS:

> A person is a CHIS if
> a) he establishes or maintains a personal or other relationship with a person for the covert purpose of facilitating the doing of anything falling within paragraph b) or c);
> b) he covertly uses such a relationship to obtain information or to provide access to any information to another person; or
> c) he covertly discloses information obtained by the use of such a relationship or as a consequence of the existence of such a relationship.[8]

There are significant reasons why CHIS, particularly informants, were crucial for countersubversion investigations in the Cold War and remain critical for counterterrorism investigations in the "War on Terror," including in Canada. In parallel to the famous acronym MICE that explains the motivations of those who spy (Money, Ideology, Compromise/Coercion, Ego/Extortion), these CHIS can be described through the acronym NERD.

N represents the nature of the target. Essentially, the more different the targets are from those tasked with spying on them, the greater the need for the informant version of CHIS. This was true during the Cold War when members of certain Eastern European ethnic groups were targeted because of their involvement in far-left radicalism, and intelligence agencies, whose agents often lacked Slavic language skills, had to recruit numerous informants from within the targeted communities. The lack of diversity within security agencies has also applied to gender in the past. Into the early 1970s, the two main domestic intelligence agencies in Canada and the United States, in part reflecting that policing and intelligence work has been historically gendered male, still did not have female agents or officers. Despite this limitation, they still managed to conduct detailed espionage against women's liberation groups, including all-female gatherings, which could not have occurred without the utilization of informants.[9] This point is even more relevant in today's increasingly multicultural world. Government agencies are not always diverse enough to have expertise in every language and/or culture. Think of cities like London, New York, and Toronto, which have citizens from every corner of the globe. It is for this reason that the Federal Bureau of Investigation has become increasingly reliant on informants for intelligence-related investigations, more so than for normal criminal work, particularly as a starting point into terrorism investigations.[10] In the United Kingdom, there has been a drive to recruit more informants from among Muslim communities because of the difficulties the police and MI5 have had in penetrating them using their own members, which is in part down to their own failures to reflect the makeup of the communities they are targeting for surveillance.[11]

E stands for ease and effectiveness, which is why CHIS are deployed. In democratic societies, it is often easier to employ informants or deploy undercover agents than to use forms of shadowing involving technology. Both the scandal that erupted in December 2005, when the *New York Times* revealed that the administration of President George W. Bush had been conducting warrantless communications interceptions, and the controversy in relation to Snowden, lack a parallel with CHIS.[12] No similar requirements exist for the deployment of informants or undercover agents.[13] The committee of Senator Frank Church (Church Committee), which in the 1970s investigated wrongdoings by American intelligence agencies, noted this anomaly with respect to informants:

> There is no specific determination made as to whether the substantial intrusion represented by informant coverage is justified by the government's interest in obtaining information. There is nothing that requires that a determination be made of whether less intrusive means will adequately serve the government's interest. There is also no requirement that the decisions of FBI officials to use informants be reviewed by anyone outside the Bureau. In short, intelligence informant coverage has not been subject to the standards which govern the use of other intrusive techniques such as wiretapping or other forms of electronic surveillance.[14]

At the time, the only loosely enforced restrictions on intelligence informants were internal ones included in the FBI's "Manual of Instructions," which it did not publicize, added the Church

Committee.[15] In the 1970s, the McDonald Commission revealed that the Royal Canadian Mounted Police (RCMP) had specific guidelines around keeping control of an informant in terms of avoiding illegal activities that reflected a criminal justice model of policing and not a security and intelligence type of investigation:

> A paid informant may think he has a license to commit any offence in order to feign the desired result. To combat this:
> 1. Do not leave him to his own devices.
> 2. Make him operate on strict instructions.
> 3. At every stage of the operation, set out his limits.
> 4. Tell him that any consideration he may get depends on whether he follows instructions.
> 5. Tell him he has no license to violate the law, but let him use all the stealth and inventiveness he can, provided he stays within the limits you set out for him.[16]

Currently, the Canadian government requires its main intelligence agency, the Canadian Security Intelligence Service (CSIS), to get special political permission, including retroactively, if necessary, when the informant version of a CHIS is utilized against sensitive targets, such as university campuses and churches and mosques, but this use still does not involve the obtaining of a warrant.[17] Since 2000, the *Regulation of Investigatory Powers Act* (RIPA) in the United Kingdom has governed the deployment of informants, including who has authority to authorize their use, but there still is no requirement to obtain a warrant.[18] A CHIS then represents a method of state surveillance that does not require the same legal approvals as does spying through technology. As a Canadian law professor put it in response to a lawsuit brought against a CHIS in 2012 by an activist who had been spied on, "the Supreme Court of Canada has been pretty clear in saying the Charter [of Rights and Freedoms] doesn't protect you from a poor choice of friends. Meaning, if you pick someone to be your friend and it happens to be an undercover cop, that's your problem."[19] A series of court decisions at various levels across Canada support this interpretation.[20] The United States Supreme Court has made similar decisions in the past, in which the court distinguished between types of surveillance. Justice William Brennan articulated the difference this way:

For there is a qualitative difference between electronic surveillance, whether the agents conceal the devices on their persons
or in the walls or under beds, and conventional police strata-
gems such as eavesdropping and disguise. The latter do not so
seriously intrude upon the right of privacy. The risk of being
overheard by an eavesdropper or betrayed by an informer or
deceived as to the identity of one with whom one deals is probably inherent in the conditions of human society. It is the risk
we necessarily assume whenever we speak. But as soon as electronic surveillance comes into play, the risk changes crucially.
There is no security from that kind of eavesdropping, no way of
mitigating the risk, and so not even a residuum of true privacy.[21]

Then there is the effectiveness that goes with CHIS. This is a particularly useful category for police forces and intelligence agencies,
since it allows them to overcome one of the main detriments of technological surveillance: vast quantities of information that cannot be
processed in a precise or timely fashion. Informants and undercover
state agents represent a precise type of surveillance that in some
ways is more difficult, although not impossible, to counteract, as it
can come in the form of a friend, colleague, or even family member.
Some targets did and do attempt to employ methods to counter informants. Moving to smaller cells with each having little knowledge of
the activities of the others is one such method. Questioning members
about their backgrounds and political convictions is another. In the
1960s, a countering method might have involved having to partake
of drugs as proof of one's counterculture credentials.[22] An additional
technique is to require serious criminal activity as a test of the commitment to the group and out of the belief that a CHIS would not
engage in such actions. Still, it is a style of information collecting
that is active instead of passive, as technological surveillance can be,
and brings a precision often missing when technology is deployed.

Nor are the various approaches to surveillance necessarily
mutually exclusive. There are ways that surveillance by CHIS can
interact with spying via technology, thus increasing both ease and
effectiveness. CHIS can use technology to spy on targeted groups
or individuals through hidden microphones and cameras, computer
spyware, GPS trackers, and other devices. CHIS can also be deployed
to investigate online criminal, hacktivist protest, and terrorism cases.
A hacker, Adrian Lamo, was responsible in 2010 for revealing to the

US government that Chelsea Manning (formerly Bradley Manning) had leaked classified records to WikiLeaks.[23] A year later, Sigurdur "Siggi" Thordarson supplied information about WikiLeaks and Julian Assange while working as an FBI informant.[24] It emerged via the media in 2012 that a well-known hacker nicknamed Sabu, involved with a hacktivist group known as LulzSec, had been working for several months as an FBI informant.[25]

R represents resources. Professional technological surveillance, in whatever form it takes, is expensive and resource-intensive. Even in the present, basic technological surveillance of a subject, which still on occasion involves physical access to the targeted group or individual's property or body, can involve up to a dozen people performing a variety of tasks.[26] All of these factors make this type of spying by the state in most democratic nations expensive, complicated, and unwieldy, and the incentive to use CHIS that much greater.

Finally, D is for destructiveness, which is the impact that the informing and spying have. It is not a coincidence that many of the alternative names applied to CHIS are negative and that those who employ them use neutral or positive terminology such as "source" or "asset."[27] Some of this negativity emanates from the nature of informing and spying, which at its heart involves betrayal, potentially at a fundamental level. But it also relates to the active role that CHIS can take as an agent provocateur, who, far from passively observing events, participates or even takes a lead role in the activities that he or she is spying on. This is the most controversial aspect of all when it comes to this type of spying, as it can lead to allegations of entrapment through manipulation of events by CHIS.[28] It also may become a featured aspect of future Canadian counterterrorism with the Harper government's Bill C-51 and the expanded ability of the CSIS to carry out disruption "measures."[29]

It is this type of human surveillance by CHIS that this chapter is concerned with. The chapter will historicize the emphasis in the domestic security and intelligence field, as opposed to ordinary crime fighting, and explore its use in contemporary Canada, ranging from counterterrorism operations to efforts against political protest. It will also situate the Canadian use within a wider American and British current context that has generated considerable controversy in both countries. Ultimately, the chapter will argue that the same controversy, although frequently muted because those targeted for this type of surveillance are frequently marginalized and thus lack a media platform or political clout to generate wider attention to their cause, will also emerge in Canada unless more effort is made to regulate and provide external scrutiny of the activities of CHIS. Inevitably, secret activity in which transparency and oversight is lacking or weakened because of the absence of direct supervision, combined with the impact on personal relationships, will lead to abuses and controversy. The catch-22 is that this type of surveillance is frequently effective and deemed necessary, particularly in a counterterrorism context, and thus its use will continue, making the emergence of scandal and controversy a given. In a real sense, then, the concerns raised by the Church Committee in the United States of the 1970s remain relevant to the Snowden era and Canada in the twenty-first century.

> The intelligence informant technique is not a precise instrument. By its very nature, it risks governmental monitoring of Constitutionally-protected activity and the private lives of Americans. Unlike electronic surveillance and wiretaps, there are few standards and no outside review system for the use of intelligence informants. Consequently, the risk of chilling the exercise of First Amendment rights and infringing citizen privacy is increased. In addition, existing guidelines for informant conduct, particularly with respect to their role in violent organizations and FBI use of intelligence informants to obtain the private documents of groups and individuals, need to be clarified and strengthened.[30]

The Canadian Historical Context

The formalized use of CHIS by the Canadian state stretches back into the nineteenth century and the rise of the modern security state. The main target in the 1860s was Irish nationalists, specifically Fenians, who launched five main cross-border attacks, which today would be labelled as terrorism, into both British North America and its successor, the fledgling country of Canada. For British North America, the main security agency was the Western Frontier Constabulary, created, according to a government official, to "find out any attempt to disturb the public peace, the existence of any plot, conspiracy, or organization whereby peace would be endangered, the Queen's Majesty insulted, or her proclamation of neutrality infringed."[31] Recruited to carry out the work of the new agency were CHIS. By 1870, there were fifty CHIS carrying out undercover work, including several who had infiltrated Irish groups.[32] The Canadian government additionally relied on British intelligence through an informant operating in the United States, although Sir John A. Macdonald remained sceptical regarding the reliability of such individuals: "A man who will engage to do what he offers to do, that is, betray those with whom he acts, is not to be trusted."[33] Later in the early twentieth century, Hindus and Sikhs became the targets of Canadian government CHIS; in turn, several informants were murdered, as was a secret agent who was killed by one of the informants whom he handled.[34]

The extensive and permanent use of CHIS in security and intelligence operations began during the First World War. In echoes of the modern counterterrorism era, the war raised the spectre of an enemy within, particularly in western Canada, which had a large "enemy alien" population drawn from parts of Europe that Canada now warred against. The immediate response on the part of the main security force in the western half of Canada, the Royal North-West Mounted Police (RNWMP), was to recruit informants who had the language and ethnic background that would allow them to move easily among those now under surveillance.[35] Later in the war, police officers from more diverse backgrounds would go undercover as well. The most famous of these was John Leopold, who was originally recruited as an informant but then became a full-time undercover Mounted Policeman because of his "ethnic" appearance and his fluency in Slavic languages. As a CHIS in the 1920s operating under the pseudonym of Jack Esselwein, he infiltrated the fledgling Communist Party of Canada and later became the most famous Mountie in Canada in the interwar period when his real identity was exposed and he testified against his former Communist comrades in an open courtroom.[36]

With the merger of the RNWMP with the Dominion Police, the security force in eastern Canada, the new Royal Canadian Mounted Police appeared in 1920. Its first commissioner, A.B. Perry, helped design the new intelligence agency and put a high priority on CHIS, although he warned that Mountie handlers should "be constantly on their guard against being purposely misled by the informants." One way to do this, he advised, was to have meetings covered by two informants operating independently from each other so that their reports could be compared against each other.[37]

The focus of CHIS for the next several decades when it came to intelligence investigations was almost exclusively on the Communist Party of Canada. This landscape began to change in the 1960s with the emergence of the New Left, Quebec nationalism, Red Power, Black Power, and other movements. The use of CHIS also emerged in the public domain in a controversial fashion that would serve as a preview of the controversy around their use in the post–Cold War, post–9/11 world. In 1961, a student at Laval University was approached by a member of the RCMP and asked to inform on two of her fellow students who were involved in the campus anti-nuclear movement. Instead, she told them about the approach and they went to the media; condemnation of the RCMP effort erupted.[38] This criticism, which the RCMP internally saw as Communist-orchestrated, led to restrictions on the ability of the RCMP to recruit informants on campus, although in practice the impact was negligible.[39] Periodically after the 1960s, controversy around specific CHIS informants would arise. In 1987, it emerged that an informant named Marc-André Boivin had supplied information on the Confederation of National Trade Unions for a number of years to the RCMP and CSIS.[40] In 1992, a journalist revealed that a well-known Quebec provincial cabinet minister in the government of Premier René Lévesque, Claude Morin, had been a paid RCMP informant in the 1970s.[41] Two years later, another journalist broke the story that Grant Bristow, prominent within Canadian far-right circles, had been in the employ of CSIS as an informant for six years.[42] In 2000, the news surfaced that the RCMP had blown up a shed at an oil site to provide credibility to an informant who was attempting to gain the confidence of a farmer who the police believed was engaged in sabotage against the oil industry.[43]

CHIS in Modern Counterterrorism

CHIS have been used and are being used not only in Canada but around the world in the context of domestic security. The post–Cold War security emphasis on counterterrorism has emphasized their significance. While technological surveillance remains important, it is not omnipotent. E-mail can be encrypted and used in different ways, with coded messages hidden within a digitized picture or messages saved in the draft section of an email account and accessed from there instead of being sent out through cyberspace. Rooms can be swept for bugs and terrorists can and do stop using telephones that are tapped or satellite telephones that reveal their location. Or, if they have to use a telephone, they speak in code with the knowledge that someone somewhere is listening in on the conversation.[44] In 1996, a US Congressional report explicitly addressed the limitations of such surveillance.

> They [technological surveillance methods] do not, however, provide sufficient access to targets such as terrorists or drug dealers who undertake their activities in secret or to the plans and intentions of foreign governments that are deliberately concealed from the outside world. Recruiting human sources — as difficult, imperfect, and risky as it is — often provides the only means of such access.[45]

Former FBI Director Robert Mueller echoes this point

> Human sources...often give us critical intelligence and information we could not obtain in other ways, opening a window into our adversaries' plans and capabilities. [They] can mean the difference between the FBI preventing an act of terrorism or crime, or reacting to an incident after the fact.[46]

Practitioners of counterterrorism have also resorted to CHIS, particularly informants, because of the nature of terrorism. By its core nature, terrorism is an activity of the feeble against the powerful. Weakness often equates with some form of marginalization, be it in terms of language, ethnicity, or religion, or a combination of all of these factors. As a result, as with other intelligence operations in the past, those countering terrorism are not usually drawn from those they are directing attention toward.[47] The increasing problem of Islamist terrorism fits into previous patterns of informant use in the Western world. Intelligence agencies and police services lack the expertise about Muslim communities in general, let alone about small terrorist cells within these groupings. Not surprisingly, then, to gain intelligence police and security agencies frequently have to recruit those on the inside or infiltrate others with a cultural and linguistic familiarity into targeted groups. In the United States, the FBI turned to informants as a solution to its lack of familiarity of Muslim communities. A November 2004 presidential directive required the Bureau to increase "human source" recruitment and control. In

2008, the FBI requested nearly US$13 million to manage its informant system, including through the creation of special software.[48] It was also during this period that the FBI recruited Philip Mudd from the CIA to play a senior role in directing its counterterrorism operations. One of his approaches was "Domain Management," which involved searching for threats within mapped ethnic communities, including through the recruitment of informants.[49]

The FBI's post–9/11 approach to counterterrorism demonstrates a fusion between the uses of informants in intelligence-type operations during the Cold War, such as the targeting of subversion, with the uses of informants in traditional crime fighting. This has led to frequent "sting" operations against alleged terrorists and the heavy involvement of informants in alleged terrorist plots. From 1999 to 2011, of 508 defendants in US terrorism cases, 48 per cent were targeted with informants, 31 per cent were arrested as part of a sting, and 10 per cent were involved in cases where the informant played a lead role in the alleged plot.[50] As will be shown later, this approach has also been used in counterterrorism cases in Canada.

CHIS and Controversy in the United States and the United Kingdom

The use of CHIS in the United States and the United Kingdom has generated different types of controversy and criticism in both countries. In the case of the former, where the CHIS emphasis is on informants, charges of entrapment through agent provocateur activities abound, although they have yet to find any traction with judges or juries in trials. The chief criticism has been that the role of the agent provocateur led to terrorist activities that otherwise would not have occurred. Take the example of Shahed Hussain, a Pakistani immigrant to the United States who arrived in the early 1990s. He eventually became an FBI informant to avoid a jail sentence and in 2004, at the behest of the Bureau, set up a sting in which he offered to sell a missile to two American Muslims for use in an attack on a Pakistani diplomat. Both men were later convicted and sentenced to fifteen years in prison. He then re-emerged in 2008 as an informant in a plot involving four men arrested for trying to blow up a New York City synagogue and shoot down a US military jet. He sold the men a phony bomb and missile, telling one of the men, "Allah didn't bring you here to work for Walmart."[51]

In another instance near Sacramento, California, an informant who received US$250,000 was heard in recordings berating an individual, who was subsequently charged with terrorism offences, for not following through on a promise to attend a terrorism training camp while in Pakistan: "You told me, 'I'm going to a camp. I'll do this, I'll do that.' You're sitting idle. You're wasting time. Be a man — do something!"[52] Then there were the Miami terrorism arrests in 2006, which the administration of President George W. Bush highlighted as the elimination of a serious plot against the United States. Seven men, involved in a bizarre religious group, were charged with various terrorism offences, including plotting to destroy the Sears Tower in Chicago. The Bureau used at least two informants pretending to be al-Qaeda operatives against them; one, who began informing about drug dealers to the New York City Police when he was sixteen, received US$40,000, while the other was paid double that amount. In the end, after two mistrials, a jury convicted five of the accused, although only one on all of the charges.[53]

In the United Kingdom, informants involved in counterterrorism have largely escaped controversy of the type experienced in the United States. A major reason for this is that informants, while still used in counterterrorism cases, do not play a public role in trials as in the American model; hence, their role largely escapes wider public scrutiny. Where controversy has erupted with respect to informants is in relation to their recruitment.[54] More widely in the UK, undercover police officers serving as CHIS in intelligence-led investigations of protest groups have received considerable critical attention. For example, there have been repeated cases of CHIS who had sexual relations with female and male activists they were spying on. In some of these situations, sexual intercourse has been part of a wider long-term relationship between the CHIS and the target. In two cases, the CHIS fathered children with the women they were simultaneously spying on.[55]

Recent Examples of CHIS Use in Canada

Trends in the development of Canada's intelligence agencies and their response to domestic security threats are similar to those in the United States and the United Kingdom. As recounted earlier, during the Cold War, CHIS played a significant role in surveillance against the Communist Party of Canada and then, particularly from the 1960s onward, against perceived and real threats from both the left and right sides of the political spectrum. That role was primarily led by the Royal Canadian Mounted Police Security Service until 1984 when it was replaced by the Canadian Security Intelligence Service. Even then the RCMP continued to play a role in national security investigations, including counterterrorism, particularly because CSIS does not have the power of arrest. At times, the provincial police forces in Canada's most populous provinces, Ontario and Quebec, would deploy CHIS in intelligence-led investigations.

Indeed, the CHIS activities of the provincial police forces, the Ontario Provincial Police (OPP) and Sûreté du Québec (SQ), have occasionally provoked debate and criticism. In the case of the latter, a well-publicized example of an undercover police officers potentially playing the role of an agent provocateur occurred in 2007 at a summit involving the leaders of Canada, the United States, and Mexico at Montebello, Quebec, when three "demonstrators" dressed as anarchists, including one carrying a rock, were confronted by other protesters. The SQ later admitted that all three men were police officers, although it denied that they were acting as agents provocateurs.[56] In Ontario, in 2010, in the lead up to the meeting of the Group of 20 (G20) conference in Toronto, at least twelve undercover police officers from a variety of forces infiltrated activist groups, including the Steelworkers Organization of Active Retirees and the Toronto Community Mobilization Network, who were preparing to carry out demonstrations. In the case of one Kitchener-Waterloo activist, who subsequently launched a lawsuit against the OPP, the undercover police officer, masquerading as a fellow activist, became a trusted friend, to the point that the CHIS would drive the target's mother to hospital for medical treatments. He later testified against his former protest comrades in a preliminary hearing. Another OPP CHIS moved in and lived with a group of activists in Guelph.[57]

The use of CHIS in post–9/11Canadian counterterrorism cases has also been evident. The most prominent involvement occurred in the so-called Toronto 18 case, in which a group of young Muslim Canadian men sought to carry out terrorist attacks within Canada, including against Prime Minister Stephen Harper. Several informants played a role in the investigation of the case, particularly two in significant roles. The most publicized was Mubin Shaikh, an openly radical Muslim, who provided weapons training to the men. The defence at the trial raised the issue of entrapment, but a judge subsequently ruled this as irrelevant. Unusually for informants, Shaikh actively courted media attention and would later publish a book about his exploits;[58] he also received nearly C$300,000 for his efforts.[59] It later emerged that a second informant played a more significant role, for which he was paid just under C$4 million along with money for debt repayments and dental work. Shaher Elsohemy, who had previously been an informant for CSIS, agreed to infiltrate the Toronto 18 plotters on behalf of the RCMP in return for a large payment. He originally asked for C$15 million, but a smaller amount was negotiated, although the payment remained controversial. He later testified against the plotters.[60]

Since then, CHIS in the form of both informants and undercover police officers have been involved in two other high-profile Canadian counterterrorism cases that at the time of writing are being tried. One involves two men accused of plotting to carry out an attack on a VIA passenger train travelling from Canada to the United States. That case, a joint American-Canadian investigation, apparently involved an FBI informant, according to American documents.[61] The other case is in British Columbia, where it is alleged that two individuals plotted to carry out a terrorist attack in the vicinity of the BC legislature in Victoria on Canada Day in 2013. The RCMP made it clear that it had used a number of investigative tools and had ensured that the explosive allegedly being constructed by the accused was harmless, prompting speculation that a CHIS had to be involved in a "Mr. Big"-style investigation, in which an undercover police officer poses as a criminal in order to encourage other criminal activity and collect evidence, or an American-style sting involving an informant or informants.[62]

Conclusion: Potential and Future Controversy

Both Canadian history and the use of CHIS in similar countries, specifically the United States and the United Kingdom, show that controversy, criticism, and potential scandal will emerge over the use of CHIS. In some respects, this is inevitable due to the nature of the work. As Julius Wachtel notes, "the individualized nature of police work makes routine oversight inconvenient, if not impossible… [t]he fluid and unpredictable nature of streetlevel encounters gives law enforcment bureaucracies limited leverage over their field personnel."[63] These circumstances are unlikely to change. Indeed, the more heavily regulated other types of surveillance become in the aftermath of the Snowden revelations, the more the potential there is for CHIS, with fewer restrictions, to be used, particularly in a Canada with a strong emphasis on counterterrorism as a security priority through new legislation. The increased use of CHIS would see a concomitant rise in the potential for controversy and scandal.

On the other hand, the option of not using surveillance by CHIS in counterterrorism cases does not really exist, for the simple reason that such intelligence collection is too valuable and the risk of not preventing potential terrorist attacks too great. CHIS use against non-violent activists is far more problematic and worthy of review because such tactics, in both the past and the present, have the appearance of being undemocratic.

There is, however, a third path, which involves greater transparency and regulation as a means of not eliminating problems but instead reducing or mitigating the circumstances that lead to scandal, controversy, and abuses. Treating human surveillance through CHIS the same as other types of intrusive surveillance, including requiring a warrant before it can be deployed, which was floated in the United States in the 1970s,[64] would be a start along this path.

Notes

1. Greg Weston, Glenn Greenwald, & Ryan Gallagher, "CSEC Used Airport Wi-Fi to Track Canadian Travellers: Edward Snowden Documents," *CBC News*, 30 January 2014, <http://www.cbc.ca/news/politics/csec-used-airport-wi-fi-to-track-canadian-travellers-edward-snowden-documents-1.2517881>; Anthony Cuthbertson, "UK Government Admits GCHQ Has Secret Warrantless Surveillance 'Arrangements,'" *International Business Times*, 29 October 2014, <http://www.ibtimes.co.uk/uk-government-admits-gchq-has-secret-warrantless-surveillance-arrangements-1472222>.

2. David Cunningham & Barb Browning, "The Emergence of Worthy Targets: Official Frames and Deviance Narratives within the FBI," (2004) 19:3 *Sociological Forum* 347.

3. David Lyon, "Surveillance as Social Sorting: Computer Codes and Mobile Bodies," in *Surveillance as Social Sorting: Privacy, Risk and Automated Discrimination*, ed. David Lyon (New York: Routledge, 2005) at 16.

4. David Lyon, "Airport Screening, Surveillance, and Social Sorting: Canadian Responses to 9/11 in Context," (2006) 48:3 *Canadian Journal of Criminology and Criminal Justice* 404.

5. See, for example, William J. Maxwell, *F.B. Eyes: How J. Edgar Hoover's Ghostreaders Framed African American Literature* (Princeton: Princeton University Press, 2015); David J. Garrow, *The FBI and Martin Luther King, Jr.* (New York: Viking, 1983); Christabelle Sethna, "High School Confidential: RCMP Surveillance of Secondary Student Activists," in *Whose National Security? Canadian State Surveillance and the Creation of Enemies*, eds. G. Kinsman, M. Steedman & D. Buse (Toronto: Between the Lines Press, 2000), 121–8; Gary Kinsman & Patrizia Gentile, *The Canadian War on Queers: National Security as Sexual Regulation* (Vancouver: UBC Press, 2010); Ward Churchill & Jim Vander Wall, *Agents of Repression: The FBI's Secret Wars Against the Black Panther Party and the American Indian Movement* (Boston: South End Press, 1988); David Cunnningham, *There's Something Happening Here: The New Left, the Klan, and FBI Counterintelligence* (Berkeley: University of California Press, 2005).

6. Jean-Paul Brodeur, "Undercover Policing in Canada: Wanting What Is Wrong," (1992) 18:1–2 *Crime, Law and Social Change* 105. See generally Gary T. Marx, "Thoughts on a Neglected Category of Social Movement Participant: The Agent Provocateur and the Informant," (1974) 80:2 *American Journal of Sociology* 402; Gary T. Marx, *Under Cover: Police Surveillance in America* (Los Angeles: University of California Press, 1988).

7. See generally Brodeur, *supra* note 6 at 109.

8. UK, United Kingdom Home Office, *Covert Human Intelligence Sources Code of Practice* (London: The Stationery Office, 2010), <www.gov.uk/government/uploads/system/uploads/attachment_data/file/97958/code-practice-human-intel.pdf>.

9. Rush Rosen, *The World Split Open: How the Modern Women's Movement Changed America* (New York: Penguin Books, 2001) at 240–60; Christabelle Sethna & Steve Hewitt, "Clandestine Operations: The Vancouver Women's Caucus, the Abortion Caravan, and the RCMP," (2009) 90:3 *Canadian Historical Review* 463.

10. Lee Romney, "The Trouble with Informants," *Houston Chronicle*, 12 August 2006.

11. Phillip Johnston, "MI5 Seeks 'Older, Wiser Women,'" *Daily Telegraph*, 10 May 2005, <http://www.telegraph.co.uk/news/uknews/1489703/MI5-seeks-older-wiser-women.html>; Michael Evans, "More Britons Are Turning to Terror, Says MI5 Director," *London Times*, 10 November 2006; Barney Calman, "Policing with Passion; Is the Met Police Still Prejudiced against Ethnic Minorities and Women?," *Evening Standard* (London), 10 July 2006.

12. James Risen & Eric Lichtblau, "Bush Lets U.S. Spy on Callers Without Courts," *New York Times*, 16 December 2005, <http://www.nytimes.com/2005/12/16/politics/16program.html?pagewanted=all&_r=0>.

13. See American Civil Liberties Union, "Unnecessary Evil: Blind Trust and Unchecked Abuse in America's Informant System," *American Civil Liberties Union*, <www.aclu.org/unnecessary-evil>.

14. US Government, *Supplementary Detailed Staff Reports on Intelligence Activities and the Rights of Americans Book III, Final Report of the Select Committee to Study Governmental Operations with Respect to Intelligence Activities, 94th Congress* (S Rep No 84-755) (Washington, DC: US Government Printing Office, 1976) at 229–30 [Church Committee Report].

15. *Ibid.*

16. Canada, Commission of Inquiry Concerning Certain Activities of the Royal Canadian Mounted Police, *Third Report: Certain R.C.M.P. Activities and the Question of Governmental Knowledge* (Ottawa: Supply and Services Canada, 1981) at 317.

17. Steve Hewitt, *Spying 101: The RCMP's Secret Activities at Canadian Universities, 1917–1997* (Toronto: University of Toronto Press, 2002) at 208–11; "Backgrounder No. 1 – The CSIS Mandate," CSIS, February 2005, <http://files.skokos.com/FC-09-3033/Letters-Sent/csis/act/__www.csis-scrs.gc.ca_nwsrm_bckgrndrs_bckgrndr01-eng.pdf>.

18. *Regulation of Investigatory Powers Act* 2000 (UK), c 23; "Covert Human Intelligence Sources," (n.d.), MI5, <https://www.mi5.gov.uk/home/about-us/how-we-operate/gathering-intelligence/covert-human-intelligence-sources.html>. See also Regulation of Investigatory Powers Act 2000 (UK), "Authorisation of Surveillance and Human Intelligence Sources," <http://www.legislation.gov.uk/ukpga/2000/23/part/II/crossheading/authorisation-of-surveillance-and-human-intelligence-sources>.

19. Jennifer Yang, "Activist Sues G20 Undercover Officer Who Was His 'Good Friend,'" *Toronto Star*, 25 April 2012, <http://www.thestar.com/news/gta/2012/04/25/activist_sues_g20_undercover_officer_who_was_his_good_friend.html>.

20. Wendy E. Dawson, *The Use of "Mr. Big" in Undercover Operations*, Course Materials (The Continuing Legal Education Society of British Columbia, 2011) at 5–7; See Edwin W. Kruisbergen, Deborah De Jong & Edward R. Kleemans, "Undercover Policing: Assumptions and Empirical Evidence," (2011) 51:2 *British Journal of Criminology* 394.

21. *Lopez v. United States*, 373 US 427 (1963) at 465, Brennan J., dissenting, cited in Richard C. Donnelly, "Judicial Control of Secret Agents" (1967) 76:5 *Yale Law Journal* 994 at 1009–10.

22. Larry Grathwohl & Frank Reagan, *Bringing Down America: An FBI Informant with the Weathermen* (New Rochelle, NY: Arlington House Publishers, 1976) at 122.

23. Glenn Greenwald, "The Strange and Consequential Case of Bradley Manning, Adrian Lamo and WikiLeaks," *Salon*, 18 June 2010, <http://

www.salon.com/2010/06/18/wikileaks_3/>; Ed Pilkington, "Hacker Who Betrayed Bradley Manning Expresses Regret over Possible Jail Term," *The Guardian*, 15 December 2011, <http://www.theguardian.com/world/2011/dec/15/hacker-adrian-lamo-bradley-manning-wikileaks>.

24. Kevin Poulsen, "WikiLeaks Volunteer Was a Paid Informant for the FBI," *Wired*, 27 June 2013. <http://www.wired.com/2013/06/wikileaks-mole/>.

25. Charles Arthur, Dan Sabbagh & Sandra Laville, "LulzSec Leader Sabu Was Working for Us, Says FBI," *The Guardian*, 7 March 2012, <http://www.theguardian.com/technology/2012/mar/06/lulz-sec-sabu-working-for-us-fbi>; Jake Davis, "Sabu, the FBI and Me: How His Light Sentence Affects the Hacking Landscape," *The Guardian*, 28 May 2014, <http://www.theguardian.com/commentisfree/2014/may/28/sabu-fbi-sentence-hackers-anonymous-lulz-sec>; Gabriella Coleman, "My Hacker, My Source, My Snitch," *Backchannel*, 10 November 2014, <https://medium.com/backchannel/my-best-hacker-source-was-snitching-for-the-feds-68414d6b552a>.

26. Jeff Sallot, "Canada Could Escape Attack, CSIS Says," *Globe and Mail*, 20 June 2006, <http://circ.jmellon.com/docs/view.asp?id=991>.; Hewitt, *supra* note 17 at 32.

27. Frank J. Donner, *The Age of Surveillance: The Aims and Methods of America's Political Intelligence System* (New York: Vintage Books, 1980) at 464.

28. Trevor Aaronson, "The Informants," 36:5 *Mother Jones* 30, <http://www.motherjones.com/politics/2011/08/fbi-terrorist-informants>.

29. Laura Payton, "C-51 Confusion Abounds As Tories Rush Anti-Terrorism Bill to Committee," *CBC News*, 22 February 2015, <http://www.cbc.ca/news/politics/c-51-confusion-abounds-as-tories-rush-anti-terrorism-bill-to-committee-1.2963569>; "Open Letter to Parliament: Amend C-51 or Kill It," *National Post*, 27 February 2015, <http://news.nationalpost.com/full-comment/open-letter-to-parliament-amend-c-51-or-kill-it>.

30. Church Committee Report, *supra* note 14 at 270.

31. Andrew Parnaby & Gregory S. Kealey, "The Origins of Political Policing in Canada: Class, Law, and the Burden of Empire," (2003) 41:2–3 *Osgoode Hall Law Journal* 211 at 215.

32. *Ibid.*; See also Reg Whitaker, Gregory Kealey & Andrew Parnaby, *Secret Service: Political Policing in Canada from the Fenians to Fortress America* (Toronto: University of Toronto Press, 2012).

33. Parnaby & Kealey, *supra* note 31 at 220–21.

34. *Ibid.* at 237–38.

35. Gregory S. Kealey, "The Early Years of State Surveillance of Labour and the Left in Canada: The Institutional Framework of the Royal Canadian Mounted Police Security and Intelligence Apparatus, 1918–26," (1993) 8:3 *Intelligence and National Security* 129; Steve Hewitt, *Riding to the Rescue:*

The Transformation of the RCMP in Alberta and Saskatchewan, 1914–1939 (Toronto: University of Toronto Press, 2006) at 83–8.

36. Steve Hewitt, "Royal Canadian Mounted Spy: The Secret Life of John Leopold/Jack Esselwein," (2000) 15:1 *Intelligence and National Security* 144.

37. Hewitt, *Riding to the Rescue, supra* note 35 at 88.

38. Steve Hewitt, "'Information Believed True': RCMP Security Intelligence Activities on Canadian University Campuses and the Controversy Surrounding Them, 1961–1971," (2000) 81:2 *Canadian Historical Review* 191.

39. *Ibid.*

40. Brodeur, *supra* note 6 at 116.

41. Steve Hewitt, *Snitch!: A History of the Modern Intelligence Informer* (New York: Continuum International Publishing Group, 2010) at 91–2.

42. Andrew Mitrovica, "Front Man," *The Walrus*, September 2004, <http://thewalrus.ca/front-man/>.

43. "RCMP Bombed Oil Site in 'Dirty Tricks' Campaign," *CBC News*, 10 November 2000, <http://www.cbc.ca/news/canada/rcmp-bombed-oil-site-in-dirty-tricks-campaign-1.188599>.

44. Craig Whitlock, "Al Qaeda Detainee's Mysterious Release," *The Washington Post*, 30 January 2006), <http://www.washingtonpost.com/wp-dyn/content/article/2006/01/29/AR2006012901044.html>; Paul Pillar, *Terrorism and U.S. Foreign Policy* (Washington: Brookings Institution Press, 2004) at 112.

45. Mark D. Villaverde, "Structuring the Prosecutor's Duty to Search the Intelligence Community for Brady Material," (2003) 88:5 *Cornell Law Review* 1471 at 1521, citing US, Commission on the Roles and Capabilities of the United States Intelligence Community, 103rd Cong, *Preparing for the 21st Century: An Appraisal of U.S. Intelligence* (Washington, DC: US Government Publishing Office, 1996) at 64, US Government Publishing Office, <www.gpoaccess.gov/int/report.html>.

46. US, Office of the Inspector General, *The Federal Bureau of Investigation's Compliance with the Attorney General's Investigative Guidelines* (Washington, DC: Office of the Inspector General, Department of Justice, 2005) at 65.

47. Amy Waldman, "Prophetic Justice," *Atlantic Monthly*, October 2006, <http://www.theatlantic.com/magazine/archive/2006/10/prophetic-justice/305234/>; Andrea Elliott, "Undercover Work Deepens Police-Muslim Tensions," *New York Times*, 27 May 2006, <http://www.nytimes.com/2006/05/27/nyregion/27muslim.html?pagewanted=all>;; Dan Eggen, "FBI Agents Still Lacking Arabic Skills," *Washington Post*, 11 October 2006, <http://www.washingtonpost.com/wp-dyn/content/article/2006/10/10/AR2006101001388.html>; See also Pamela Hess, "Intel Agencies Seek Help Recruiting Immigrants," *USA Today*, 17 May 2008, <http://usatoday30.usatoday.com/news/

washington/2008-05-16-intel-recruiting_N.htm>. Steve Hewitt, *The British War on Terror: Terrorism and Counter-Terrorism on the Home Front since 9/11* (London: Continuum, 2008).

48. Aaronson, *supra* note 28.

49. Scott Shane & Lowell Bergman, "F.B.I. Struggling to Reinvent Itself to Fight Terror," *New York Times*, 10 October 2006, <http://www.nytimes.com/2006/10/10/us/10fbi.html?pagewanted=all&_r=0>; Aaronson, *supra* note 28. See also Philip Mudd, *Takedown: Inside the Hunt for Al Qaeda* (Philadelphia: University of Pennsylvania Press, 2013)

50. Aaronson, *supra* note 28.

51. Aaronson, *supra* note 28 (quoting Shahed Hussain); William K. Rashbaum & Kareem Fahim, "Informer's Role in Bombing Plot," *New York Times*, 22 May 2009, <http://www.nytimes.com/2009/05/23/nyregion/23informant.html?pagewanted=all>; Deborah Hastings, "Terrorism Arrests: Snitch, Sting, Then Controversy," *Associated Press*, 24 May 2009; Brendan Lyons, "Mosque Welcomed in Informant," *Albany Times Union*, 8 August 2004. See also Dave Gilson, "FBI Spies and Suspects, in Their Own Words," *Mother Jones*, 10 August 2011, <http://www.motherjones.com/politics/2011/08/fbi-sting-greatest-hits>.

52. Don Thompson, "Tapes: FBI Informant Pushed Suspect into Al-Qaida Camp," *Los Angeles Daily News*, 1 March 2006; Lee Romney, Eric Bailey & Josh Meyer, "Sighting of Terrorist in Lodi Questioned," *Los Angeles Times*, 15 March 2006, <http://articles.latimes.com/2006/mar/15/local/me-lodi15>. See Waldman, *supra* note 47.

53. Mark Hosenball, "Terror Plot Takedown," *Newsweek*, 3 July 2006, <www.newsweek.com>; Bob Norman, "Have Terror, Will Travel," *New Times Broward-Palm Beach*, 22 November 2007, <www.browardpalmbeach.com>; Kirk Semple, "U.S. Falters in Terror Case Against 7 in Miami," *New York Times*, 14 December 2007, <http://www.nytimes.com/2007/12/14/us/nationalspecial3/14liberty.html>; Damien Cave & Carmen Gentile, "Five Convicted in Plot to Blow Up Sears Tower," *New York Times*, 12 May 2009, <http://www.nytimes.com/2009/05/13/us/13miami.html>.

54. Robert Verkaik, "Exclusive: How MI5 Blackmails British Muslims," *The Independent*, 21 May 2009, <http://www.independent.co.uk/news/uk/home-news/exclusive-how-mi5-blackmails-british-muslims-1688618.html>; Vikram Dodd, "Terrorism Act: 'They asked me to keep an eye on the Muslim community,'" *The Guardian*, 23 May 2011, <http://www.theguardian.com/uk/2011/may/23/terrorism-act-muslim>; Aviva Stahl, "Grassing: The Use and Impact of Informants in the 'War on Terror,'" 23:2 *Statewatch* 23, <www.statewatch.org>.

55. Rob Evans & Paul Lewis, "Undercover Police Had Children with Activists," *The Guardian*, 20 January 2012, <http://www.theguardian.com/uk/2012/jan/20/undercover-police-children-activists>. Also see

Paul Lewis & Rob Evans, *Undercover: The True Story of Britain's Secret Police* (London: Faber and Faber, 2013).

56. "Quebec Police Admit They Went Undercover At Montebello Protest," *CBC News*, 23 August 2007, <http://www.cbc.ca/news/canada/quebec-police-admit-they-went-undercover-at-montebello-protest-1.656171>; CanadiansNanaimo, "Police Provocateurs stopped by union leader at anti SPP protest," posted 20 August 2007. https://www.youtube.com/watch?v=St1-WTc1kow.

57. Adrian Morrow & Kim Mackrael, "Publication Ban Lifted on Identities of Undercover G20 Officers," *Globe and Mail*, 22 November 2011, <http://www.theglobeandmail.com/news/toronto/publication-ban-lifted-on-identities-of-undercover-g20-officers/article4184061/; Adrian Morrow & Kim Mackrael, "Undercover Officers Knew of Plans for Downtown Mayhem during G20," *Globe and Mail*, 23 November 2011, <http://www.theglobeandmail.com/news/toronto/undercover-officers-knew-of-plans-for-downtown-mayhem-during-g20/article555130/?page=all>; Tim Groves & Zach Dubinsky, "G20 Case Reveals 'Largest Ever' Police Spy Operation," *CBC News*, 22 November 2012, <http://www.cbc.ca/news/canada/g20-case-reveals-largest-ever-police-spy-operation-1.1054582>; Yang, *supra* note 19.

58. Anne Speckhard & Mubin Shaikh, *Undercover Jihadi: Inside the Toronto 18 – Al Qaeda Inspired, Homegrown Terrorism in the West* (Bassendean, Australia: Advance Press, 2014).

59. Tom Regan, "Is Using Informants in Terror Cases Entrapment?," *Christian Science Monitor*, 13 July 2006; Colin Freeze, "RCMP Agent Concedes Key Role in Set-Up, Running of Terrorist Training Camp," *Globe and Mail*, 31 January 2009; Isabel Teotonio, "No Entrapment, Court Rules in Terror Case," *Toronto Star*, 24 March 2009, <http://www.thestar.com/news/crime/2009/03/24/no_entrapment_court_rules_in_terror_case.html>. See John Miller & Cybele Sack, "The Toronto — 18 Terror Case: Trial by Media? How Newspaper Opinion Framed Canada's Biggest Terrorism Case," (2010) 10:1 *International Journal of Diversity in Organizations, Communities and Nations* 279.

60. Colin Freeze & Omar El Akkad, "Was Imam Another Informant in Toronto Terror Plot?," *Globe and Mail*, 16 January 2007, <www.theglobeandmail.com>; Colin Freeze, "How a Police Agent Cracked a Terror Cell," *Globe and Mail*, 2 September 2009, <www.theglobeandmail.com>; Michael Friscolanti, "Vindication for an Undercover Informant," *Maclean's*, 20 January 2010, <www.macleans.ca>; "Informant's motives Questioned in Toronto 18 Trial,", *CBC News*, 25 January 2010, <www.cbc.ca/news>; Blake Mobley, *Terrorism and Counterintelligence: How Terrorist Groups Elude Detection* (New York: Columbia University Press, 2013) at 218–19.

61. Colin Freeze, "U.S. officials: Train Terror Suspect Suggested Bacteria Plot," *Globe and Mail*, 9 May 2013, <www.theglobeandmail.com>.
62. Steven Chase et al, "RCMP Thwarts Alleged Plot to Bomb B.C. Legislature on Canada Day," *Globe and Mail*, 2 July 2013, <www.theglobeandmail.com>; Bob Mackin, "What Role Did RCMP Play in BC Bomb Plot?," *The Tyee*, 4 July 2013, <thetyee.ca/news>; Bill Tieleman, "Accused's Lawyer Believes Leg Bomb Plot Involved RCMP Sting," *The Tyee*, 13 August 2013, <thetyee.ca>. See generally Dawson, *supra* note 20 for more on "Mr Big" tactics.
63. Julius Wachtel, "From Morals to Practice: Dilemmas of Control in Undercover Policing," (1992) 18 *Crime, Law and Social Change* 137.
64. Federal Bureau of Investigation, *Exhibit 33: Request for Information Concerning This Bureau's Operation of Informants in the Internal Security Field, Church Committee* (Washington, DC: Congress, 1975).

PART II

LEGAL ISSUES

CHAPTER III

Foreign Intelligence in an Inter-Networked World: Time for a Re-Evaluation

Tamir Israel

The recent and dramatic expansion of foreign intelligence surveillance activities, revealed definitively in a trove of documents made public by former NSA analyst Edward Snowden, can be traced to a few drivers. First and foremost, technical changes have made an immense amount of data practically accessible and analyzable in ways that have no precedent in human history. Most of our activities have migrated to digital networks, raising distinct implications in the foreign intelligence-gathering context. Digital networks do not route in direct lines.[1] Moreover, most digital interactions are intermediated through one or more entities, often based in foreign jurisdictions. Cloud-based data is often stored redundantly on multiple servers, each in its own jurisdiction. Foreign intelligence agencies can now clandestinely monitor the world's communications from their own territory, without the practical impediments inherent in sending agents to foreign lands. Additional technical interoperability between foreign intelligence partners, particularly within the Five Eyes partnership (Australia, Canada, New Zealand, the United Kingdom, and the United States) (hereafter FVEY) has facilitated an unprecedented integration of foreign intelligence capacities, extending the monitoring and analysis capacities.[2] Finally, technical advances in data *storage* make retention of vast amounts of information possible in ever-growing volumes.[3]

At the same time, foreign intelligence has been rapidly shifting its focal point from foreign states and their agents (the Cold War "spy vs. spy" paradigm that characterized much of the history of Western foreign intelligence agencies) to a "spy on everyone" mindset driven by a terrorist-based threat matrix and a new collect-it-all mentality.[4] This operational shift has had tangible impacts as agencies begin to push the limits of their already broad powers and their ever increasing technical capacities to collect, analyze, and keep "everything."

These shifts in technical capacities and intelligence culture have been accompanied by broadly framed legal powers that do little to check excesses that might result. Canada's foreign intelligence agency, the Communications Security Establishment (CSE), derives its legal mandate and surveillance authorization framework from Part V.1 of the *National Defense Act (NDA)*.[5] The framework is modelled on the same rationale and general structure as that of other FVEY agencies — open-ended powers limited primarily by an obligation to limit the exposure of domestic individuals and a need to show some nexus to a foreign intelligence objective.[6]

The analysis below argues that the core limitations placed on CSE in its foreign intelligence mandate are ineffective at constraining its activities.[7] Before embarking on this substantive assessment, however, we first describe shortcomings in CSE's control structure, which exacerbate the inherent breadth of its legal restrictions by focusing too heavily on oversight.

Oversight and Accountability: Loose Assurances of Legality from behind a Veil of Secrecy

CSE is subjected to minimal legal control, even when measured by the standard of its FVEY partners.[8] The NSA, for example, operates under similarly broad legal restrictions, but is subjected to some non-partisan legislative and loose judicial control.[9] CSE's legal restrictions can in essence be reduced to four primary constraints. It relies on ministerial authorizations (to intercept private communications) or ministerial directives as lawful authority for its privacy invasive activities. Its activities must be in pursuit of its mandate, statutorily defined in the NDA (the *Privacy Act* also limits it to collecting information relevant to its mandate).[10] It is statutorily prevented from directing its activities at Canadians. It cannot, of course, violate the *Charter*. The substantive scope of each is explored in more detail in the following sections. Here, we examine how the executive branch essentially interprets and applies these legal restraints on its own, with no external controls from either the judiciary or legislative branch of government. The executive is effectively left as the primary if not sole arbiter of its own legal restraints. Against this backdrop, official defence of CSE often amounts to publicly compelling, yet ultimately meaningless, statements that CSE "operates within the law."

As in many contexts, the modern technological era poses great challenges, as legal concepts struggle to keep pace with rapidly evolving and highly complex contexts. This leads to many ambiguities that are central to the scope and nature of the legal restraints imposed on CSE. Determination of these ambiguities can significantly change the scope of permitted activities. While *Charter* privacy protections should develop in a technologically neutral manner,[11] understanding the implications of shifting practices in new technological mediums can be a difficult exercise, confounding attempts at oversight and control.[12] In the absence of rigorous and adversarial challenge, these ambiguities and complexities are often resolved in favour of the foreign intelligence agency that is implementing the powers in question.

Even in the presence of judicial control (but lacking adversarial input and with only a loose review mandate), understanding the evolving technical landscape has been difficult. The Foreign Intelligence Surveillance Court (FISC), for example, found in 2011 that the NSA Internet surveillance program it had been regularly approving for five years was significantly broader in scope than it had understood: "[The Government] disclosed... for the first time that NSA's upstream collection of Internet communications... may contain data that is wholly unrelated to the tasked selector."[13] The "Upstream" program referred to is one of the NSA's most expansive electronic surveillance mechanisms.[14] It, along with its sister program PRISM, harvests billions of transactions from communications networks daily, most of which are retained for thirty days, with hundreds of millions retained longer term.[15] Since 2006, FISC had believed it was approving interception of discrete communications of specific targets. In 2011, it realized entire Internet transactions were being collected, indiscriminately sweeping up mass amounts of domestic and untargeted data alongside each discrete target, yet the program had been regularly approved for five years without this central understanding. A process open to adversarial input would have forced FISC to confront this factual inaccuracy far sooner.[16]

Similar issues have arisen with respect to CSE's activities. The Federal Court found in *Re X* that it had significantly underestimated the scope of activities undertaken by CSE when authorized to assist Canadian Security Intelligence Service (CSIS) monitor communications of Canadians abroad.[17] Since 2009, the court had understood it was authorizing the monitoring of such communications as they transited through Canadian-based networks.[18] However, CSE was secretly tasking its FVEY partners' formidable intercept capacities in conjunction with this "from home" surveillance.[19] The government's defence of its omission was that it required no authorization in this context. It is an interpretation that highly favours its position and robs the court of the ability to evolve the law to account for new realities, such as the increasingly expansive scope of FVEY surveillance capabilities. However, this legal interpretation is not patently unreasonable.[20] It should not be a surprise that the government, on its own initiative and in the absence of adversarial input, reached this conclusion, or that it will reach similar conclusions in the future.

These examples demonstrate that even with the presence of nominal judicial scrutiny, applying legal restraints to the activities of foreign intelligence agencies has proven a challenge. Far from robust mechanisms for rigorous adversarial challenge, CSE operates without the prospect of even sparse external control. Given the clandestine nature of CSE's intelligence-gathering mandate, some secrecy is required. However, this does not mean CSE can be relieved of all public accountability and the rule of law. The application, interpretation, and implementation of the four legal constraints referred to above occurs primarily on the basis of internal legal opinions from the Department of Justice. Neither this underlying legal reasoning nor the ministerial authorizations and directives and CSE activities that are based on this reasoning are made public. Additionally, CSE is free from any parliamentary control or even scrutiny.[21] Canadians are left to trust, but can never verify legality.

Its primary oversight mechanism is the CSE commissioner, an autonomous former judge with independent budget appropriation.[22] The commissioner assesses CSE's activities for compliance with the various legal restrictions placed on it. Having access to secret CSE activities, internal documents, and even privileged opinions, the commissioner can provide a critical independent voice in internal CSE and ministerial decision making. In addition, the commissioner's annual reports can provide an avenue to enhanced public debate around CSE activities. However, the commissioner's recommendations are not binding and are often ignored on issues of central importance.[23] Further, the commissioner's annual reports are cryptic, rarely providing meaningful insight into specific CSE activities.[24] They typically focus more on describing the commissioner's own oversight activities, with specific issues addressed at a high level of generality. As the commissioner never publicizes the legal reasoning underpinning his oversight (receipt of privileged communications may even prevent this),[25] there is no opportunity for the academic or legal community to challenge these without significant guesswork or a whistle-blower.

Problems with the existing framework abound. For example, CSE was granted the power to incidentally intercept private communications of Canadians under ministerial authority. Several commissioners disagreed with CSE's legal interpretation of this authority, arguing it unjustifiably broadened what CSE can do.[26] Successive commissioners were nonetheless obligated to assess the legality of CSE's activities based on its own prevailing interpretation. In his final report, Commissioner Lamer noted that his "one regret" was leaving his position "without a resolution of the legal interpretation issues that have bedevilled this office since December 2001."[27] CSE is often publicly defended with assertions that no commissioner had ever found CSE activities to be in violation of the law.[28] The value of these assessments is significantly undermined as they are premised on legal interpretations that the commissioners themselves found inadequate. It is concerning that meaningful details regarding the nature of the disagreements in question only emerged in the public reports in 2008 — six years after they were first identified.[29] Even then, the object of the dispute was disclosed, but not the substance or legal basis of the disagreement.

Another example arises from *Re X*. In late 2013, Commissioner Décary's first post-Snowden annual report mentioned that CSIS had provided incomplete information to the Federal Court when it sought a new legal framework for CSE assistance in monitoring Canadians abroad in 2009.[30] The missing information in question led to a judicial reformulation of the legal framework for CSE/CSIS assistance.[31] Some have pointed to this as an example of a *functioning* CSE oversight system. However, CSE/CSIS did not comply with Commissioner Décary's recommendation to provide the court with more information. Mr. Justice Mosley, who had issued the initial 2009 framework authorization, read the report on his own volition and mandated CSIS/CSE to provide the information.[32] Justice

Mosley had no obligation to read this report and, had it not come to his personal attention, the reconsideration is not likely to have occurred. Moreover, this particular scenario implicated CSE in its (c) assistive mandate (see also note 7). CSIS must obtain prior judicial authorization to seek CSE assistance in intercepting private communications. Had a comparable scenario arisen with respect to CSE's independent foreign intelligence activities, there would be no Federal Court judge with jurisdiction to proactively assess the issue in this manner. In addition, important details that Justice Mosley found necessary for his assessment came from the Security Intelligence Review Committee's (tasked with reviewing CSIS) annual report, which provides significantly more substantive operational details.[33]

The Privacy Commissioner of Canada also has oversight powers with respect to CSE operations. However it, too, can only issue recommendations and only with respect to limited protections encoded in the *Privacy Act*. Both the Privacy and CSE commissioners provide valuable input into CSE's internal assessment processes, enhancing its attempts to properly account for important counter-interests such as fundamental rights and freedoms. Many of the recommendations that these bodies provide CSE are adopted voluntarily. However, a system that relies almost solely on secret internal policies and non-binding recommendations is not one constrained by law. Key disagreements over central legal ambiguities remain unresolved and colour all the assessments carried out by these bodies. In effect, the oversight occurs against a yardstick defined by CSE itself, "put[ting] at risk the integrity of the review process."[34] Such a system is not capable of ensuring that the extraordinary powers granted to CSE are being employed in a proportionate manner.

Ministerial Authorizations and Directives: Lack of Any Meaningful Control

Compounding the general secrecy that pervades CSE's accountability regime is a general lack of external control. The Minister of National Defence ("Minister") is the only entity empowered to legally control CSE, which relies on ministerial authorizations and directives as lawful authority for its surveillance activities.[35] The Minister is also able to issue further discretionary operational directives that are binding on CSE.[36] Neither Parliament nor the courts nor any independent tribunal play any role in controlling CSE. Like any government action, CSE's activities can, of course, be challenged in court, as can its underlying statutory framework.[37] However, such challenges will by necessity be rare, as CSE's activities and the ministerial authorizations and directives that underpin them remain shrouded in secrecy. Also, CSE activities rarely appear in judicial proceedings. In the absence of a whistle-blower, adversarial legal challenge to CSE's expansive *activities* is unlikely.

Section 8 of the *Charter* requires that the state obtain prior authorization issued by an "entirely neutral and impartial" arbiter.[38] The purpose of section 8 is "to protect individuals from unjustified state intrusions upon their privacy," and this requires that a neutral arbiter determine whether a particular intrusion is justified, whenever possible. The minister is, in the words of one expert commentator, "many things, but a disinterested judicial officer he is not."[39] CSE receives its foreign intelligence target priorities from the minister (and the rest of cabinet). Specifically, the minister is responsible for establishing CSE's foreign intelligence-gathering priorities.[40] That the minister is at once the arbiter of investigative priorities *and* the legitimacy of investigative techniques used to achieve those priorities is deeply problematic. The minister of national defence would naturally be guided by a range of public policy and expediency concerns when setting CSE's intelligence priorities, rendering him incapable of acting judicially when determining whether a particular privacy invasive activity is or is not justified.[41]

Prior judicial authorization is the default requirement for constitutional privacy invasion, but the particular circumstances of a given context can justify departures from this general rule.[42] Diminished expectations of privacy, exigent situations, and investigative contexts where secrecy is necessary can all justify modifications from the standard procedural requirements.[43] However, in each of these instances, there must be some mechanism for meaningful judicial review and adversarial challenge.[44] Similarly, some (but not all) of CSE's intelligence-gathering activities relate to national security. However, the heightened concerns inherent in national security may not, in the absence of demonstrable practical challenges, justify forgoing judicial authorization with respect to digital interactions that attract high expectations of privacy.[45] In this context, the information obtained by these privacy invasive activities may result in adverse consequences for individuals (such as placement on a no-fly list or worse), but affected individuals are not likely to ever discover CSE intelligence as the source of such impacts. The surveillance itself is highly surreptitious despite its far-reaching scope. Judicial review is a highly unlikely prospect.

Nor do the circumstances in question justify excluding the judiciary from the process. Ministerial authorizations were chosen in lieu of judicial authorization because it was presumed that Canadian courts lack the jurisdiction to authorize surveillance activities occurring in foreign territories.[46] This is no longer a sustainable premise. Indeed, Bill C-44, which became law on April 23, 2015, explicitly grants Canadian judges the ability to "authorize activities outside Canada to enable [CSIS] to investigate a threat to the security of Canada."[47] CSE is permitted to assist CSIS in carrying out these extraterritorial investigations.[48] A similar provision could readily be employed to ground judicial authorization of CSE surveillance activities abroad. CSIS is tasked with a similar investigative mandate and operates under prior judicial authorization.[49] There is no practical reason not to impose some form of judicial control onto CSE.

The provisions guiding CSE's authorization are equally problematic, and so broad that even a court would have difficulty constraining CSE's activities through them. The minister may authorize CSE to "intercept private communications in relation to an activity or class of activities" if satisfied that Canadian privacy is protected, that the information could not be otherwise obtained, and that the anticipated value of the intelligence justifies the interception.[50] Because authorization occurs on the basis of "activities or classes of activities," consideration of whether the "particular interests that could be compromised" by the authorized surveillance justify it or not occurs at a high level of generality and fails to account for specific privacy interests.[51] The lack of a clear reasonable grounds standard to measure the authorization justification framework exacerbates this breadth.[52] Courts have recognized that national security investigations may require a different kind of specificity than traditional criminal investigations, tailored to the anticipatory nature of the investigations.[53] However, Canadian courts have *not* accepted the proposition that national security concerns can justify a lower standard for invading high expectations of privacy.[54] The breadth of the current standard allows CSE almost limitless latitude in determining the scope of its privacy-violating activities.

As broad as the legislated authorization standard is, CSE has interpreted it to be even broader — the Minister need only authorize "classes of communications interception activities," as opposed to interceptions of private communications in relation to specific activities or targets. Commissioners have noted that this interpretation is not supported by the statute and unduly expands CSE's authorization regime.[55] It allows the Minister of National Defence to frame his authorizations so broadly that only three are required for CSE's entire foreign intelligence interception program.[56] This alone speaks to their expansive breadth and lack of specificity.

Commissioners have also pointed to CSE's misinterpretation of the term "interception" as having obscure "legal and operational significance."[57] We know that most FVEY interception programs rely on network level filtering — all network traffic and phone calls are continually searched for matches on tasked keywords.[58] CSE itself has over two hundred sensors filtering network traffic around the world, and is further able to task other FVEY agency interception resources.[59] Some FVEY agencies only consider an interception to occur when network traffic is "accessed." Filtering conducted by ISP equipment (under order from the agency) is not engaged.[60] Another argument sometimes presented by FVEY agencies is that "interception" only occurs (and privacy is only implicated) when specific communications are acquired and retained. For example, the commissioner recently described CSE's wiretapping activities only in terms of "accidentally collected" and "retained" private communications, while ignoring how many private communications were "searched" for keywords.[61] Either argument greatly skews the privacy analysis by disregarding significant analytical activity — the private communications of millions can be scoured for selectors, yet only the "hits" count. Non-collected communications monitored for keywords are clearly "searched," if only to confirm that they do *not* include the keyword in question.[62] Simply knowing that one's communications are being scanned for certain words can have a serious chilling effect.

CSE's legal framework is also flawed in its application to "metadata," data *about* a communication. CSE is operating under the assumption that metadata is not considered a "private communication."[63] As a result, CSE's activities (its own collection as well its use of FVEY resources) are different in character and scope if it classifies data as "metadata" or "content." Metadata does not fall under the ministerial authorization regime, which only regulates interception of private communications. Instead, under a single ministerial directive, CSE gathers "huge amounts" of metadata, "on large numbers of people."[64] Internet metadata is often difficult to distinguish from "content": a Facebook ID provides you with access to the profile itself; a URL permits you to see the web page or other resource viewed; the URL for an online search will include the search query.[65] Even traditional phone metadata can be highly revealing of the objects of the call itself.[66] Whereas most definitions of metadata exclude data that would reveal the purpose of the communication it relates to, CSE defines it broadly.[67] It includes URLs of web resources, Facebook identifiers, search queries, and even document-authoring information.[68] There is no basis for treating such metadata differently from content; they equally implicate our private lives.[69]

Attempts to moderate the inherent breadth of CSE's lawful authorization come in the form of targeting and minimization limitations. These involve general processes (explored below) designed to limit impact on Canadian privacy, not to target surveillance on intelligence targets.[70] Even if effective, such mechanisms would never be reassuring, as CSE would still be able to monitor all communications indiscriminately and will have infiltrated the infrastructure necessary to do so. Its powers are so broad that they disregard the privacy of millions around the world in order to obtain small iotas of potentially useful information. For example, one Government Communications Headquarters, or GCHQ, input into a joint FVEY resource collected millions of Yahoo customer private video chats, without regard to whether specific accounts were targets or not.[71] GCHQ explored expanding this intake to include video/audio cameras increasingly found in living rooms.[72] One sample of NSA-acquired and retained communications data revealed medical records, resumes, children's academic transcripts, sensitive pictures, and embarrassing comments of innocent individuals.[73] The ratio of targeted to non-targeted individuals whose data was collected and retained in this sample was 1:9 (not counting irrelevant information on targets). Once collected, mining of this dataset is determined by CSE itself, not the minister, and not on the basis of any individualized suspicion of wrongdoing. While the *Privacy Act* imposes a "relevance" requirement, other agencies have defined this to mean a "two-to-three degree of separation" model of suspicion, which scales rapidly on digital networks.[74] Moreover, while the NSA relevance criteria are at least tied to a particular investigation, CSE's relevance is only tied to its general foreign intelligence mandate.

Even as the sensitivity of digital data has increased over the past decade, FVEY agencies have decided that "all" communications are relevant to their mandate because they generate general intelligence capacities that are useful.[75] Doubtless, these various programs have had some investigative value in important efforts to prevent serious threats to life and limb. But their formulation makes no attempt to account for the disproportionate impact this approach has on our private digital lives. The prevailing "collect everything" mindset is not effectively mitigated by minimal steps to limit subsequent access and use. As explored in the next section, the near-limitless mandate that governs the use of these collected treasure troves is, on the one hand, far broader than the existential terrorist threat that is often its public face and, on the other, poses a direct threat to democracy as we know it.

Foreign Intelligence: A Mandate with Few Limits and Substantial Potential for Abuse

Defences of the incredibly broad powers granted to CSEC and its Five Eyes counterparts often focus on the need to prevent serious terrorist or other existential threats; however, this is a "misleadingly narrow sales pitch."[76] The term *foreign intelligence* itself is defined in broad terms as information "about the capabilities, intentions or activities of a foreign individual, state, organization or terrorist group, as they relate to international affairs, defence or security."[77] It couples a strong focus on counterterrorism with an enduring interest in political intentions and a general need for situational awareness.[78] Substantively, this has evolved to include a broad range of objectives and intelligence agencies have used their powers to further political or economic objectives and, fundamentally, as a vehicle for advancing *any* national interest.[79] The mandate is problematic for its all-inclusiveness, but also for its application to the intentions of foreign individuals who are neither representatives of a foreign power nor agents of a terrorist organization. As the need to act within its mandate (and restrict collection to mandate-relevant intelligence) is one of the central substantive limitations on CSE's surveillance activities, this breadth of purpose and application is concerning.

Expansive foreign intelligence powers are increasingly used to gain domestic economic and political advantages. Information is gathered to "assist a [FVEY] member government engaged in

sensitive international negotiations — be they diplomatic or economic."[80] Foreign intelligence agencies are playing a bigger role in
advising the government on economic decision making.[81] A recent
government focus on international trade agreements is expected to
lead to even greater government "demands for information on...
economic/prosperity issues."[82] It can also include situational awareness of various economic and political issues that Canadian cabinet
ministers decide are priorities.[83] This has included, for example, use
of extensive FVEY surveillance capacities to spy on the Brazilian
ministry in charge of mining rights, to spy on economic meetings
such as the G20 summits in London and Toronto, to seize data from
the lawyer of a foreign government in the midst of negotiations, to
insert malicious spyware targeting trade institutions within the EU,
to directly exploit private networks used by businesses such as banks
and telecommunications companies, and to spy on other countries
in preparation for a summit on environmental issues.[84] It has even
included targeting of UN Secretary General Ban Ki-Moon for the
less than life-preserving objective of obtaining his talking points
in advance of a meeting with President Obama.[85] These objectives
accompany the more serious national security concerns, and the
same investigative techniques (the same databases, in fact) fuel both.
Moreover, FVEY mandates also include "understanding the global
communications infrastructure," a broad and open-ended objective
that appears to permit random and unfettered experiments on collected data.[86]

    With respect to terrorism, it has long been recognized that an
unchecked security investigative mandate poses a serious threat
to core democratic values. This threat arises from the open-ended
nature of security investigations and the close proximity between
security concerns and unpopular (but important) political views,
making privacy protections all the more important in this context.[87]
The inherent breadth of the security concept, which necessarily
adopts an open-ended threat model, renders attempts to prevent
detrimental impact difficult.[88] Recent examples have confirmed that
the temptation to use expansive security-based powers for other
objectives is difficult to resist. Australia was recently rebuked for
spying on communications between East Timor and its lawyer in the
course of an arbitration dispute, putatively for national security.[89]
Canada's own domestic experience with security intelligence confirms this — decades of abuse of security power harmed legitimate

political activities, forcing Parliament to sever security intelligence investigations from the RCMP's mandate and vest these in an independent agency, CSIS.[90] CSE itself is expressly empowered to assist domestic agencies with their own respective investigations, and repurposes its vast intelligence holdings when doing so.[91] Far from taking steps to address these problems, CSE's foreign intelligence mandate heightens the threat by overtly combining political and economic objectives alongside security.

Historically, the inherent breadth and heightened human rights risk inherent in the foreign intelligence concept were tempered by a focus on foreign powers and their agents.[92] In the wake of 9/11, this focus was broadened to include not only terrorist organizations and their agents but any information about the "intentions" of any "foreign individual" in relation to "international affairs." We have since seen the formidable powers of FVEY agencies levelled at individual financial transactions conducted through text messaging;[93] prominent Muslim community leaders with no terrorist affiliation;[94] civil society groups engaged in public advocacy on human rights issues;[95] and journalists critical of the US government's response to 9/11.[96] Some FVEY agencies have carried out cyber attacks designed to disrupt online discussion forums used by hacktivists and political dissidents.[97]

This is problematic because the integrated nature of modern digital networks not only places most individual interactions within reach of FVEY surveillance systems, but also leads to policy resolution that increasingly occurs on the international stage. Much of this now falls within the potential purview of foreign intelligence agencies, as it relates to the "intentions" of "foreign individuals" in relation to "international affairs." As argued in the next sections, this integration not only means that the wide net cast by foreign intelligence agencies captures significant swaths of domestic data, but also seriously questions the ongoing legitimacy of the prevailing foreign intelligence paradigm, rooted in a disregard for the privacy rights of foreigners. In particular, the migration of political debate to the international stage and the focus on "individuals" who are neither "foreign powers" nor "agents" of terrorist groups suggests that the same hazards historically recognized in the domestic security context are present — and must be addressed — on the international stage.

Five Eyes on the World's Communications: A Global Problem with No Global Solution

Perhaps the most substantive legal check on CSE's surveillance capacities is the prohibition on "directing" its activities at Canadians and the requirement to minimize the impact of its activities on Canadians' privacy if their data is collected incidentally.[98] This approach is more effective as a rhetorical tool than at protecting Canadians' privacy.[99] Nor is it acceptable to ignore the privacy of non-Canadians. The prohibition on directing CSE activities at Canadian persons (defined as any person in Canada or Canadian abroad) expressly permits the targeting of communications *known* to include those of Canadians, while prohibiting the *purposive* targeting of Canadian individuals. For CSE, to direct at or target means "to single out."[100] In the traditional phone context, this means that if you are directing your wiretap at someone outside of Canada and that person phones a Canadian, that call is fair game as an incidental collection.[101] On digital networks, however, traffic routing is "all intermixed together," meaning that any mass-scale collection of foreign communications is guaranteed to include significant amounts of Canadian data.[102]

With respect to interception of private communications ("content"), CSE filters communications streams en masse at key Internet traffic points.[103] It likely uses metadata selectors or keywords (e-mail addresses, telephone numbers, IP addresses with a probability of foreignness) to scan all communications passing through its network filters; all hits are collected.[104] Other agencies filter both the designated "to/from" fields of communications *and* their text-based content ("about" communications), meaning that an e-mail, text, or Facebook message referencing a targeted phone number would be collected.[105] CSE's definition of metadata selectors in this context might be broad enough to include URLs, Facebook account identifiers, or document-authoring information, in which case these, too, would be hits if present in an e-mail text or attachment.[106] The minister only authorizes "classes of monitoring activities," so CSE selects targeting keywords and applies them to monitored communications streams by itself.[107] With respect to private communications incidentally acquired, CSE must minimize the impact on Canadians by expeditiously determining whether these are "essential" to foreign intelligence.[108] In 2013, sixty-six private communications of Canadians were retained for current and future use.[109] The number likely does not represent discrete communications, but rather communications streams (all text messages between 613-555-5555 and <foreign number>).[110] Moreover, this only represents *retained* communications. The reported NSA 1:9 intake relevance ratio suggests that an additional 594 Canadian communications (streams) were collected, analyzed, and eventually discarded.[111] By comparison, the RCMP's extensive domestic mandate rested in its entirety on 700 intercepted communications in 2012.[112]

Metadata is not only collected and used to identify what content to collect, but increasingly for its own intelligence value. This is governed by different rules. CSE cannot "direct metadata analysis at Canadians" but, critically, the statutory obligation to expeditiously identify and delete Canadian data not deemed "essential" only applies to "private communications" (i.e., *not* metadata).[113] Instead, post-collection minimization procedures for metadata are anaemic, limited to suppressing identifying details of Canadians in derived intelligence reports.[114] Neither the deletion of metadata known to belong to Canadians,[115] nor the placement of meaningful restrictions on its analysis is required; CSE analysts can access Canadian metadata without even seeking senior management approval.[116]

It is clear CSE has a lot of Canadian metadata at its disposal. It adopts a permissive definition of "directed at Canadians" that allows extensive use of this metadata. One revealed CSE program in particular involved an analytical model designed to "track" individuals by correlating identifiers (Facebook and Google cookie IDs, e-mail addresses) associated with geolocated Wi-Fi network IP addresses.[117] A metadata packet timestamped at 11 a.m. containing "canuck@ maple.ca" and an IP address known to be used by a particular cafe's Wi-Fi network is an accurate indicator of canuck's location. No metadata was collected for the program, meaning that the extensive underlying metadata set is indicative of CSE's regular holdings.[118] The program description notes that in one tested Canadian city over 300,000 active IDs associated with two sets of public Wi-Fi networks were identified in a short two-week period — a lot of Canadian metadata.[119] Despite the fact that the test program was clearly directed at people within Canada ("at Canadians"), its defenders argued it was not "directed at Canadians" because it did not "identify any individual Canadian."[120] This approach is inconsistent with the *Privacy Act* definition of personal information by which CSE claims to be bound, and which has been held to clearly apply to similar data analytics.[121] If CSE does not consider this program to be "directed at Canadians," then there are few limits on the extensive analysis it can make of its Canadian metadata.[122]

This permissive approach to Canadian metadata is particularly problematic in light of CSE's access to FVEY resources. Active integration of CSE and other FVEY resources, including tasking intercept capacities and access to shared databases through interoperable interfaces has been underway since at least 2010.[123] Some CSE analytic programs make highly integrated use of FVEY metadata databases.[124] The FVEY agencies that create these databases are not legally prevented from targeting Canadians in their acquisition programs and, in fact, many operate under the assumption that their constitutional privacy obligations have no extraterritorial application. The databases and capacities in question are therefore generated without any legal obligation to respect the human rights of Canadians. When using these databases, CSE remains bound by the prohibition on "directing its activities at Canadians." However, with respect to metadata at least, CSE appears to consider it appropriate to analyze Canadian-rich datasets in its foreign intelligence programs. Moreover, CSE uses its entire metadata resources (inclusive of FVEY resources) when assisting domestically empowered agencies such as the RCMP and CSIS under its (c) mandate, without distinction as to how the underlying data was collected.[125] Recently introduced Bill C-51 seeks to dramatically expand this domestic element of CSE's activities by granting CSIS an open-ended digital disruption mandate, which will be implemented through CSE assistance, with all the FVEY resources at its disposal.[126]

This round robin — whereby each agency operates under no legal restrictions when spying on the citizens of its FVEY allies, and the spoils of the exercise are shared by all — raises a number of issues. While it is indisputable that privacy is an internationally recognized human right, FVEYs argue that their obligations to respect this right stop at their respective territorial borders. Additionally, some have argued that the context of foreign intelligence in particular operates as a categorical "exception" to privacy. On these bases, each FVEY agency deems itself free to spy on the world's communications networks as long as they do not target domestic citizens. Neither of these arguments is sustainable in the modern era. Digital communications networks are too intertwined for the status quo — where everything "foreign" is fair game — to continue.

While historical limitations on extraterritorial privacy obligations were steeped in principles of comity, the ability to spy on political leaders and citizens of allies without restriction does more to undermine than "facilitate interstate relations and global co-operation."[127] It also increasingly raises the same human rights implications on the international stage that have led to the strict regulation of national security surveillance domestically.[128] Resolution and debate of political issues increasingly happens on the global stage. The need for interoperability of digital networks is a particular driver for international resolution of domestic political issues at a range of supra-national governance bodies (Internet Governance Forum, Organization for Economic Co-operation and International Telecommunication Union).[129] Trade agreements increasingly address a range of domestic issues, and there are ongoing attempts to imbue new hemisphere-wide bodies with significant control over e-commerce.[130] Further, many domestic policy issues are now a matter of *integrated* international debate, as individuals from around the world discuss these matters on international online platform.[131] Even legal disputes are increasingly resolved on the international stage, where the historically permissive foreign intelligence approach permits states to spy on their legal adversaries.[132] There is evidence that the prevailing mass foreign surveillance model is already having a chilling effect on the ability of reporters and civil society advocates in both their domestic and international efforts.[133] It is also having an adverse impact on transborder data flows more generally, raising concerns regarding storage of data abroad.[134] All told, the "Wild West" approach to foreign surveillance is antithetical to comity in that it undermines "peaceable interstate relations and the international order" as well as the most fundamental of our democratic rights.[135]

The need for robust extraterritorial protection of human rights has been gaining significant attention in recent times. The Maastricht Principles open by noting that globalization has made territorial limits on human rights obligations inherently inconsistent with the universality of human rights, adopting a framework focused on state actors and causation with foreseeable impact as its primary touchstone.[136] With respect to communications surveillance specifically, there is growing recognition that current extraterritorial foreign intelligence surveillance is no longer consistent with human rights.[137] The High Commissioner on Human Rights in particular noted that granting minimal protection to "external communications" constitutes impermissible discrimination in the application of human rights obligations to foreigners.[138] Technical acts of interception or data access abroad increasingly constitute exercises of effective control of the state's regulatory jurisdiction, implicating jurisdiction.[139] An unprecedented UN General Assembly resolution has now recognized that surveillance is having negative impacts on human rights "including extraterritorial surveillance and/or interception of communications."[140] Finally, the International Court of Justice issued an order prohibiting Australia from monitoring any communications between East Timor and its legal advisors regarding any proceedings before it.[141]

The right to privacy under the *Charter* has always protected *people* not *places*.[142] Canadian courts have recognized, however, practical and legal challenges in attempts to apply *Charter* standards to Canadian officials invoking foreign invasive state search powers abroad.[143] Requiring Canadian agents operating in another country to follow Canadian search and seizure standards could constitute a violation of sovereignty. Canadian agents are therefore typically permitted to follow foreign investigative standards when acting abroad. However, this rule is premised on two key assumptions: that Canadian agents operating abroad are restrained by *some* legal framework (that of the foreign country) and that Canadian courts retain some control through the ability to exclude evidence gathered abroad in a manner that is inconsistent with fundamental justice.[144] Neither applies here. CSE's foreign surveillance does not "rely on [foreign] state compulsion" to invade the privacy of foreign citizens — it neither operates under foreign laws nor is constrained by them.[145] As the fruits of its surveillance are rarely used in court, the threat of exclusion is non-existent. More importantly, however, the leeway granted to foreign investigations ends where violations of fundamental and internationally protected human rights begin.[146] By explicitly failing to account for foreigners' individual privacy rights *in any way at all*, CSE's legal framework fails to strike a proportionate balance and constitutes a violation of the right to privacy.[147] The *Charter* must constrain CSE's activities in some manner, as nothing else can. Notably, as a matter of comity, allowing CSE to disregard the privacy of foreign citizens implicitly allows all other states to disregard the privacy of our own.

CSE's participation in the FVEY network is more complex. Courts have recognized that the *Charter* does not apply to the activities of foreign agencies assisting Canadian counterparts, nor is there any direct mechanism to compel foreign agencies to operate by *Charter* standards.[148] The *Charter* does apply, at minimum, to CSE participation in a process clearly violative of fundamental human rights, if there is a sufficient causal connection between CSE and the resulting violation.[149] FVEY resource sharing is highly integrated, with CSE likely able to directly task at least some FVEY monitoring resources.[150] Such direct tasking often requires no intervention or approval by the agency hosting the resource once general arrangements are in place, giving CSE practical control. CSE has repeatedly stated Canadian law binds its use of such capacities, if only with respect to the protection of Canadians.[151] Canadian law is therefore practically capable of restricting CSE use of FVEY resources. The FVEY cooperative is premised on a foundation of disregard for the privacy rights of foreigners and participants are not meaningfully constrained by their domestic laws.[152] Each time CSE tasks the FVEY network, it takes the risk that another agency will act independently on the information, leading to unconstitutional "detention or harm."[153] CSE has direct and explicit knowledge based on its own legal advice that tasking FVEY partners involves "the breach of international law by the requested second parties."[154] Canadian law should restrict CSE's use of these resources so as to respect the rights of non-Canadians.[155] Arguably, the *Charter* requires it.

While CSE cannot obligate its FVEY partners to adopt *Charter*-compliant information-gathering activities, it *can* more effectively constrain its own intelligence gathering and tasking of FVEY resources to reflect the privacy of affected targets. Those could include a reasonable grounds standard, for example, or the application of caveats.[156] It can also lead by example, or engage its allies in discussions geared towards an alliance that respects the privacy rights of all individuals.[157] However, domestic governments will not undertake such changes on their own initiative. Governments rarely act to curtail their own surveillance powers. As it will generally be politically palatable to placate domestic populations with reassurances that extraordinary powers are directed externally, there is an element of discrimination inherent in this system, which impacts minimally on voters.[158] The impetus for any form of effective change to this framework can only come from the *Charter* and the Courts entrusted with protecting the fundamental values enshrined within it.

Conclusion

The last decade has seen a dramatic expansion in the integration of communications networks, as well as in the portion of our daily lives that have become digital. Changes to the threat model and the operational approaches of foreign intelligence agencies have placed all of these interactions in the digital sphere within the unfettered and limitless scope of agencies whose legal frameworks were developed in a Cold War, spy-vs.-spy context that is categorically inapplicable to daily interactions of individuals, in Canada or abroad. The oversight of these entities, while important, has proven to be an ineffective check on the broad powers granted to CSE and its counterparts. At the same time, globalization and interconnectivity have moved the discussion of central political and democratic issues, once primarily in the domain of domestic politics, onto the international stage and within the granted purview of these agencies. Most importantly, the unprecedented scope of individual data collection these agencies have undertaken raises serious questions as to the underlying proportionality of the prevailing model and demands an urgent re-evaluation.

Notes

1. The New Transparency, "What Is IXmaps?," <https://vimeo.com/67102223>, at 1:56 minutes; Ron Deibert, "Why NSA Spying Scares the World," *CNN*, 12 June 2013, <cnn.com>.
2. Nick Hopkins, "The UK Gathering Secret Intelligence via Covert NSA Operation," *Guardian*, 7 June 2013, <http://www.theguardian.com/technology/2013/jun/07/uk-gathering-secret-intelligence-nsa-prism>. ("... the service has been made available to spy organisations from other countries").
3. Brian Fung, "The NSA's Giant Utah Data Center Will Probably Hold a Bunch of Spam," *Washington Post*, 15 October 2013, <http://www.washingtonpost.com/blogs/the-switch/wp/2013/10/15/the-nsas-giant-utah-data-center-will-probably-hold-a-bunch-of-spam/>.
4. Ellen Nakashima & Joby Warrick, "For NSA Chief, Terrorist Threat Drives Passion to 'Collect it All', Observers Say," *Washington Post*, 14 July 2013, <http://www.washingtonpost.com/world/national-security/for-nsa-chief-terrorist-threat-drives-passion-to-collect-it-all/2013/07/14/3d26ef80-ea49-11e2-a301-ea5a8116d211_story.html>.
5. Bill C-36, *Anti-Terrorism Act*, 2001, 1st Sess, 37th Parl, 2001 (as assented to 18 December 2001).
6. Privacy International, "Eyes Wide Open," Version 1.0, *Privacy International*, 26 November 2013, <privacyinternational.org>, at 38 *et seq*.

7. CSE operates under a tri-partite mandate: providing foreign intelligence to the government (its (a) or foreign intelligence mandate); providing advice and services aimed at protecting the government electronic infrastructure (its (b) or IT defence mandate); and providing technical/operational assistance to federal investigative agencies (its (c) or assistive mandate): *National Defence Act*, RSC 1985, c N-5, [NDA] at ss. 273.64(1) (a)-(c). This chapter focuses on CSE's (a) mandate, touching on its other mandates only tangentially. Jane Bailey, "Systemic Government Access to Private-Sector Data in Canada," (2013) 2:4 *Oxford Journals, International Data Privacy Law* 207.

8. Colin Freeze, "Former U.S. Spymaster Praises American Intelligence Oversight, but Envies Canadian System's 'agility'," *Globe and Mail*, 1 May 2014, <http://www.theglobeandmail.com/news/national/former-us-spymaster-praises-american-intelligence-oversight-but-envies-canadian-systems-agility/article18357209/>.

9. Cindy Cohn & Mark Jaycox, "NSA Spying: The Three Pillars of Government Trust Have Fallen," *EFF Deeplinks*, 15 August 2013, <eff.org>.

10. *Privacy Act*, RSC 1985, c P-21, ss 4, 7 and 8.

11. *R v TELUS Communications Co.*, [2013] 2 SCR 3 [*TELUS*], generally, and per Abella, J., at 4.

12. *Proceedings of the Standing Senate Committee on National Security and Defence*, 1st Sess., 38th Parl, No. 13 (13 June 2005), at 19–20; Canada, Office of the Communications Security Establishment Commissioner, *Annual Report 2006–2007*, May (Ottawa: Public Works and Government Services Canada, 2007), <http://www.ocsec-bccst.gc.ca/ann-rpt/2006-2007/ann-rpt_e.pdf> [OCSEC 2007], at 4: "… there is an ever-widening knowledge gap between the general public and evolving technologies."

13. [*Name Redacted by the Court*], 2011 US Dist LEXIS 157706, (US FISC, 2011)[FISC11], at 5, 33–34. The mis-characterization began in 2006: [*Name Redacted by the Court*], 2012 US Dist LEXIS 189344, (US FISC, 2012), at 2.

14. Upstream intercepts data from communications cables, PRISM obtains it from providers: Snowden Disclosure, "PRISM/US-984XN Overview," April 2013, <snowdenarchive.cjfe.org>, at 3. Collectively, they intake approximately 220 billion items of Internet [DNI] and telephone [DNR] metadata in a given month: Glenn Greenwald & Ewan MacAskill, "Boundless Informant: The NSA's Secret Tool to Track Global Surveillance Data," *Guardian*, 11 June 2013, <http://www.theguardian.com/world/2013/jun/08/nsa-boundless-informant-global-datamining>.

15. UPSTREAM harvests in-transit metadata and keeps it in a 30 day "buffer" for NSA analysts to query and decide what to keep ("content" buffers are 3 days): NSA, "XKEYSCORE," Snowden Disclosure, 25 February

2008, <snowdenarchive.cjfe.org>[XKS]. In 2011, 250 million data points were persistently retained: *FISC11, supra* note 13 at 36, footnote 24.

16. See *Jewel v National Security Agency*, Docket #: 4:08-cv-04373, Initial Complaint, 18 September 2008, <eff.org>. The *Jewel* complaint asserts similar facts regarding the same NSA Internet monitoring program that were ultimately uncovered by FISC in the 2011 decision (*supra* note 13).

17. *Canadian Security Intelligence Service Act (Can.)(Re)*, [2013] FTR 125 [*Re X FC2013*] aff'd in *X (Re)*, [2014] 377 DLR (4th) 735 [*Re X FCA*] leave to appeal granted, [2014] SCCA No 481.

18. *Re X FC2013, supra* note 17 at 1–2 and 37.

19. *Re X FC2013, supra* note 17 at 55.

20. *R v Hape*, [2007] 2 SCR 292 [Hape]; *Schreiber v Canada (Attorney General)*, [2002] 3 SCR 269 [Schreiber].

21. Wesley Wark, "Electronic Communications Interception and Privacy: Can the Imperatives of Privacy and National Security be Reconciled?," March 2012, <cips.uottawa.ca> [Wark] at 5.

22. Canada, OCSEC, *Annual Report 2010–2011*, June (Ottawa: Public Works and Government Services Canada, 2011), <ocsec-bccst.gc.ca> [OCSEC 2011], at 6.

23. Canada, OCSEC, *Annual Report 2007-2008*, May (Ottawa: Public Works and Government Services Canada, 2008), <ocsec-bccst.gc.ca> [OCSEC 2008], at 2-3.

24. *Supra* note 21 at 15.

25. Canada, CSE, "CSE Commissioner's Review of [Redacted] Activities [Redacted]," Response to *Access to Information Act* request, 30 December 2010, <https://cippic.ca/uploads/ATI-OCSEC-review_of_CSE_meta-data_activities.pdf>, [Metadata Review] at note 8; *Re X FC2013 supra* note 17 at 70–74.

26. Canada, OCSEC, *Annual Report 2009-2010*, June (Ottawa: Public Works and Government Services Canada, 2010), <ocsec-bccst.gc.ca> [OCSEC 2010], at 4.

27. Canada, OCSEC, *Annual Report 2005–2006*, April (Ottawa: Public Works and Government Services Canada, 2006), <ocsec-bccst.gc.ca> [OCSEC 2006].

28. CBC News, "Project Levitation and Your Privacy," *CBC News*, 28 January 2015, <cbc.ca>, quoting Associate Minister of National Defence Julian Fantino; CSE, "Response from the Communications Security Establishment to CBC's Questions," *CBC News*, 28 January 2015, <https://documentcloud.org/documents/1509928-response-from-the-communications-security.html>.

29. OCSEC 2008, *supra* note 23. Prior to 2008, there were cryptic references to interpretive disagreements, with no details: *supra* note 21 at 15.

30. Canada, OCSEC, *Annual Report 2002–2013*, June (Ottawa: Public Works and Government Services Canada, 2013), <ocsec-bccst.gc.ca> [OCSEC 2013] at 25.

31. *Re X FC2013, supra* note 17.

32. *Re X FC2013, supra* note 17 at 53.

33. *Re X FC2013, supra* note 17 at 110–15.

34. Canada, OCSEC, *Annual Report 2008–2009,* June (Ottawa: Public Works and Government Services Canada, 2009), <ocsec-bccst.gc.ca> [OCSEC 2009].

35. NDA, *supra* note 7, section 273.65 governs CSE interception of private communications through ministerial authorizations. As CSE cannot invade constitutionally protected privacy expectations without lawful authority (*R v Collins,* [1987] 1 SCR 265 at 23) its privacy invasive activities that do not include interception can operate further to ministerial directives issued under section 273.62(3).

36. NDA, *supra* note 7, ss 273.62(3) and 273.66.

37. *Lyster v Attorney General of Canada,* BCSC File No T-796-14, Statement of Claim, 1 April 2014, <bccla.org>; *Clapper v Amnesty International USA,* 568 US __ (2015) (US Supreme Court).

38. *Hunter v Southam Inc,* [1984] 2 SCR 145 at 160–62 [*Hunter*]; *R v Vu,* [2013] 3 SCR 657 [*Vu*] at 46.

39. Craig Forcese, "A Tale of Two Controversies: Thoughts on CSEC's Headline Act(s)," *National Security Law Blog,* 16 October 2013, <http:// craigforcese.squarespace.com/national-security-law-blog/2013/10/16/a-tale-of-two-controversies-thoughts-on-csecs-headline-acts.html>.

40. NDA, *supra* note 7, s 273.64(1)(a); OCSEC, "Frequently Asked Questions," 8 December 2014, <http://ocsec-bccst.gc.ca/new-neuf/faq_e.php>: "Establishing intelligence priorities is a prerogative of the executive arm of government."

41. *Canada (Minister of National Revenue) v Coopers and Lybrand Ltd,* [1979] 1 SCR 495 at 507–8: (Minister "governed by many considerations, dominant among which is the public interest and his duty as an executive officer of the government"); *Hunter, supra* note 38 at 162–65: (Commission guided by public policy and expediency).

42. *R v Grant,* [1993] 3 SCR 223 at 239–40; *R v Simmons,* [1988] 2 SCR 495 [*Simmons*] at 47.

43. *Simmons, supra* note 42 at 49 (lower privacy expectations at borders); *R v Tse,* [2012] 1 SCR 531 [*Tse*] at 18 (exigency); *Ruby v Canada (Solicitor General),* [2002] 4 SCR 3 [*Ruby*] at 40, 44; *Charkaoui v Canada (Citizenship and Immigration),* [2007] 1 SCR 350 at 27.

44. *Simmons, supra* note 42 at 50–51: (warrantless searches must be less intrusive, based on specific grounds, and challengeable "before any person can be searched"); *Tse, supra* note 43 at 84–85; *Ruby, supra* note 43 at 42.

45. *Mahjoub (Re),* 2013 FC 1096, [*Mahjoub*] at 32-34, 38-39; *Atwal v Canada,* [1988] 1 FCR 107 (FCA)[*Atwal*] at 35, 45-46; *Re X FCA, supra* note 17 at

86–87; *Re X* FC2013, *supra* note 17 at 99–100; *United States v US District Court*, 407 US 297 (1972) (US Supreme Court) [US 1972] (domestic security surveillance cannot be sole discretion of executive branch of government).

46. Senate, "Fundamental Justice in Extraordinary Times: Main Report of the Special Senate Committee on the *Anti-Terrorism Act*" (February 2007) [Senate 2007] at 77: ("warrants from Canadian courts have no jurisdiction outside of Canada"). <http://www.parl.gc.ca/Content/SEN/Committee/391/anti/rep/rep02feb07-e.pdf>.

47. Bill C-44, *Protection of Canada from Terrorists Act*, SC 2015, c. 9, April 23, 2015, at 8(2).

48. This reform is a direct response to *Re X* FC2013, *supra* note 17.

49. *Mahjoub, supra* note 45.

50. *NDA, supra* note 7 at 273.65.

51. *Vu, supra* note 38 at 47.

52. Senate 2007, *supra* note 46 at 78, Recommendation 18.

53. *Atwal, supra* note 45 at 24, 35–36.

54. *Atwal, supra* note 45 at 35.

55. OCSEC 2008, *supra* note 23 at 4; OCSEC 2010, *supra* note 26 at 4.

56. Authorizations are valid for up to twelve months, typically renewed annually (NDA, *supra* note 7 at s 273.68). In 2014 the six long-standing authorizations were "reformatted" into three (without any corresponding substantive changes): Canada, OCSEC, *Annual Report 2013–2014*, June (Ottawa: Public Works and Government Services Canada, 2014) [OCSEC 2014], at 39.

57. OCSEC 2008, *supra* note 23 at 4.

58. Privacy and Civil Liberties Oversight Board, "Report on the Surveillance Program Operated Pursuant to Section 702 of the Foreign Intelligence Surveillance Act" (2 July 2014) [PCLOB FAA702], at 7. Open Rights Group, "GCHQ and Mass Surveillance," *OpenRightsGroup.org*, 11 March 2015, <https://www.openrightsgroup.org/ourwork/reports/gchq-and-mass-surveillance>, at 6–8.

59. *Re X* FC2013, *supra* note 17 at 55, 105. EONBLUE is CSE's primary interception program: CSE, "CSEC SIGINT Cyber Discovery: Summary of Current Effort," *Snowden Disclosure*, November 2010, <snowdenarchive.cjfe.org> [Cyber Discovery], at 13–14. EONBLUE is an "XKEYSCORE" input (*Ibid.*, at 18), an NSA-developed resource allowing interoperability in intercept, search, and storage capacities across FVEY agencies: XKS, *supra* note 15. See also Christopher Parsons, "Canadian SIGINT Summaries," *Technology, Thoughts & Trinkets*, 6 February 2015, <https://christopher-parsons.com/writings/cse-summaries/> [Parsons].

60. Siobhan Gorman & Jennifer Valentino-Devries, "New Details Show Broader NSA Surveillance Reach: Programs Cover 75% of Nation's

Traffic, Can Snare Emails," *Wall Street Journal*, 30 August 2013: "The NSA defines access as 'things we actually touch,'... telecom companies do the first stage of filtering ... based on the NSA's criteria." <http://online.wsj.com/news/articles/SB10001424127887324108204579022874091732470>.

61. OCSEC 2014, *supra* note 56 at 40. *X, Re*, [2010] 1 FCR 460 [*Re X FC2009*] at 58 suggests an "interception" occurs when the "substantive content of the communication" is acquired in Canada, not when it is otherwise processed in a redacted manner abroad.

62. *R v Kang-Brown*, [2008] 1 SCR 456 (dog sniffing luggage indicates whether bag does or does not contain drugs constituting a search). *TELUS, supra* note 11.

63. Metadata Review, *supra* note 25 at 5: "Metadata is not [redactions] a private communication."

64. Greg Weston, "Spy Agency CSEC Needs MPs' Oversight, Ex-Director Says," *CBC News*, 7 October 2013, <http://www.cbc.ca/news/politics/spy-agency-csec-needs-mps-oversight-ex-director-says-1.1928983>.

65. Tamir Israel, "Rogers' Use of Deep Packet Inspection Equipment," *CIPPIC*, 2 December 2009, <cippic.ca>, at 14–16.

66. *ACLU v. Clapper*, Case No. 14-42, *Amici Curiae* Brief of Experts in Computer and Data Science, 13 March 2014, (US 2nd Cir 2014).

67. *Criminal Code*, RSC 1985, c C-46, recently enacted section 487.011(c) defines "transmission data" as data that "does not reveal the substance, meaning or purpose of the communication." CSE does not include this caveat: Metadata Review, *supra* note 25 at 10.

68. CSE, "LEVITATION and the FFU Hypothesis," *Snowden Disclosure*, <snowdenarchive.cjfe.org> [LEVITATION], at 5–6 (URLs), 15 (FacebookID), 3 (search term analytics); XKS, *supra* note 15 at 17 (document-authoring information).

69. *R v Spencer*, [2014] 2 SCR 212 at 45–47, 50 (Online identifiers attract high expectations of privacy where revealing otherwise anonymous online activities).

70. Metadata Review, *supra* note 25 at 16.

71. Spencer Ackerman & James Ball, "Optic Nerve: Millions of Yahoo Webcam Images Intercepted by GCHQ," *The Guardian*, 28 February 2014, <http://www.theguardian.com/world/2014/feb/27/gchq-nsa-webcam-images-internet-yahoo> [OPTICNERVE].

72. *Ibid.* See also Matt Kwong, "Samsung SmartTV an 'Absurd' Privacy Intruder," *CBC News*, 10 February 2015, <http://www.cbc.ca/news/technology/samsung-smarttv-an-absurd-privacy-intruder-ann-cavoukian-says-1.2950982>.

73. Barton Gellman, Julie Tata & Ashkan Soltani, "In NSA-Intercepted Data, Those Not Targeted Far Outnumber the Foreigners Who Are," *The*

Washington Post, 5 July 2014) [Gellman], <http://www.washingtonpost.com/world/national-security/in-nsa-intercepted-data-those-not-targeted-far-outnumber-the-foreigners-who-are/2014/07/05/8139adf8-045a-11e4-8572-4b1b969b6322_story.html>.

74. Privacy and Civil Liberties Oversight Board, "Report on the Telephone Records Program Conducted Under Section 215 of the USA PATRIOT Act and on the Operations of the Foreign Intelligence Surveillance Court," 23 January 2014, [PBCLOB 215] at 28–29, 60–65.

75. *Ibid.* at 61–63.

76. Scott Shane, "No Morsel Too Miniscule for All-Consuming NSA," *New York Times*, 2 November 2013, <http://www.nytimes.com/2013/11/03/world/no-morsel-too-minuscule-for-all-consuming-nsa.html> [Shane].

77. *NDA, supra* note 7 at s. 273.61.

78. *Supra* note 21 at 9; *Proceedings of the Standing Senate Committee on National Security and Defence*, 2nd Sess, 41st Parl, No 2 (3 February 2014) [Senate 2014] at 41, 66. <http://www.parl.gc.ca/content/sen/committee/412/SECD/pdf/02issue.pdf>.

79. Glenn Greenwald, "Documents from No Place to Hide," *GlennGreenwald.net*, <http://glenngreenwald.net/#BookDocuments>, at 95–96.

80. James Cox, "Canada and the Five Eyes Intelligence Community," *Strategic Studies Working Group Papers* (18 December 2012) [Cox], at 7.

81. Senate 2014, *supra* note 78 at 38.

82. Canada, SIRC, "Bridging the Gap: Recalibrating the Machinery of Security Intelligence and Intelligence Review," *Annual Report 2012–2013* (Ottawa: Public Works and Government Services Canada, 2014) [SIRC 2013], at 20.

83. Senate 2014, *supra* note 78 at 38.

84. Colin Freeze & Stephanie Nolen, "Charges That Canada Spied on Brazil Unveil CSEC's Inner Workings," *Globe and Mail*, 7 October 2013, <http://www.theglobeandmail.com/news/world/brazil-spying-report-spotlights-canadas-electronic-eavesdroppers/article14720003/>; Greg Weston et al., "New Snowden Docs Show US Spied during G20 in Toronto," *CBC News*, 1 December 2013, <http://www.cbc.ca/news/politics/new-snowden-docs-show-u-s-spied-during-g20-in-toronto-1.2442448>; Ewen MacAskill et al., "GCHQ Intercepted Foreign Politicians' Communications at G20 Summit," *Guardian*, 17 June 2013, <http://www.theguardian.com/uk/2013/jun/16/gchq-intercepted-communications-g20-summits>; David Sanger & Thom Shanker, "NSA Devises Radio Pathway into Computers," *New York Times*, 14 January 2014, http://www.nytimes.com/2014/01/15/us/nsa-effort-pries-open-computers-not-connected-to-internet.html; NSA, "Intro to the VPN Exploitation Process," *Snowden Disclosure*, 13 September 2010, <snowdenarchive.cjfe.org>, at 40; Ryan Gallagher, "Operation Socialist," *The Intercept*, 12 December 2014, <firstlook.org>.

NSA, "UN Climate Change Conference in Copenhagen — Will the Developed and Developing World Agree on Climate Change?" *Snowden Disclosure*, 7 December 2009, <snowdenarchive.cjfe.org>.

85. Shane, *supra* note 76.

86. Jean-Pierre Plouffe, "Statement by CSE Commissioner the Honourable Jean-Pierre Plouffe re: January 30 CBC Story," *Office of the CSE Commissioner*, 31 January 2014, <ocsec-bccst.gc.ca>. (CSE can use domestic metadata to conduct analytical experiments); OPTICNERVE *supra* note 71 (GCHQ experiments with intercepted video chats to improve facial recognition).

87. *US 1972, supra* note 45: "History abundantly documents the tendency of Government… to view with suspicion those who most fervently dispute its policies." <http://openjurist.org/407/us/297>.

88. *Report of the Special Rapporteur on the Promotion and Protection of the Right to Freedom of Opinion and Expression, Frank La Rue*, UNHRC, 23rd Sess, UN Doc A/HRC/23/40 (2013) [*La Rue*], <ohchr.org>: "The concept is broadly defined and is thus vulnerable to manipulation by the State."

89. *Questions Relating to the Seizure and Detention of Certain Documents and Data (Timor-Leste v Australia)*, Order of March 3, 2014 [*Timor-Leste*].

90. Canada, SIRC, "Reflections," Security Intelligence Review Committee, Ottawa, 2005, <sirc-csars.gc.ca>, at 7.

91. Colin Freeze, "Spy Agency's Work with CSIS, RCMP Fuels Fears of Privacy Breaches," *Globe and Mail*, 31 January 2014, <http://www.theglobeandmail.com/news/politics/spy-agencys-work-with-csis-rcmp-fuels-fears-of-privacy-breaches/article16623147/>.

92. The NSA's statutory obligation to direct its activities only at "foreign powers and their agents" was removed: Tamir Israel, Katitza Rodriguez, & Mark Rumold, "U.S. Foreign Intelligence: From Carte Blanche Surveillance to Weak [Domestic] Protections," *EFF Deeplinks*, 15 June 2013, <eff.org/>.

93. NSA, "Content Extraction Enhancement for Target Analytics," *Snowden Disclosure*, 9 June 2011, <snowdenarchive.cjfe.org>, at 8.

94. Glenn Greenwald & Murtaza Hussain, "Meet the Muslim-American Leaders the FBI and NSA Have Been Spying On," *The Intercept*, 9 July 2014, <firstlook.org>.

95. Luke Harding, "Edward Snowden: US Government Spied on Human Rights Workers," *Guardian*, 8 April 2014, <http://www.theguardian.com/world/2014/apr/08/edwards-snowden-us-government-spied-human-rights-workers>.

96. Jonathan Easley, "Snowden: NSA Targeted Journalists Critical of Government After 9/11," *The Hill*, 13 August 2013, http://thehill.com/blogs/blog-briefing-room/news/316751-snowden-nsa-targeted-journalists-critical-of-government-after-911.

97. Mark Schone et al., "Snowden Doc Shows UK Spies Attacked Anonymous Hackers," *NBC News*, 5 February 2014, <http://www.nbc-news.com/feature/edward-snowden-interview/exclusive-snowden-docs-show-uk-spies-attacked-anonymous-hackers-n21361>.

98. *NDA, supra* note 7 at s 273.64(2).

99. Michael Geist, "Why Better Oversight Won't Fix Internet Surveillance and the New Anti-Terrorism Bill," *MichaelGeist.ca*, 10 February 2015, <michaelgeist.ca> [Geist].

100. Metadata Review, *supra* note 25, at footnote 17: "To target (verb) means: "To single out [redactions]."

101. Senate 2014, *supra* note 78 at 63.

102. *Ibid.* at 71. PCLOB FAA702, *supra* note 58 at 7 (MCT); Gellman, *supra* note 73; Geist, *supra* note 99.

103. EONBLUE monitors communications streams for keywords at backbone data speeds: Cyber Discovery, *supra* note 59 at 13–14. Parsons, *supra* note 59.

104. CSE has confirmed it uses metadata in part to help it target non-Canadians in its content acquisition programs: OCSEC 2014, *supra* note 56 at 21. Content is also buffered for three days, and it remains unclear whether buffers are generated before or after the targeting criteria are applied.

105. PBCLOB FAA702, *supra* note 58 at 7.

106. *Supra* note 68.

107. After it had proven impossible to properly restrain NSA analyst searches, FISC recently mandated prior judicial approval for any search selectors to be used on one of its telephone metadata databases: PCLOB 215, *supra* note 74 at 52.

108. *NDA, supra* note 7 at s 273.65(2)(d).

109. OCSEC 2014, *supra* note 56 at 66.

110. PCLOB FAA702, *supra* note 58 at 39–41 (Internet transactions not discrete communications).

111. Gellman, *supra* note 73.

112. Canada, "2013 Annual Report on the Use of Electronic Surveillance," (Ottawa: Public Safety Canada, 2014), at Table 7.

113. *NDA, supra* note 7 at s. 273.65(2)(d), only applies to "the interception of private communications." CSE does not consider this to include metadata (*supra* note 63).

114. Metadata Review, *supra* note 25 at 5, footnote 7.

115. Senate 2014, *supra* note 78 (CSE Chief John Foster), at 71: "We will keep [all collected] metadata… If it is Canadian, then we… make sure we protect the privacy of that information and how we use it."

116. Metadata Review, *supra* note 25 at 5.

117. Greg Weston et al., "CSEC Used Airport Wi-Fi to Track Travellers," *CBC News*, 30 January 2014, <http://www.cbc.ca/news/politics/

csec-used-airport-wi-fi-to-track-canadian-travellers-edward-snowden-documents-1.2517881>; Bruce Schneier, "CSEC Surveillance Analysis of IP and User Data," *Schneier on Security*, 3 February 2014, <schneier.com>.

118. Senate 2014, *supra* note 78 at 54–55: "It's part of our normal global collection."

119. CSE, "IP Profiling Analytics & Mission Impacts," *Snowden Disclosure*, 10 May 2012, <http://cbc.ca/news2/pdf/airports_redacted.pdf>, at 4, 23.

120. Senate 2014, *supra* note 78 at 56.

121. The *Privacy Act* definition of "identifiable Canadian individual" that CSE uses (OCSEC 2014, *supra* note 56 at 42) applies to the type of large scale analytics demonstrated here because the identifiers (IP addresses, etc.) at the heart of the program are traceable back to an individual: PIPEDA Report of Findings #2009-010, September 2009, at 47–49; Office of the Privacy Commissioner of Canada, "Policy Position on Behavioural Advertising," *OPC Guidelines*, 6 June 2012); Yves-Alexandre de Montjoye et al., "Unique in the Crowd: The Privacy Bounds of Human Mobility," *Scientific Reports* 3:1376 (25 March, 2013), <http://www.nature.com/srep/2013/130325/srep01376/full/srep01376.html>.

122. An active CSE program that analyzes metadata to identify individuals who have viewed certain documents on file upload sites includes Canadian outputs, anonymized in the subsequent intelligence reports, but not in the underlying database: LEVITATION, *supra* note 68 at 12.

123. LEVITATION, *supra* note 68 at 18.

124. LEVITATION, *supra* note 68 at 15 uses MARINA, an NSA metadata database, to query Facebook IDs.

125. Metadata Review, *supra* note 25, at 15, second bullet. *Re X* FC2013, supra note 17.

126. Bill C-51, *Anti-Terrorism Act*, 2015, 2 Sess, 41st Parl, 2015 (1st reading) (30 January 2015) at Clauses 42–44.

127. *Hape, supra* note 20 at 50. Laura Poitras et al., "A is for Angela: GCHQ and NSA Targeted Private German Companies and Merkel," *Der Spiegel*, 29 March 2014, <spiegel.de>; Canadian Press, "Harper 'Very Concerned' about Reports of Canada Spying on Brazil," *Toronto Star*, 8 October 2013, <http://www.thestar.com/news/world/2013/10/08/harper_very_concerned_about_reports_of_canada_spying_on_brazil.html>.

128. *Hape, supra* note 20 at 51.

129. Milton Mueller, *Ruling the Root: Internet Governance and the Taming of Cyberspace* (Boston: MIT Press, 2002); Jeremy Malcolm, "The Role of Governments in Internet Governance," *Consumers International*, 28 May 2013, <http://www.diplomacy.edu/sites/default/files/May%202013%20IG%20webinar%20PDF%20-%20Dr%20Jeremy%20Malcolm.pdf>.

130. Maira Sutton, "It Doesn't Matter Who Does the Lobbying: Trade Agreements Aren't the Place for Internet Regulations," *EFF Deeplinks*,

19 December 2014, <eff.org>; Jane Kelsey & Burcu Kilic, "Briefing on US TISA Proposal on E-Commerce, Technology Transfer, Cross-border Data Flows and Net Neutrality," *PSI* (17 December 2014), <http://www.world-psi.org/sites/default/files/documents/research/briefing_on_tisa_e-commerce_final.pdf>.

131. Nahed Eltantawy & Julie West, "Social Media in the Egyptian Revolution: Reconsidering Resource Mobilization Theory" (2011) 5 *International Journal of Communication* 1207; Hillary Rodham Clinton, US Secretary of State, "Remarks on Internet Freedom" *US Department of State*, 21 January 2010, <state.gov>.

132. *Timor-Leste, supra* note 89.

133. Human Rights Watch, "With Liberty to Monitor All: How Large-Scale US Surveillance Is Harming Journalism, Law and American Democracy," *Human Rights Watch*, (July 2014): 22–23; <http://www.hrw.org/sites/default/files/reports/usnsa0714_ForUPload_0.pdf>; and Access et al., "Letter to General Keith Alexander and the Honorable Michael Froman,"12 November 2013, <http://www.consumerfed.org/pdfs/cso-letter-on-nsa-surveillance-11-12-13.pdf>.

134. Parliament of the European Union, "Inquiry on Electronic Mass Surveillance of EU Citizens," *Committee on Civil Liberties, Justice and Home Affairs (LIBE)* (2013–2014), <http://europarl.europa.eu/document/activities/cont/201410/20141016ATT91322/20141016ATT91322EN.pdf>, at 46–47; Claire Cain Miller, "Revelations of NSA Spying Cost US Tech Companies," *New York Times*, 21 March 2014, <http://www.nytimes.com/2014/03/22/business/fallout-from-snowden-hurting-bottom-line-of-tech-companies.html>.

135. *Hape, supra* note 20 at 50–52.

136. Maastricht Principles on Extraterritorial Obligations of States in the Area of Economic, Social and Cultural Rights, (28 September 2011), Principles 8(a) and 9(b).

137. La Rue, *supra* note 88 at 64; International Principles on the Application of Human Rights to Communications Surveillance, (July 2013) Final Version, *Necessary and Proportionate*, <https: necessaryandproportionate.org>, [IPAHRCS].

138. UN High Commissioner for Human Rights, "The Right to Privacy in the Digital Age," UNHRC, 27th Sess., UN Doc A/HRC/27/37 (2014) [High Commissioner], at 36.

139. *Ibid.* at 34–35.

140. "The Right to Privacy in the Digital Age," GA Res 68/167, UNGAOR, 68th Sess, UN Doc A/RES/68/167; Colum Lynch, "Inside America's Plan to Kill Online Privacy Rights Everywhere," *Foreign Policy*, 20 November 2013, <foreignpolicy.com>; Ewen MacAskill & James Ball, "UN Surveillance Resolution Goes Ahead Despite Attempts to Dilute Language," *The*

Guardian, 21 November 2013, <http://www.theguardian.com/world/2013/nov/21/un-surveillance-resolution-us-uk-dilute-language>.

141. *Timor-Leste, supra* note 89 at 52.

142. *Hunter, supra* note 38 at 159; *Hape, supra* note 20 at 94, 159–61.

143. *Hape, supra* note 20.

144. *Ibid.* at 111–12, 169.

145. *Hape, supra* note 20 at 74, 160–74, *Canadian Security Intelligence Service Act (Re)*, [2008] 4 FCR 230 at 51.

146. *Ibid.* at 52; *Canada (Justice) v Khadr*, [2008] 2 SCR 125 at 18 [*Khadr8*]; *Canada (Prime Minister) v Khadr*, [2010] 1 SCR 44 [*Khadr10*].

147. *Hape, supra* note 20 at 100.

148. *Hape, supra* note 20 at 112.

149. *Khadr8, supra* note 146 at 18; *Khadr10, supra* note 146 at 14, 19; *Hape, supra* note 20 at 52, 175.

150. Likely including direct access to existing databases as well as capacity to directly send keywords to some FVEY network monitoring equipment: *supra* notes 59 and 124. Contrast *Hape, supra* note 20 at 74.

151. *Cox, supra* note 80 at 7.

152. *Re X FC2009, supra* note 61 at 77.

153. SIRC 2013, *supra* note 82 at 19.

154. *Re X FC2013, supra* note 17 at 105; *Khadr10, supra* note 146, at 20, 24; *Wakeling v United States of America*, 2014 SCC 72 at 80.

155. *Hape, supra* note 20 at 46 and 169; *Timor-Leste, supra* note 89.

156. *Supra* notes 53, 54; IPAHRCS, *supra* note 137; High Commissioner, *supra* note 138 at 21 *et seq.* and note 14.

157. High Commissioner, *supra* note 138 at 33; *Hape, supra* note 20 at 112.

158. High Commissioner, *supra* note 138 at 36.

CHAPTER IV

Lawful Illegality: What Snowden Has Taught Us about the Legal Infrastructure of the Surveillance State

Lisa M. Austin

Introduction

The Snowden revelations have revealed to us, with impressive documentation, the technical infrastructure of contemporary state surveillance. What is less obvious, but of great importance, is the revelation of the legal infrastructure of this surveillance. In this chapter I argue that this infrastructure is best understood as one of "lawful illegality."

One aspect of the lawful illegality of surveillance is the conflicting reactions of citizens and authorities when surveillance programs are revealed. Members of the public, upon learning what some national security authority is doing, protest that it must be illegal. The national security authority, and government, claim that everything they do is lawful. The label "lawful illegality" captures this conflict between the perspective of the state and the perspective of ordinary citizens.

It is likely the case that spy craft has always operated within a space of conflicted legality. For example, state security agencies might have lawful authority under their domestic law to engage in actions abroad that might breach the domestic laws of other nations or international legal norms.[1] But what has become so clear in the wake of the Snowden revelations is the dramatically changed landscape of state surveillance. Ideas of what is included in "national security" have broadened, and targets now include ordinary individuals and not simply foreign states and foreign agents. The line between criminal offences and national security offences has blurred, both domestically and internationally. Effective state action against terrorism requires cooperation between national security authorities, law enforcement authorities, and border officials, both within a state and across borders, as well as sophisticated technologies that make use of a global and interconnected communications infrastructure.[2] This changed landscape reveals a deeper tension than simply conflicting perspectives of legality. My claim in this chapter is that there is a serious rule of law problem.

The rule of law requires the commitment that state action itself be subject to the law. In this chapter I claim that the issues of secrecy, complexity, and jurisdiction work together to create "lawful" paths for state surveillance for national security purposes that are nevertheless in deep tension with a general commitment that this surveillance be subject to the oversight and accountability demanded by the rule of law. Throughout, I illustrate these issues with a set of examples largely taken from the Snowden revelations, with a Canadian perspective. These examples are not meant to provide an exhaustive overview of the issues, but to highlight the importance of attending to these larger questions of legality if we are going to move forward and design a better system of oversight.

Illegality and Emergencies

In the aftermath of 9/11, there was a significant rule-of-law debate regarding the role of law in fettering executive discretion in times of emergency. This framework of "emergencies" remains important in public discourse concerning surveillance. For example, United States Supreme Court Justice Scalia commented upon the possibility that the Supreme Court would ultimately decide upon the constitutionality of some of the American surveillance programs.[3] The legal question, he said, is about "balancing the emergency against the intrusion [on the individual]." He also suggested that the court was the "least qualified" institution to decide this issue. This lack of expertise, one can infer, concerns the court's qualification to judge the demands of emergencies, not the demands of the Fourth Amendment; whatever judgment emergencies require, the executive and not the courts are the experts.

As David Dyzenhaus has argued, some of the post-9/11 debate regarding emergencies and the rule of law concerns the different responses one might take to the existence of either legal black holes or legal grey holes. A black hole is where the legislature seeks to carve out a space of no-law; a grey hole is "one in which there is the facade or form of the rule of law rather than any substantive protections."[4] The space created by such holes is a space for executive discretion and the need for such space derives from the perceived exceptional nature of national emergencies, where it is difficult to anticipate in advance what that emergency will be and how one should respond.[5]

This framework of emergencies, with its themes of uncertainty and unenforceability, is both helpful and unhelpful when applied to state surveillance. It is helpful in that the exceptional nature of terrorism has deeply influenced contemporary methods of state surveillance. One aspect of the exceptional nature of terrorism is indeed its unpredictability. It is difficult to anticipate who will engage in acts of terrorism: agents of foreign powers, members of existing and known terrorist organizations, affiliates abroad, or homegrown extremists? It is difficult to anticipate where an attack will take place, whether many civilians will be at risk, the potential scale of an attack, and so on. Another aspect of the exceptional nature of terrorism is the type of risk it is seen to be — not just a risk of potentially catastrophic harm, but a deep political threat to the state. For example, the United States considers itself to be at "war" against al-Qaeda.[6] The extraordinary nature of the threat of terrorism also underpins the US response of seeking to prevent future terrorist attacks, with a "never again" mentality.[7]

However, focusing on the exceptional nature of emergencies can distract us from the most salient features of the state surveillance methods Snowden has revealed to the world: they are in fact a rational, systematic, planned response to the perceived need to prevent terrorist attacks. In other words, the framework of emergencies concerns whether what is needed is a discretionary space for executive authority — either legal black holes or legal grey holes — to nimbly respond to exceptional circumstances that cannot be foreseen in advance. But state surveillance premised on the idea of collecting the "haystack" to find the "needle" is not about preserving discretion at all. It is about applying rational analytic methods to the problem of preventing certain kinds of threats that have been identified at least at some level of generality (e.g., terrorist threat).[8] The proper frame of the rule of law challenge is not about the question of whether executive discretionary authority in relation to emergencies can and should be constrained by the reason of the law; instead, it is about whether mass surveillance as a mode of rational social ordering is in conflict with the deepest commitments of law as a mode of rational social ordering.

When we talk about the legality of surveillance, therefore, we need to focus less on the spaces of discretion and more on the systematic features of surveillance that put strain on our traditional understandings of the rule of law. In particular, I want to flag three issues. The first is the issue of secrecy and the degree to which it is demanded by the national security context. My claim is that it creates pressure for unilateral, rather than objective and public, interpretations of the law. The second is the issue of legal complexity, especially as it relates to law reform initiatives. Where there is an increased blurring between regular law enforcement, border control, and terrorism investigations, as well as increasingly complex relationships between private sector communications intermediaries and the state, gaining a clear public understanding of proposed changes to lawful access laws or the full significance of legal cases before the courts is extremely difficult. The third is the issue of jurisdiction and the extent to which national boundaries and questions of status (like citizenship) affect the lawfulness of surveillance. In particular, I argue that instead of providing us with the tools for accountability, status and jurisdiction allow for the leveraging of national boundaries to create an international surveillance regime with questionable accountability.

Secrecy and Unilateralism

One of the most basic understandings of the rule of law is that government itself is subject to law. As already noted, one of the remarkable things about the Snowden revelations is that the response of both the intelligence agencies and the governments involved has largely been to claim that they are acting in a lawful manner. What has become clear, however, is that these claims of lawfulness are often unilateral in the sense that they are either claims of a one-sided interpretation of the law or claims of deference to that one-sided interpretation within an accountability framework that is structurally biased. Secrecy is a key ingredient to this unilateralism. However, such unilateralism lies in tension with our deeper commitments to legality, which demands that law reflect a "public" perspective and not that of an entity who is supposed to be regulated by that law.

In Canada, the Communications Security Establishment's claims of the lawfulness of its metadata program, for example, turn out largely to be a claim that there is a plausible legal interpretation that shows CSE's activities to be both within its statutory authority and consistent with the Canadian *Charter of Rights and Freedoms*. The problem is that the plausible legal interpretation is one provided by the government itself and its conclusion of lawfulness is far from obvious to an outside observer. As we have seen from the public controversy surrounding the disclosures regarding CSE's alleged collection of communications metadata at public Wi-Fi spots, many well-informed commentators express incredulity regarding how such activities are lawful under either the *National Defence Act* or the Canadian *Charter of Rights and Freedoms*.[9]

CSE does not make its legal interpretation public, so its claims of lawfulness rest not just on its own legal interpretation but, importantly, on a secret interpretation. CSE itself often points to the independent oversight of the CSE commissioner as part of the accountability framework within which it operates.[10] This suggests that the CSE commissioner is able to independently assess the lawfulness of CSE's activities. However, we know from the annual reports of past CSE commissioners that where there is a difference of views regarding legal interpretation, it is CSE's view that prevails. For example, in his 2005–2006 annual report, Commissioner Lamer stated,

> With respect to my reviews of CSE activities carried out under ministerial authorization, I note that I concluded on their lawfulness in light of the Department of Justice interpretation of the applicable legislative provisions. I have pointed out elsewhere that there are ambiguities in the legislation as now drafted, a view that I share with my predecessor, the Hon. Claude Bisson, O.C., a former Chief Justice of Quebec. Currently, two eminent lawyers, the Deputy Minister of Justice and my independent Legal Counsel disagree over the meaning of key provisions that influence the nature of the assurance that I can provide.[11]

Similar statements have been made by subsequent commissioners.[12] Without an accountability mechanism that allows for the government's interpretation of the law to effectively be contested as well as for a final determination by an objective body, like a court, then "lawfulness" turns out to simply mean a claim to operate within one's own interpretation of the law. Oversight, on this model, means independent assurance that one's activities conform to one's own interpretation of the law. To be subject merely to one's own interpretation of the law looks a lot like getting to be one's own judge, and it lies in deep tension with the ideal of law as an objective constraint on state power.

This unilateralism is exacerbated by several other layers of secrecy that remove a number of potential informal constraints that can operate to ensure balanced, rather than biased, legal advice. People seek legal advice because they want to do things and need to find out how to do them legally. There is a natural pressure, in such a context, to provide a permissive interpretation of the law. Many factors typically operate to provide a countervailing pressure, but most of these depend upon the understanding of the parties involved that the actions taken pursuant to that legal advice will be public and can be called into question by those affected by them. If there is reason to think that those affected can argue that the actions taken are in fact contrary to law, then there is a risk of legal liability that will factor into the original advice offered. More generally, public scrutiny through the press and academia provides another set of informal constraints, albeit less direct. But state surveillance operations, both in terms of general programs and in terms of particular operations, are secret. If surveillance is secret, then the people likely affected by the surveillance are in no position to contest it, and this removes one of the informal constraints that can operate to provide balance in determining the lawfulness of the surveillance. In other words, the layers of secrecy surrounding state surveillance structurally enable one-sided legal advice.

If the legal opinions establishing lawfulness are secret, if the activities at issue are secret, if the legal opinions are ones that even those tasked with oversight must defer to, then the "lawfulness" of surveillance is very one-sided indeed. The systematic effect of this on civil liberties should not be underestimated. David Cole has argued, for example, that post-9/11 civil society groups have been one of the most important guardians of constitutional and rule-of-law values, and not the more "formal mechanisms of checks and balances" in the United States.[13] Such groups cannot perform this function when they have no way of knowing the legal opinions and actions of the state, apart from what they learn from whistle-blowers.

We also need to view this unilateralism in the context of what two different whistle-blowers have told us about how the government might in different ways exert pressure for favourable legal interpretations.

The first whistle-blower is Edgar Schmidt, a retired Justice Department lawyer who is taking the Canadian government to court, seeking a declaration regarding what he considers to be unlawful practices in relation to the Department of Justice's review of proposed legislation and regulations. In his statement of claim, he argues,

> Since about 1993, with the knowledge and approval of the Deputy Minister, an interpretation of the statutory examination provisions has been adopted in the Department to the effect that what they require is the formation of an opinion as to whether any provision of the legislative text being examined is manifestly or certainly inconsistent with the Bill of Rights or the Charter and, in the case of proposed regulations, whether any provision is manifestly or certainly not authorized by the Act under which the regulation is made.[14]

This has yet to be tested in court. However, these allegations highlight some of the ways in which institutional cultures can develop in a manner that promotes, not bad faith interpretative practices, but at least a practice of "sharp elbows," where legal interpretation is routinely pushed as far as possible in the government's favour.[15]

The other whistle-blower is Edward Snowden. In a statement to the European Parliament, Snowden outlined the National Security Agency's (NSA) role in law reform in Europe. His remarks are worth quoting at length:

> One of the foremost activities of the NSA's FAD, or Foreign Affairs Division, is to pressure or incentivize EU member states to change their laws to enable mass surveillance. Lawyers from the NSA, as well as the UK's GCHQ, work very hard to search for loopholes in laws and constitutional protections that they can use to justify indiscriminate, dragnet surveillance operations that were at best unwittingly authorized by lawmakers. These efforts to interpret new powers out of vague laws is an intentional strategy to avoid public opposition and lawmakers' insistence that legal limits be respected, effects the GCHQ internally described in its own documents as "damaging public debate."

In recent public memory, we have seen these FAD "legal guidance" operations occur in both Sweden and the Netherlands, and also faraway New Zealand. Germany was pressured to modify its G-10 law to appease the NSA, and it eroded the rights of German citizens under their constitution. Each of these countries received instruction from the NSA, sometimes under the guise of the US Department of Defense and other bodies, on how to degrade the legal protections of their countries' communications. The ultimate result of the NSA's guidance is that the right of ordinary citizens to be free from unwarranted interference is degraded, and systems of intrusive mass surveillance are being constructed in secret within otherwise liberal states, often without the full awareness of the public.[16]

We have no evidence so far that Canada has been subject to such pressure, but Snowden's remarks highlight another cause for concern regarding secrecy and the unilateralism it enables — that a strategy of promoting legal interpretations enabling surveillance, rather than seeking to clarify the law through law reform, might be a strategy of actually avoiding public debate. The result is a claim of "lawfulness" that has not just lost its connection to the public point of view, but has sought to actively sever it.

Complexity and Lawful Access

In addition to secrecy, and sometimes working in conjunction with it, legal complexity undermines accountability. One aspect of this complexity, within Canada, is the different institutions that deal with national security concerns, including the RCMP, Canadian Security Intelligence Service (CSIS), and CSE. Oversight of each is handled differently, with limited ability to coordinate between oversight bodies even in relation to the ways in which these bodies cooperate and assist one another.[17] However, the complexity that I want to highlight here concerns law reform itself, given these interrelationships. That is, even if the state pursues public law reform rather than secret legal interpretations, it is often difficult to understand the full implications of legal changes. Instead of understanding themselves as participants in an open, transparent, and public debate, lawyers concerned about civil liberties need to approach proposed legislation with a "hacker" mentality, looking for non-obvious ways to read the legislation in order to locate the little-understood legal vulnerabilities the government might exploit behind its wall of secrecy and protective official statements.

For example, Canada's ongoing debates regarding lawful access reform generally focus on the ordinary law enforcement context, and yet this reform has difficult-to-understand implications for surveillance in the national security context as well.

Since 9/11, the federal government has sought to pass lawful access legislation. One of the more recent failed iterations, Bill C-30, would have created a mandatory warrantless access regime for some kinds of metadata. In particular, both CSIS and Canadian police services could designate particular individuals who would be authorized to require any telecommunications service provider to provide them with identifying subscriber information. This included the

> [n]ame, address, telephone number and electronic mail address of any subscriber to any of the service provider's telecommunications services and the Internet protocol address and local service provider identifier that are associated with the subscriber's service and equipment.[18]

At the time, critics were concerned that this effectively amounted to a mandatory identification regime, undermining Internet anonymity.[19] The federal government claimed, controversially, that such mandatory identification was required to fight crimes such as child pornography.[20] After a great deal of public controversy over the warrantless access regime, Bill C-30 was shelved.

However, now that we have learned more details regarding some of the ways in which CSE and the NSA have built tracking tools, we can see how mandatory warrantless access to some forms of subscriber data could also enable the tracking of individuals. Bill C-30 did not place any kind of constraint on requiring access to this information, except in relation to who could require it.[21] It is true that Bill C-30 would not have allowed CSE to ask for subscriber information. However, part of CSE's mandate is to provide technical assistance to other Canadian authorities, including CSIS and the RCMP, who could get access to this data and who would face no legal impediment to setting up a regime of bulk access to this data.

As computer security expert Bruce Schneier writes, "If the NSA has a database of IP addresses and locations, it can use that to locate users."[22] We know from the recent CSE disclosures that the ability to track individuals in real time through the use of various forms of metadata, including IP addresses, was known to the government at least as early as May 2012.[23] Bill C-30 received first reading in February 2012 and was shelved amidst public protest in February 2013.[24] Therefore, it is perfectly conceivable that the federal government knew that Bill C-30 could enable the deployment, by either CSIS or the RCMP, with the assistance of CSE, of the kind of real-time tracking tools recently revealed. However, such capabilities were not part of the federal government's public discussion of Bill C-30.

In November 2013, the federal government reintroduced lawful access reform as part of its cyberbullying legislation, and in December 2014 these reforms became law.[25] The new lawful access provisions do not include mandatory warrantless access to subscriber information. However, this did not mean that the issue disappeared. Rather, it shifted to the courts in relation to the question of voluntary, rather than mandatory, warrantless access to subscriber information.[26] A number of lower court decisions suggested that it is permissible for the state to get warrantless access to some forms of subscriber information where this information is voluntarily provided by the service provider and where that service provider has a service agreement with its customer indicating that it might share this information with the state.[27] Although many were concerned that legally permissible warrantless access to subscriber information was facilitating large-scale data collection by the state, it is important to note that the legal cases were being argued within a very specific and narrow context — a specific criminal investigation into child pornography — where these broader implications for how such cases might be interpreted to enable very different forms of surveillance were not at all part of the public discussion. In June 2014 the Supreme Court of Canada weighed in and decided, in *R v. Spencer*, that anonymity is an aspect of informational privacy protected by the *Charter of Rights and Freedoms* and that the police require a warrant to obtain subscriber information, even when telecommunication providers are willing to voluntarily provide it.[28] While *Spencer* shuts down many forms of warrantless access, its scope is unclear. For example, the decision emphasized that the police were trying to link a specific person to specific online activities that were being monitored and it is unclear what kind of protections would extend to "bulky" surveillance contexts where lots of data is collected but remains anonymous (the haystack) in order to help track or locate others (the needle).

Just as the warrantless access issue moved from one of mandatory access to one of voluntary access, the new lawful access provisions make the terms of voluntary access easier. Where a person voluntarily shares information with authorities, so long as she "is not prohibited by law from disclosing" the information, no order is required and there is no criminal or civil liability for providing this information.[29] The Canadian government has suggested that this simply provides "greater certainty" to what is already the case, without providing information as to the contexts in which it seeks voluntary access.[30] It is matched by proposals to amend the federal government's private sector data protection legislation in order to make it easier for organizations to share information with the state, also with virtually no public discussion regarding how this might enable forms of state surveillance.[31]

At a 2014 conference on surveillance, former chief of CSE, John Forster, in response to a question from the audience, indicated that CSE could access its metadata database for the purposes of carrying out its assistance mandate, but that it would then be constrained by whatever legal requirements applied to the institution it was providing assistance to.[32] In other words, if CSE was assisting the RCMP, then its assistance would be governed by the terms of the RCMP's warrant. For those concerned about the domestic implications of broad state surveillance capabilities, this means that the warrant requirements need to be scrutinized with this assistance in mind. Seen in this light, some of the new lawful access reforms are important. For example, there are new production orders for "transmission data" as well as "tracking data" on a standard of reasonable suspicion.[33] The government's rationale is that this is analogous to what we already permit in relation to the use of tracking devices and number recorders.[34] The thought is that since a reasonable suspicion standard was enough when we had to install devices on telephone landlines to determine the numbers phoned, it is enough now to unlock the metadata associated with modern communications. However, we cannot arrive at public understanding of these provisions unless we understand the full context of their use.

What the Snowden revelations have shown us so clearly is that the issue is not about types of information, but *systems* of information and *methods* of analysis. Creating a system of orders and warrants

that presumes meaningful distinctions between subscriber information, transmission data, and content is one that cannot provide the
public with a clear understanding of what authorities can actually
do and what the privacy implications are. The challenge here is quite
serious, as it is not clear that our current constitutional jurisprudence provides us with appropriate legal tools. Our constitutional
privacy jurisprudence focuses on types of information, and specifically whether the information meets the "biographical core" test for
identifying a reasonable expectation of privacy. What we need are
methods of oversight that help us focus on systems and methods.

Jurisdiction and Borderless Communications

When we consider questions of accountability and oversight, we most
often do so within a national framework. Canadian commentators, for
example, point to systems of oversight south of the border and argue
that in comparison our own framework is inadequate and in need
of reform.[35] The framing of the question is then how to ensure that
Canadian surveillance activities occur within a framework of law,
or that Canadians and persons within Canada receive the protection
of the law. However, I argue that it is also important to question the
extent to which national jurisdiction remains a meaningful category
in relation to questions of oversight. As I outline in this section, in the
context of a global communications infrastructure, ideas of national
law and status categories (like non-US person) are currently more
likely to create the legal "loopholes" that enable broad surveillance
than to create forms of accountability and oversight.

Our increasingly borderless system of communication is one
that follows the technical imperatives of the nature of information.
It is widely agreed that the classic point of departure for information
theory is Claude Shannon's 1948 paper "The Mathematical Theory of
Communication," which purported to provide a theory that would
allow one to measure information and system capacity for storage
and transmission of information.[36] As he so strikingly outlines in
his introduction, the "semantic aspects" of communication — the
meaning of messages — "are irrelevant to the engineering problem."
"Information," on this model, is not something that is dependent
on the context of disclosure or of receipt. One can see how, despite
developments in information theory and practice in the intervening
decades, this still captures an important aspect of information and

communications technology (ICT). ICT easily shifts information from one context to another partly because what information *is*, is seen to be independent of these contexts. This logic is further extended in the context of the so-called digital revolution in ICT, which has largely erased the differences between different mediums of transmission and led to an ever-greater proliferation of networking.

The basic "logic" of information, therefore, is that it does not respect context. This is one of the reasons that ICT raises so many privacy concerns. Both privacy norms and justifications for the breach of privacy norms depend upon many contextual factors, yet ICT facilitates practices that render those contextual factors irrelevant.[37] Disclosing information in a context and for a purpose different than the context and purpose for which it was initially collected is one example; taking information that is relatively innocuous in one context and aggregating it to create revealing profiles is another. Geographical borders are another "contextual" feature that ICT increasingly renders irrelevant in many practical details. With so many of our personal and professional activities mediated by the Internet, many of us physically sit in one jurisdiction and at the same time talk, shop, write, and read in an entirely different jurisdiction. The rapid adoption of cloud computing has meant that we can now be in one jurisdiction, but have what are essentially our own personal digital archives stored in another jurisdiction (or multiple jurisdictions).

Several NSA surveillance programs exploit these features of modern communications technology through leveraging the fact that much of the world's Internet traffic passes through the United States and that many of the most central players in cloud computing are US companies, giving it a "home-field advantage."[38] Although the NSA's Internet surveillance programs operated extra-legally in the aftermath of 9/11,[39] they now operate within a legal infrastructure that allows them to take advantage of US dominance of the Internet. Prior to 2008, US authorities could only conduct surveillance on non-US person targets outside of the United States by showing reasonable and probable grounds that the target was a foreign power or an agent of a foreign power, and by obtaining an order from the Foreign Intelligence Surveillance Court (FISC).[40] With the passage of the *FISA Amendments Act* (FAA) in 2008,[41] FISC can approve surveillance of non-US persons outside of the United States without individualized orders.[42] These changes have provided the legal basis for NSA programs like PRISM, which involve obtaining communications data from Internet companies such as Microsoft and Google.

From an American perspective, these legal changes remove obstacles to the timely acquisition of important intelligence information while not compromising US constitutional guarantees, since the US constitution is widely held to not apply to non-US persons abroad.[43] However, from the perspective of a non-US person this can enable state surveillance on standards that fall below their own domestic statutory and constitutional guarantees. Consider Canada. A Canadian using Gmail, for example, has her email routed through the United States and stored on US servers, making it vulnerable to collection under the FAA. Under s. 702, the Attorney General (AG) and the Director of National Intelligence (DNI) are permitted to jointly authorize the targeting of individuals located outside of the United States "to acquire foreign intelligence information."[44] This is not an individualized warrant regime. FISC approves annual certifications for the collection of categories of foreign intelligence information and the AG and DNI can then determine which individuals to target, without any additional oversight.[45] Foreign intelligence information includes information that "relates to...conduct of the foreign affairs of the United States."[46] Such a broad definition can easily include things like political speech, for example; while there are protections in FAA for freedom of expression, these all apply to US persons only.[47] There are also a variety of "minimization" provisions to reduce the privacy impact of authorized surveillance, but these provisions also only apply to US persons.

Canadians do not face a similar threat of surveillance from the Canadian state. For example, the *National Defence Act* does not allow CSE to target Canadians, much less to do so on such lax standard. Canadians can be targeted by CSIS or the RCMP, and then CSE can assist through its assistance mandate, but such targeting is then subject to both the warrant requirements that apply to these agencies as well as our *Charter* guarantees. Of course, CSE has a controversial metadata program that has raised numerous questions regarding both its statutory authorization and its constitutionality. The Snowden revelations have also shown that the CSE is tracking millions of Internet downloads every day, which will inevitably include Canadian Internet activity.[48] Nonetheless, what is important here is that, in relation to non-US persons, FAA permits access to content as well as metadata with fairly limited statutory restrictions and no constitutional restrictions at all. Canadians who use US-based cloud computing therefore are subject to US state surveillance on standards that, if applied within Canada, would be clear violations of our statutory and constitutional rights.

Many have also claimed that these standards are clear violations of international human rights standards. This debate is ongoing, but the official position of the US government is that the protections of the International Convention on Civil and Political Rights only extend to individuals *both* within its territory and within its jurisdiction.[49] The split that cloud computing makes possible — that an individual would be outside its territory but her information subject to US jurisdiction — also creates a space where international human rights norms (arguably) do not apply.

There has been pressure to amend US law in order to erase this distinction between US and non-US persons. The President's Review Group offered one of the most serious attempts to justify some form of such a distinction. The justification they offer is not based upon the reach of the Fourth Amendment, but an understanding of democratic community. It is worth reproducing at some length:

> To understand the legal distinction between United States persons and non–United States persons, it is important to recognize that the special protections that FISA affords United States persons grew directly out of a distinct and troubling era in American history. In that era, the United States government improperly and sometimes unlawfully targeted American citizens for surveillance in a pervasive and dangerous effort to manipulate domestic political activity in a manner that threatened to undermine the core processes of American democracy. As we have seen, that concern was the driving force behind the enactment of FISA.
>
> Against that background, FISA's especially strict limitations on government surveillance of United States persons reflects not only a respect for individual privacy, but also — and fundamentally — a deep concern about potential government abuse within our own political system. The special protections for United States persons must therefore be understood as a crucial safeguard of democratic accountability and effective self-governance within the American political system. In light of that history and those concerns, there is good reason for every nation to enact

> special restrictions on government surveillance of those persons
> who participate directly in its own system of self-governance.[50]

The justification for the distinction therefore remains rooted in ideas of the importance of national jurisdiction and traditional ideas of the significance of the state and its coercive powers. This just underscores the fundamental tension: we have a global communications network where increasingly borders do not matter, we have surveillance practices responding to this reality, and yet we seek to justify and hold surveillance powers to account through asserting that borders matter. Even the idea that concerns about abuse of state authority are restricted to the context of domestic political activity is difficult to accept when so many of us frequently cross borders for both personal and professional reasons. The Canadian example of Maher Arar is a stark reminder of this: Arar was apprehended by US authorities while in transit in New York and removed to Syria, where he was tortured.[51]

Apart from the issue of Canadians crossing the border and becoming directly subject to US jurisdiction, there is the issue of information sharing between the United States and Canada, as well as with other allies. If US authorities can collect information about Canadians on lower standards than are permitted within Canada, and then share this information with Canadian authorities, then this effectively creates an end-run around our constitutional guarantees even if it is, on some level, "lawful." Although we do not know enough about Canadian practices to assess the seriousness of this worry, recent evidence suggests it is not that far-fetched.

In a controversial 2014 Federal Court decision, many important details came to light regarding the Canadian government's understanding of information sharing practices between its allies.[52] The case concerned whether when obtaining a warrant from the Federal Court, CSIS needed to disclose the fact that it would seek assistance from CSE under CSE's assistance mandate, and that CSE would task foreign allies with this assistance. Justice Mosley's concern was not with the flow of information from foreign allies to Canadian authorities, but the other way around — that asking for assistance means that the targets of surveillance could face an increased risk of detention or harm from those foreign allies.[53] The issues are legally complex, and the case is being appealed to the Supreme Court of Canada. Here, I merely want to underscore a number of important details that bear on the question of whether Canadian authorities can obtain information about Canadians that was collected under foreign domestic laws that violate our own constitutional standards.

Partly at issue was a 2007 Federal Court decision that held that the Federal Court did not have the jurisdiction to issue a warrant for surveillance activities abroad.[54] CSIS argued that, in light of this decision,

> they turned to the general authority to investigate threats to the security of Canada set out in s.12 of the [CSIS] Act. They reached the conclusion, through the advice of their legal counsel, that a warrant was not required for CSIS to engage the assistance of the second parties through CSEC [CSE] to intercept the private communications of Canadians outside the country.[55]

It was also CSE's position that no warrant was required for this foreign assistance, that only domestic law of the foreign nation would apply.[56] Accordingly, "they could request that a foreign agency do within its jurisdiction that which CSIS and CSEC could not do in Canada without a warrant."[57] Consistent with this, the Deputy Attorney General of Canada has taken the position that CSIS can ask CSE to task foreign allies to conduct surveillance abroad so long as such surveillance is in accord with the foreign ally's domestic legislation and does not raise serious human rights concerns.[58]

This view partly rests on cases like *R v. Hape*, which have held that when Canadian authorities conduct surveillance on Canadians in other countries the *Charter* does not apply.[59] However, there remains uncertainty as to whether Canadian authorities require some form of lawful authority to conduct surveillance abroad, including engaging the assistance of its allies, even if the *Charter* does not apply.[60] Indeed, the federal government has introduced reforms that would allow CSIS to obtain a warrant with extraterritorial effect.[61] There are also questions as to whether the broad powers legally argued for have actually been exercised.[62] Nonetheless, it shows that there is a plausible legal interpretation that suggests the following asymmetry: there are circumstances where Canadian authorities can ask US authorities to intercept the communications of Canadians on standards that fall far below the level of rights protection afforded to Canadians under our own domestic legislation and constitutional guarantees. In doing so, they would not be acting unlawfully, given the interpretation of the law just outlined.

What these various examples underscore is that we cannot simply focus on domestic institutions and domestic laws if we are to bring surveillance practices within an effective regime of oversight and accountability. Some form of international treaty is likely required with international oversight bodies. Early in the lifecycle of the Snowden revelations there was speculation about the existence of "no spy" agreements between members of the Five Eyes alliance,[63] protecting the citizens of each country from spying from other members. Although there seem to be informal practices and conventions, the United States has publicly and emphatically denied any formal agreements.[64] Whatever we might think about these relationships "based on decades of familiarity, transparency, and past performance between the relevant policy and intelligence communities," these are not legal protections.[65] They are secret, of uncertain scope, can be discarded in the interests of national sovereignty,[66] exist to protect the interests of the state and not the citizens of that state, and are in no way subject to independent oversight.

Conclusion

It is clear that Canada needs to provide a better system of accountability and oversight for our national security agencies and activities. However, in doing so we need to stop thinking that the issue is illegal activity on the part of our national security agencies, such that the answer is to create a system where we can ensure that they follow the law. Instead, I have argued that we need to start from the proposition that our national security agencies do, in good faith, understand themselves to be acting within the law. If we do that, then we can start to appreciate that the relationship between the surveillance state and the rule of law is much more complex, and the possibility of reform more challenging, than is sometimes clear from reactions to the Snowden disclosures. If we look closely, we will see that surveillance does indeed operate according to a legal infrastructure. The problem is that that infrastructure is one of lawful illegality.

Acknowledgements

I would like to thank David Dyzenhaus and Kent Roach for comments on portions of an earlier draft. I would also like to thank Kent Roach and Hamish Stewart for ongoing discussions regarding the Snowden revelations. All errors are, of course, mine.

Notes

1. For a good discussion of extraterritorial intelligence gathering, see Craig Forcese, "Spies without Borders: International Law and Intelligence Collection," (2011) 5 *Journal of National Security Law & Policy* 179.
2. This was very clear from the remarks of Stephen Rigby, national security advisor to the prime minister and PCO, Michel Coulombe, director of CSIS, and John Forster, chief of CSE, at the hearing of the Senate Committee on National Security and Defence, 3 February 2014. See *Proceedings of the Standing Senate Committee on National Security and Defence*, <http://www.parl.gc.ca/Content/SEN/Committee/412/secd/02ev-51162-e.htm?Language=E&Parl=41&Ses=2&comm_id=76>.
3. Lawrence Hurley, "Supreme Court Will Likely Rule on NSA Programs, Antonin Scalia and Ruth Bader Ginsburg Suggest," Reuters, 17 April 2014, <http://www.huffingtonpost.com/2014/04/17/supreme-court-nsa_n_5170559.html>.
4. David Dyzenhaus, *The Constitution of Law: Legality in a Time of Emergency* (Cambridge: Cambridge University Press, 2006) at 3.
5. *Ibid.* See also Adrian Vermuele, "Our Schmittian Administrative Law," (2009) 122:4 *Harvard Law Review* 1095; Evan J. Criddle, "Mending Holes in the Rule of (Administrative) Law," (2010) 104:3 *Northwestern University Law Review* 1271.
6. President Barak Obama, Address (Speech delivered at the National Defense University, 23 May 2013), The White House, <http://www.whitehouse.gov/the-press-office/2013/05/23/remarks-president-national-defense-university>.
7. John Ashcroft, *Never Again: Securing America and Restoring Justice* (New York: Center Street, 2006); Juliette Kayyem, "Never Say 'Never Again': Our Foolish Obsession with Stopping the Next Attack," *Foreign Policy*, 11 September 2013, <http://foreignpolicy.com/2012/09/11/never-say-never-again/>.
8. As Roach has argued, this debate is not about emergencies per se so much as the rights of terrorist suspects. See Kent Roach, "Ordinary Laws for Emergencies and Democratic Derogations from Rights," in *Emergencies and the Limits of Legality*, ed. Victor V. Ramraj (Cambridge: Cambridge University Press, 2012) at 229.

9. Greg Weston, Glenn Greenwald & Ryan Gallagher, "CSEC Used Airport Wi-Fi to Track Travellers: Edward Snowden Documents," *CBC News*, 30 January 2014, <http://www.cbc.ca/news/politics/csec-used-airport-wi-fi-to-track-canadian-travellers-edward-snowden-documents-1.2517881>.

10. See, for example, the remarks of John Forster, chief of CSE, *supra* note 2.

11. Canada, Office of the Communications Security Establishment Commissioner, *Annual Report 2005–2006* (Ottawa), <http://www.ocsec-bccst.gc.ca/ann-rpt/archives_e.php>, at 9. This disagreement was not about the metadata program.

12. Canada, Office of the Communications Security Establishment Commissioner, *Annual Report 2006–2007* (Ottawa), <http://www.ocsec-bccst.gc.ca/ann-rpt/2006-2007/cover_e.php>, at 2; Canada, Office of the Communications Security Establishment Commissioner, *Annual Report 2008–2009* (Ottawa), <http://www.ocsec-bccst.gc.ca/ann-rpt/2008-2009/cover_e.php>, at 2; Canada, Office of the Communications Security Establishment Commissioner, *Annual Report 2012–2013* (Ottawa), <http://www.ocsec-bccst.gc.ca/ann-rpt/2012-2013/cover_e.php>, at 7–8 (Commissioner Décary discussing his disappointment that the government has not made the legislative amendments called for as a response to this dispute. The commissioner also noted that 92 per cent of the commissioners' recommendations since 1997 have been implemented, at 3).

13. David Cole, "Where Liberty Lies: Civil Society and Individual Rights After 9/11," (2011) 57 *Wayne Law Review* 1203 at 1204–5.

14. Federal Court, Edgar Schmidt, and the Attorney-General of Canada, Statement of Claim, Court File No. T-2225-12, *Voices-Voix* <http://www.slaw.ca/wp-content/uploads/2013/01/Edgar_Schmidt_Statement_of_Claim.pdf>, at para. 12, emphasis in original.

15. Lon Fuller argues that a "strong commitment to the principles of legality compels a ruler to answer to himself, not only for his fists, but for his elbows as well." Lon L. Fuller, *The Morality of Law* (New Haven, CT: Yale University Press, 1969) at 159.

16. Edward Snowden, Address (Delivered at the European Parliament, 7 March 2014), <http://www.europarl.europa.eu/document/activities/cont/201403/20140307ATT80674/20140307ATT80674EN.pdf>.

17. This was recently highlighted in the Office of the Privacy Commissioner of Canada, *Special Report to Parliament: Checks and Controls: Reinforcing Privacy Protection and Oversight for the Canadian Intelligence Community in an Era of Cyber-Surveillance*, (Ottawa: 28 January 2014), <https://www.priv.gc.ca/information/sr-rs/201314/sr_cic_e.asp>.

18. Bill C-30, *An Act to enact the Investigating and Preventing Criminal Electronic Communications Act and to amend the Criminal Code and other Acts*, 1st Sess., 41st Parl., 2011–2012, cl 16.

19. Lisa M. Austin & Andrea Slane, "What's in a Name? Privacy and Citizenship in the Voluntary Disclosure of Subscriber Information in Online Child Exploitation Investigations," (2011) 57 *Criminal Law Quarterly* 486.

20. Fred Chartrand, "Vic Toews Accuses Bill's Opponents of Siding with Child Pornographers," *Toronto Star* (Toronto), 13 February 2012, <http://www.thestar.com/news/canada/2012/02/13/vic_toews_accuses_bills_opponents_of_siding_with_child_pornographers.html>.

21. Bill C-30, *supra* note 18.

22. Bruce Schneier, "Finding People's Locations based on Their Activities in Cyberspace," *Schneier on Security* (blog), 13 February 2014, <https://www.schneier.com/blog/archives/2014/02/finding_peoples.html>.

23. Communications Security Establishment Canada, *IP Profiling Analytics & Mission Impacts*, 10 May 2012, <http://www.cbc.ca/news2/pdf/airports_redacted.pdf>.

24. Laura Payton, "Government Killing Online Surveillance Bill," *CBC News*, 11 February 2013, <http://www.cbc.ca/news/politics/government-killing-online-surveillance-bill-1.1336384>.

25. Bill C-13, *An Act to amend the Criminal Code, the Canada Evidence Act, the Competition Act and the Mutual Legal Assistance in Criminal Matters Act*, 2nd Sess., 41st Parl., 2013, cl 20 (first reading 20 November 2013, royal assent 9 December 2014).

26. *R. v. Spencer*, 2014 SCC 43, 375 DLR (4th) 255, 438 Sask R 230, (CanLII).

27. *R. v. Ward*, 2012 ONCA 660, 112 OR (3d) 321, (CanLII). Cases like this suggest that the agreement is just one factor in the reasonable expectation of privacy analysis, rather than a decisive factor.

28. *Supra* note 25.

29. This is the new section 487.0195 of the *Criminal Code*.

30. Government of Canada, Department of Justice, news release, "Myths and Facts Bill C-13, Protecting Canadians from Online Crime Act," November 2013, <http://news.gc.ca/web/article-en.do?nid=832399>.

31. Bill S-4, *An Act to amend the Personal Information and Electronic Documents Act and to make a consequential amendment to another Act*, 2nd Sess. 41st Parl. (first reading 17 June 2014).

32. *The Electronic Surveillance State: Canada's Position, Global Implications & The Question of Reform*, The Canadian International Council, Toronto Branch, 1 March 2014. The question was mine.

33. These are the new sections 487.015, 487.016, and 487.017 of the *Criminal Code*.

34. *Criminal Code*, RSC 1985, c C-46, ss 492.1 (tracking warrant) and 492.2 (number recorder).

35. Weston, Greenwald & Gallagher, *supra* note 9.

36. Claude E. Shannon, "The Mathematical Theory of Communication," (1948) 27 (July) Bell System Technical J 379 and (1948) 27 (October) Bell

System Technical J 623. Reprinted in Claude E. Shannon & Warren Weaver, eds., *The Mathematical Theory of Communication* (Urbana: University of Illinois Press, 1949) at 3.

37. Lisa M. Austin, "Privacy and the Question of Technology," (2003) 22:2 *Law and Philosophy* 119.

38. Glenn Greenwald & Ewen MacAskill, "NSA Prism Program Taps into User Data of Apple, Google and Others," *The Guardian*, 7 June 2013, <http://www.theguardian.com/world/2013/jun/06/us-tech-giants-nsa-data>.

39. James Risen & Eric Lichtblau, "Bush Lets U.S. Spy on Callers without Courts," *New York Times*, 16 December 2005, <http://www.nytimes.com/2005/12/16/politics/16program.html?pagewanted=all>.

40. *Foreign Intelligence Surveillance Act of 1978*, Pub L No 95-511, 92 Stat 1783; US, Senate Committee on Intelligence, 112th Cong, *Report on FAA Sunsets Extension Act of 2012* (S Doc No 112-174) (Washington, DC: US Government Printing Office, 2012) at 16. A "United States person" includes US citizens, permanent residents, unincorporated associations that include a substantial number of US citizens and permanent residents, and corporations incorporated in the United States. See 50 USC § 1801 (i).

41. *FISA Amendments Act of 2008*, Pub L No 110-261, 122 Stat 2463.

42. *Report on FAA Sunsets Extension Act*, *supra* note 40 at 3. At the same time, the FAA increased the protections provided to US persons located outside of the United States, primarily through providing for judicial review.

43. *Ibid.* at 16.

44. *Supra* note 39.

45. President's Review Group on Intelligence and Communications Technologies, "Liberty and Security in a Changing World," *The White House* (blog), 18 December 2013, <http://www.whitehouse.gov/blog/2013/12/18/liberty-and-security-changing-world>, at 135, emphasis in original.

46. See 50 USC § 1801 (e).

47. The President's Review Group reports that section 702 is only used to intercept communications where the foreign intelligence information at issue is "related to such matters as international terrorism, nuclear proliferation, or hostile cyber activities" (*supra* note 43 at 152–3). However, the language of section 702 and the definition of foreign intelligence information does not contain any such limitations.

48. Amber Hildebrandt, Michael Pereira, & Dave Seglins, "CSE Tracks Millions of Downloads Daily: Snowden Documents," *CBC News*, 27 January 2015, <http://www.cbc.ca/news/canada/cse-tracks-millions-of-downloads-daily-snowden-documents-1.2930120>.

49. Charlie Savage, "U.S., Rebuffing U.N., Maintains Stance That Rights Treaty Does Not Apply Abroad," *New York Times*, 13 March 2014, <http://www.nytimes.com/2014/03/14/world/us-affirms-stance-that-rights-treaty-doesnt-apply-abroad.html?_r=0>.

50. President's Review Group, *supra* note 43 at 153–4, emphasis in original.

51. Commission of Inquiry into the Actions of Canadian Officials in Relation to Maher Arar, *Report of the Events Relating to Maher Arar* (Ottawa: 2006), <http://epe.lac-bac.gc.ca/100/206/301/pco-bcp/commissions/maher_arar/07-09-13/www.ararcommission.ca/eng/26.htm>.

52. X *(Re)*, 2013 FC 1275, [2010] 1 FCR 460, 369 DLR (4th) 157, (CanLII), affirmed 2014 FCA 249.

53. *Ibid.* at paras. 115, 122.

54. Reasons for Order and Order (22 October 2007), Justice Blanchard. The public redacted version is *Canadian Security Intelligence Service Act (Re)*, 2008 FC 301, [2008] 4 FCR 230, 356 FTR 56, (CanLII).

55. X *(Re)*, *supra* note 49 at para. 94.

56. *Ibid.* at para. 58.

57. *Ibid.* at para. 60.

58. *Ibid.* at para. 34.

59. *Ibid.* at para. 29; *R. v. Hape*, 2007 SCC 26, [2007] 2 SCR 292, 280 DLR (4th) 385, (CanLII).

60. X *(Re)*, *supra* note 49 at para. 30.

61. See section 8 of Bill C-44 *An Act to amend the Canadian Security Intelligence Service Act and other Acts*, 2nd Sess. 41st Parl.

62. *Ibid.* at para. 112. "I am satisfied that the Service and CSEC chose to act upon the new broad and untested interpretation of the scope of s 12 only where there was a 30-08 warrant in place." The original 30-08 warrants under discussion were issued for surveillance within Canada on targets who were then travelling abroad, so additional warrants were then sought (at para. 36).

63. The members are the United States, Canada, the United Kingdom, Australia, and New Zealand.

64. The President's Review Group, *supra* note 43 at 175; Jennifer Epstein, "U.S. Doesn't Have 'No-Spy' Agreement with Foreign Countries, Obama Says," *Politico*, 11 February 2014, <http://www.politico.com/story/2014/02/nsa-spying-foreign-countries-103382.html>.

65. The President's Review Group, *ibid.* at 175.

66. X *(Re)*, *supra* note 49 at para. 17.

CHAPTER V

Law, Logarithms, and Liberties: Legal Issues Arising from CSE's Metadata Collection Initiatives

Craig Forcese

Introduction

The year 2013 was the year of the spy. Edward Snowden — "leaker" or "whistle-blower" depending on one's perspective — ignited a mainstream (and social) media frenzy in mid-2013 by sharing details of classified US National Security Agency (NSA) surveillance programs with the UK *Guardian* and *Washington Post* newspapers.[1]

For related reasons, 2013 was also the year in which the term metadata migrated from the lexicon of the technologically literate into the parlance of everyday commentary. The NSA, it would appear, collects and archives metadata on millions of Internet and telecommunication users.[2] This information has been compared to "data on data" — that is, it is the contextual information that surrounds the content of an Internet transaction or communication. As the *Guardian* explains, "examples include the date and time you called somebody or the location from which you last accessed your email. The data collected generally does not contain personal or content-specific details, but rather transactional information about the user, the device and activities taking place."[3]

The NSA revelations fuelled media, academic, and other speculation about whether similar surveillance programs exist in Canada. That attention focused on Canada's NSA equivalent (and close alliance partner), the Communications Security Establishment (CSE). In

2013, journalists unearthed tantalizing clues concerning a Canadian metadata project.[4] In early 2014, a Snowden document pointed to some sort of CSE metadata collection project implicating travellers accessing a Wi-Fi network at a Canadian airport.[5]

These disclosures prompted questions about the legal basis for any collection initiative, and the extent to which CSE was governed by robust accountability mechanisms. They also sparked a constitutional lawsuit brought by the BC Civil Liberties Association.[6]

The Canadian government remained largely inert faced with these concerns, hewing to a policy of limited comment rather than more open debate.[7] The government's clear expectation has been that the controversies ignited by Snowden would eventually expire, if starved of oxygen. By the time of this writing, this hope appears not to have been realized. Mr. Snowden's chief journalistic partner, Glen Greenwald, has adopted a strategy of "serial" releases of Snowden documents, including a regular trickle of Canada-specific materials on various surveillance issues.[8] This dribble of material — although single-sourced, decontextualized, and often difficult to understand — has kept the matter in the public eye.

Meanwhile, CSE and its partner the Canadian Security Intelligence Service (CSIS) have been caught in a seemingly unrelated surveillance controversy by exceeding the legal limits on surveillance imposed by Federal Court warrants.[9] Together, these events have created more than a whiff of scandal surrounding Canada's surveillance activities. The undoubtedly unfair impression left by the timing and frequency of these controversies is of recidivist skullduggery by the Canadian spy services.

The purpose of this chapter is not, however, to rehearse these events or assess the merits or demerits of Canada's national security surveillance actions. Instead, I focus on a narrower, but in my view, even more fundamental question: By reason of technological change and capacity, have the state's surveillance activities now escaped governance by law? This is a broad question with a number of facets, and this article examines the specific sub-issue of metadata and its relationship with conventional rules on searches and seizures.

I proceed in two main parts. In Part I, I trace what is currently known about CSE's metadata activities. In Part II, I examine two specific legal questions raised by these activities: first, the extent to which metadata are "private communications" that attract special statutory privacy protections; and, second, whether CSE metadata collection is consistent with section 8 of the *Canadian Charter of Rights and Freedoms*.[10] The discussion in this chapter is provisional, by dint of imperfect information about CSE activities. Based on what we do know, however, I argue that the privacy standards that CSE must meet in relation to metadata are much more robust than the government seems to have accepted to date.

Canada's Metadata Surveillance Initiatives

It is, of course, impossible to outline in anything close to full form CSE's metadata collection initiative. Nevertheless, enough is now on the public record that something may be said about it. It is important, however, to begin with a brief discussion of metadata and its implications for privacy. I then turn to a review of CSE and its functions so that readers may contextualize the more specific information on metadata collection. Finally, this section traces what is known about CSE's metadata operations.

Metadata in Context

In a 2013 report, the Privacy Commissioner of Ontario defined "metadata" as "information generated by our communications devices and our communications service providers, as we use technologies like landline telephones, mobile phones, desktop computers, laptops, tablets or other computing devices. It is essentially information about other information, in this case, relating to our communications."[11] The commissioner compared metadata to "digital crumbs" that reveal "time and duration of a communication, the particular devices, addresses, or numbers contacted, which kinds of communications services we use, and at what geolocations."[12]

This information is stored by communications providers for differing periods of times, and is amendable to compilation, linking, and tracing. Metadata can be used to paint a quite intimate portrait: work and sleep habits, travel patterns, and relationships with others. From these data, observers may develop detailed inferences about places of employment, patterns and means of travel, frequency of visits to doctors and pharmacies, visits to "social or commercial establishments," religious and political affiliations, and the like.[13]

Reviewing this kind of information may be more invasive of privacy than even intercepting the actual content of communications. MIT computer scientist Daniel Weitzner considers metadata "arguably

more revealing [than content] because it's actually much easier to analyze the patterns in a large universe of metadata and correlate them
with real-world events than it is to through a semantic analysis of all
of someone's email and all of someone's telephone calls."[14]

Metadata associated with Internet use may also reveal notable amounts of personal information. A study by the Privacy
Commissioner of Canada concluded that subscriber information
such as IP addresses[15] may "provide a starting point to compile a
picture of an individual's online activities, including: online services
for which an individual has registered; personal interests, based on
websites visited; and organizational affiliations."[16]

Even more concerning than the direct privacy implications of
metadata is the amalgamation of these data with other information,
a process that some have colloquially called "Big Data." Big Data can
be defined as "the storage and analysis of large and/or complex data
sets using a series of [computer-based] techniques."[17] Big Data may
involve the linking of discrete and separate pieces of information
together to create a "mosaic" portrait of a person's life.

An Overview of CSE's Mandates

By law, CSE's mandate includes acquiring and using "information
from the global information infrastructure for the purpose of providing foreign intelligence" ("Mandate A") and providing "technical
and operational assistance to federal law enforcement and security
agencies in the performance of their lawful duties" ("Mandate C").[18]
In other words, it is principally an electronic eavesdropping agency
that collects what is known as "signals intelligence," SIGINT.

However, to perform any spying, CSE must be lawfully authorized to do so — that is, it must be able to lawfully access the electronic
data. CSE may spy on foreigners and on Canadians, but the rules that
apply to each of these scenarios are radically different. Put bluntly, for
foreign spying there are no real legislated rules. For spying that may
implicate Canadians, there are several legislated provisos.

1. Mandate A and Lawful Access

First, under its Mandate A, CSE can collect "foreign intelligence" — that is, "information or intelligence about the capabilities,
intentions or activities of a foreign individual, state, organization
or terrorist group, as they relate to international affairs, defence or

security."[19] Much (probably almost all) of this foreign intelligence is just that: foreign. There is no Canadian or person in Canada implicated in the intercepted communication. Here, the law does not prescribe any specific rules on intercept authorizations.

On the other hand, CSE's rules insist that its foreign intelligence activities "not be directed at Canadians or any person in Canada; and... shall be subject to measures to protect the privacy of Canadians in the use and retention of intercepted information."[20]

Squaring this expectation with the reality of webbed communication is challenging. In a world where telecommunications systems are webbed together, even "foreign intelligence" may have a Canadian nexus. For instance, it may be that a telephone call sent to or originating in Canada might be intercepted. Similarly, CSE surveillance may capture the communication of a Canadian located overseas. As the government acknowledges, "the complexity of the global information infrastructure is such that it is not possible for CSE to know ahead of time if a foreign target will communicate with a Canadian or person in Canada, or convey information about a Canadian."[21]

CSE's law recognizes that "there may be circumstances in which incidental interception of private communications or information about Canadians will occur."[22] The law permits the Minister of National Defence to issue a "ministerial authorization" authorizing CSE to collect "private communications." The minister may issue this authorization only where satisfied, among other things, that the interception is directed at foreign entities outside of Canada and privacy-protecting measures are in place in the event that Canadian communications are captured. [23]

"Private communication" in CSE's law is defined with reference to Part VI of the *Criminal Code*, described further below.[24] Part VI makes it a crime to intercept a "private communication" in most instances, when done without authorization. Under its law, the ministerial authorization exempts CSE from this criminal culpability.[25] The authorization presumably also makes an intercept "lawfully made," and excuses the government from the civil liability that otherwise exists for intercepting "private communications."[26]

Under these circumstances, it is obviously critical that the government agency have a clear-eyed view of what constitutes "private communication" and that it act assiduously in obtaining the required authorization for its intercept.

In practice, ministerial authorizations have been issued on a "just in case" basis — that is, because one can never be sure that the communications intercepted will lack a Canadian nexus, authorizations are sought regularly to make sure CSE remains on-side with the law. Compared to warrants issued by judges in police investigations (and those in investigations by CSIS), ministerial authorizations are general. As described by the commissioner charged with review of CSE in his 2011–12 annual report, ministerial authorizations "relate to an 'activity' or 'class of activities' specified in the authorizations... The authorizations do not relate to a specific individual or subject (the whom or the what)."[27]

The minister issued a total of seventy-eight authorizations between 2002 and 2012.[28] For 2011, six authorizations existed, and CSE intercepted private communication in relation to only one of these authorizations.[29]

2. Mandate C and Lawful Access

In addition, CSE may also assist other government agencies, such as CSIS or the RCMP, in intercepting information and providing technological wherewithal that these other agencies may not have. Given the mandate of most of these bodies, these intercepts would usually involve Canadians or communications within Canada. Such domestic intercepts would only be legal if the other agency (typically CSIS or RCMP) themselves had lawful authority for the intercept.

In practice, that legal authority depends on a judge pre-authorizing the intercept by judicial warrant or authorization. CSE, in other words, would only spy on Canadians on behalf of CSIS or the RCMP where these agencies themselves were lawfully permitted to perform the surveillance.[30] The legal authority exercised by the requesting agency creates a safe harbour for CSE.

As this book goes to press, Parliament is debating a massive overhaul of CSIS's powers in Bill C-51, permitting that agency to engage in "measures" to reduce threats to the security of Canada. These measures could easily reach offensive use of Internet abilities, to corrupt computer systems or bring down websites. Mandate C assistance to CSIS may, in other words, soon invest CSE in more than surveillance of Canadian computer traffic and systems.

Metadata Collection by CSE

I turn now to a description of CSE's metadata collection initiatives under its Mandate A. This assessment relies on often deeply redacted documents obtained mostly by *Globe and Mail* journalist Colin Freeze, under the *Access to Information Act*.

1. *2004 to 2008*

On 14 March 2004, the Minister of National Defence issued a "ministerial directive" to CSE, pursuant to his power to do so under the *National Defence Act*.[31] While the full title of this directive is redacted from documents released under the access law, it clearly concerned (at least in part) collection by CSE of telecommunications metadata under that agency's Mandate A.

The public document is deeply censored and details on the initiative (including the definition of metadata) are deleted. The directive does, however, specify that CSE "will not direct program activities at Canadians or at any person in Canada." It also obliged the agency to apply its existing privacy protection procedures to the "use and retention of communications and data." CSE could share metadata with other agencies but "subject to strict conditions to protect the privacy of Canadians, consistent with the standards governing CSE's other programs."

The minister replaced this initial instrument with another directive, dated 9 March 2005 and entitled "Ministerial Directive, Communications Security Establishment Collection and Use of Metadata."[32] The public version of document again excises a full definition of metadata, but states that metadata "means information associated with a telecommunication to identify, describe, manage or route that telecommunications or any part of it."

Again, the ministerial directive tasked CSE with metadata collection under its foreign intelligence mandate (Mandate A),[33] and repeated language on compliance with existing privacy protections. These privacy strictures were apparently enumerated in detail, but the actual protections are redacted from the document. The directive also acknowledged the responsibility of CSE's review body, the commissioner of the CSE. CSE's law charges this commissioner with, among other things, reviewing "the activities of the Establishment to ensure that they are in compliance with the law."[34]

The commissioner undertook such a review, dated January 2008, in order to "identify and understand the nature of CSE's metadata activities and to assess their compliance with the ministerial directive and with the laws of Canada" and CSE's "own operational policies, procedures and practices."[35] Much of the commissioner's report is redacted. It is clear, however, that legal advice provided by the Department of Justice undergirded CSE's metadata collection process. For reasons excised from the public document, the commissioner concluded that at least some metadata collection activities under the directive did not require ministerial authorization,[36] presumably because they did not implicate "private communications."

However, there are other passages in the commissioner's report that suggest that some metadata was collected pursuant to a ministerial authorization, "as it is possible that a private communication could be intercepted."[37] Indeed, the commissioner recommended that CSE "re-examine and re-assess its current position and practice that requires that only those private communications recognized [redaction] be accounted for."[38]

2. 2008 to Present

The commissioner's report and other commissioner documents also raised doubts as to whether CSE acted properly in conducting metadata collection under its Mandate A that should, in fact, have been sought under Mandate C, assistance to security and law enforcement agencies. In his report, the commissioner asks, "is CSE's (a) mandate the appropriate authority to conduct [redaction] in the context of a criminal or national security investigation of a Canadian in Canada?"[39] The commissioner ultimately called on CSE to re-examine and reassess the legislative authority used to conduct at least some of its (presumably) metadata activities.[40]

The position was contested by CSE, apparently on the strength of legal advice obtained from the Department of Justice.[41] However, in a follow-up letter to the Minister of National Defence, the commissioner noted his view that the issue was not the interpretation of Mandates A and C, but which mandates applied in which context. He underscored the significance of the distinction between Mandate A and C: deciding which applies "is important because it determines the legal requirement (e.g., ministerial authorization vs. a court warrant) in cases where activities may be 'directed at' a Canadian."[42]

Despite these differences of opinion, the commissioner's concerns were apparently enough to prompt CSE to suspend its metadata initiative during the period April 2007 to October 2008. CSE recommenced the project thereafter, but apparently with changes. According to ministerial media lines, the initial suspension "was initiated by the Chief of CSEC in order to make absolutely certain that the activities in question were compliant with Canadian privacy laws as well as with CSEC's own policies and procedures....In consultation with the Department of Justice an internal review determined that these activities were indeed in compliance with the law but I felt that certain CSEC policies should be clarified. This was done and CSEC resumed these activities."[43]

A December 2010 report by the CSE commissioner examined CSE's re-commenced metadata activities from October 2008 to October 2009. According to a 2011 CSE briefing note, that report concluded that activities "were appropriately authorized under part (a) of the mandate," and the commissioner no longer had concerns as to whether activities should instead be conducted under Mandate C.[44]

The 2005 ministerial directive itself changed in late 2011.[45] According to briefing notes prepared in support of the 2011 change, CSE concluded that something redacted (but in context, perhaps metadata) "does not represent a reasonable threshold for privacy concerns and therefore current privacy protection measures are adequate."[46] It is also clear that metadata were not, in CSE's view, "a communication."[47] Indeed, in its Ops-Manual, CSE writes that "metadata" "does not require an MA [ministerial authorization],"[48] which could only be true if CSE viewed metadata as outside the scope of private communication. These conclusions are relevant to the legal analysis that follows in Part II of this article.

The government's position on some privacy questions may since have shifted, at least in a small way. In February 2014, it specified that metadata refers to "information associated with a telecommunication to identify, describe, manage or route that telecommunication or any part of it as well as the means by which it was transmitted, but excludes any information or part of information which could reveal the purport of a telecommunication, or the whole or part of its content."[49] It seems also to acknowledge that collection of at least some metadata may give rise to a reasonable expectation of privacy, although interference with this expectation is reasonable because, in part, of ministerial authorizations.[50]

Metadata and the Law

I turn now to legal issues raised by the metadata program described at the beginning of this chapter under Canada's Metadata Surveillance Initiatives. To encapsulate the apparent government position suggested by the documents described above, the government may not regard metadata as constituting a "private communication." Exactly why this is so is unknown but may reflect the government view that metadata are not communication per se. While its position may be shifting, it may also not view metadata as giving rise to a "reasonable expectation of privacy" or their collection as constituting an unreasonable search and seizure.

These findings are crucial. If metadata are private communications, then their collection must be supported by a ministerial authorization in order to be exempted from application of the criminal law (and civil liability exposure). If any of CSE's activities (with metadata or elsewhere) give rise to a reasonable expectation of privacy, *Charter* section 8 issues arise, with serious implications not only for the collection process but also more generally for the constitutionality of CSE's ministerial authorization regime.[51]

Metadata May Be "Private Communication"
In both CSE's law and Part VI of the Criminal Code, "private communication" means

> any *oral communication*, or any *telecommunication*, that is made by
> an originator who is in Canada or is intended by the originator
> to be received by a person who is in Canada and that is made
> under circumstances in which it is reasonable for the originator
> to expect that it will not be intercepted by any person other than
> the person intended by the originator to receive it.[52]

This definition may be apportioned into key constituent elements. First, the provision pertains to a communication — whether "oral" or a "telecommunication." Second, the "originator" must have an expectation that the communication is, in fact, private — that is, that it will not be shared with a third-party intermediary. In this respect, the courts have sometimes spoken about a reasonable expectation of privacy,[53] creating a link of sorts between "private communication" and the threshold for Charter section 8 protections. Third, the communication must be in Canada, or the communication must be intentionally directed at a person who is in Canada. I discuss each of these elements in turn.

1. *Metadata Falls within the Meaning of "Telecommunication"*

Enacted in 1974, Part VI predates modern communications technologies. The concept of "private communications" has, however, been the subject of judicial construals over the decades, as technology changes.

Private communication includes "telecommunication," a concept that most people once would have associated with voice communication over telephone wires. However, the federal *Interpretation Act* prescribes a broader understanding, defining "telecommunication" as "the emission, transmission or reception of signs, signals, writing, images, sounds or intelligence of any nature by any wire, cable, radio, optical or other electromagnetic system, or by any similar technical system."[54]

In *R. v. Telus Communications*,[55] a plurality of the Supreme Court of Canada relied on the *Interpretation Act* to conclude that "text messages" — a written form of electronic communication — were clearly a "telecommunication" for the purposes of Part VI of the *Criminal Code*. Lower courts have reached similar conclusions. In *R. v. Mills*, the Newfoundland and Labrador Provincial Court held that "private communication" included "emails and chat messages."[56]

These cases concerned intercept of content-rich data — actual communications. However, in *Telus*, the plurality saw Part VI's rules on intercept of private communication as reaching the "state acquisition of informational content — the substance, meaning, or purport — of the private communication. *It is not just the communication itself that is protected, but any derivative of that communication that would convey its substance or meaning.*"[57] Likewise, in *Lyons v. The Queen*, the court concluded that Part VI was not "'wiretapping' legislation, nor eavesdropping legislation, nor radio regulation. It is the regulation of all these things and 'any other device' that may be used to intercept intelligence reasonably expected by the originator not to be intercepted by anyone other than the intended recipient."[58]

As suggested earlier, metadata meets these thresholds precisely; it is derivate of the communication, but from it much substance can be inferred. In other words, it communicates "intelligence," which the *Interpretation Act* makes part of "telecommunication." Indeed, intelligence is exactly why the security services seek to collect it.

The Supreme Court has also signalled its concerns with metadata in other contexts, other than Part VI. It has noted that the accumulation of metadata on computer systems is one reason why privacy protections on computer searches should be robust. In the court's words

> Word-processing programs will often automatically generate temporary files that permit analysts to reconstruct the development of a file and access information about who created and worked on it. Similarly, most browsers used to surf the Internet are programmed to automatically retain information about the websites the user has visited in recent weeks and the search terms that were employed to access those websites. Ordinarily, this information can help a user retrace his or her cybernetic steps. In the context of a criminal investigation, however, it can also enable investigators to access intimate details about a user's interests, habits, and identity, drawing on a record that the user created unwittingly.[59]

All of this is to say that metadata constitute revealing, personal information from which potentially intimate content data can be inferred. There is good reason, therefore, to posit the inclusion of metadata as telecommunication and therefore as private communication.

2. *Precedent Tends to Support Metadata's Inclusion in "Telecommunication"*

This conclusion is bolstered, to a point, by case law that deals with close analogues to metadata: information collected by telephone number recorders (TNRs). TNRs record the "telephone number or location of the telephone from which a telephone call originates, or at which it is received or is intended to be received."[60] Collection of this information is now regulated by a separate *Criminal Code* provision.[61] Both before and after the introduction of this provision, however, cases considered the applicability of Part VI to TNR information. These cases fall into three camps.

First, a minority of cases concludes that the data recorded by TNRs are not captured by the definition of private communication because Part VI only protects content-rich communications. In the eyes of these judges, private communication involves the exchange of information between originator and recipient, not the "the fact that a means of communication has been engaged."[62]

These decisions are difficult to reconcile with the concept of telecommunications noted above, and indeed tend to disregard the *Interpretation Act*.[63] Not surprisingly, therefore, a second set of cases has viewed TNR data as "private communication,"[64] plain and simple. Yet a third, more recent category of cases has agreed that data created by these devices are telecommunications under Part VI, but that the concept of private communication has no bearing where the communicator "knows some or all of it will or might be collected by the phone company in the normal course of business."[65] Put another way, the fact that the data is obtained by the authorities from a third-party intermediary changes its character to something other than a private communication.

3. *Collection from Third-Party Intermediaries Does Not Always Remove Metadata from the Class of "Private Communications"*

The metadata collected by CSE may often be obtained from third-party communication service providers. It is important, therefore, to examine closely the question of third-party intermediaries and its relevance to the concept of private communications. In this regard, I believe there is reason to doubt whether the view expressed by this third class of cases in relation to TNR data applies to the broader range of metadata telecommunications.

a) Past cases on this issue have been about which privacy regime applies, not about negating the application of any privacy regime
First, it is important to underscore that Parliament has now created a separate warrant regime for telephone number recorders. The recent cases that have excluded TNR data from "private communication" have not, therefore, had to decide between "privacy protection or no privacy protection." Instead, they have dealt with the issue in the context of "*which* privacy protection."

In *Lee*, for example, the Alberta trial court concluded that Part VI was inapplicable because of the third-party intermediary, but emphasized that this "is not to say the originator does not have some expectation of privacy in the TNR data." In fact, Parliament had enacted special provisions on TNR that "may be taken to reflect Parliament's recognition there is a reasonable expectation of privacy in TNR data, albeit a somewhat diminished expectation." The court then observed that the "TNR device nowadays may well capture more than telephone numbers, date and time of telephone contact and nearest cellular telephone tower. It may also record passwords, pin numbers, or other number-based codes keyed in using the number pad on the telephone. The very fact contact was made between certain telephone numbers may reveal some aspects of lifestyle."[66]

The existence of a transparent, TNR-specific judicial authorization regime places that issue on a dramatically different footing than the subject of this chapter: intercept of potentially even more revealing metadata by CSE without any third-party authorization *whatsoever*. If an intercept is not private communication, CSE may act without any advance, third-party scrutiny. Since this is fully lawful, the commissioner's review will not detect any defect in this behaviour. Put another way, defining metadata as outside the ambit of private communication would give exclusive intercept authority to an intelligence service whose conduct will never come to light or be second-guessed, except through happenstance.

I hypothesize, therefore, that a court would be much more reluctant to define metadata as falling outside the ambit of private communication when the result is a carte blanche for an intelligence service. By way of rough analogy, the Supreme Court has condemned past construal of the law that "by-passes any judicial consideration of the entire police procedures and thereby makes irrelevant the entire scheme in Part IV.1 of the Code."[67] All of this is to say that the third class of TNR court decisions is distinguishable from the subject matter of this chapter.

b) The reasonable originator would not be aware of the full scope of third-party access to metadata
Second, it is clear that under the definition of private communication, "it is the originator [of the communication's] state of mind that is decisive."[68] Put another way, the "private" nature of the communication turns on whether the "sender of such communications can reasonably expect that they will not be intercepted by any person other than the persons intended to receive them."[69] The existence of a third-party intermediary goes to the reasonableness of the originator's expectation of privacy.

This is exactly the issue raised by the third class of TNR cases. A reasonable originator should properly realize that TNR data in the possession of service providers is not confidential information — not least, it is used for billing purposes. However, what an originator should believe about a telephone company's access to TNR data is quite different than what he or she should reasonably believe about other, more arcane forms of metadata.

It is not clear as a factual matter that a reasonable observer would, or should, appreciate the full extent of the metadata attached to a modern communication, undertaken with different devices. Nor does it seem plausible, as communications technologies proliferate and converge, that a reasonable originator should be expected to appreciate the precise degree to which a third-party intermediary may be privy to this metadata.

For instance, would a reasonable observer be able to distinguish between conventional telephone calls, voice calls made over a cell service, voice calls made over a VoIP system, and voice calls made over a peer-to-peer service such as Skype? These different technologies may produce different sorts of metadata, and there may be differences in the extent to which a third-party intermediary may record and have access to this data. Moreover, service providers (an increasingly varied and international class) may differ in the extent to which they collect and archive this information, or adhere to whatever policies they do have. As an empirical matter, the "reasonable originator" probably lacks the technological literacy to really understand what is and can be collected about his or her communication by a third-party intermediary.

Of course, in the wake of the Snowden revelations, that reasonable originator might now be adjudged a paranoid originator. Faced with revelations about the scope of government intercepts and the extent to which communication companies do (or are compelled to) cooperate, an argument might be made that no reasonable originator should assume privacy in *any* of their telecommunication.

Put another way, the invasiveness of government surveillance and the evolution of the technology that allows this surveillance has the effect of redefining the expectations of the reasonable person. If these developments (and whatever notoriety is attached to them) are in turn used to determine the scope of the reasonable person's expectations, the result is a vicious spiral that further and further erodes the scope of private communications. The end result is that the concept of private communication is rendered moot, which makes a mockery of Parliament's obvious intent to protect the integrity of telecommunication privacy.

It would also run counter the position articulated by the Supreme Court in its *Charter* section 8 jurisprudence. There, the court has rejected the idea that "as technology developed, the sphere of protection for private life must shrink."[70] In a *Charter* section 8 case involving an intercepted conversation with an informer, the Court held,

> No justification for the arbitrary exercise of state power can be made to rest on the simple fact that persons often prove to be poor judges of whom to trust when divulging confidences or on the fact that the risk of divulgation is a given in the decision to speak to another human being. On the other hand, the question whether we should countenance participant surveillance has everything to do with the need to strike a fair balance between the right of the state to intrude on the private lives of its citizens and the right of those citizens to be left alone.[71]

Neither paranoia nor ubiquitous state surveillance set the standard for the reasonable person.[72] The reasonable expectation of privacy is a normative concept that does not vary with naïveté and the risk that people's privacy expectations may be dashed. As the Supreme Court observed in yet another section 8 case, "in an age of expanding means for snooping readily available on the retail market, ordinary people may come to fear (with or without justification) that their telephones are wiretapped or their private correspondence is being read... Suggestions that a diminished subjective expectation of privacy should automatically result in a lowering of constitutional protection should therefore be opposed."[73] It stands to reason that a similar logic applies to Part VI and private communication.

c) The explosion of data in the hands of third parties should not undermine privacy protections
Third, a plurality of the Supreme Court in *Telus* resists using the modern ubiquity and permanence of data in hands of third-party service providers to undermine the scope of privacy protections in Part VI. There, it emphasized that

> the communication process used by a third-party service provider should not defeat Parliament's intended protection for private communications... This Court has recognized in other contexts that telecommunications service providers act merely

as a third-party 'conduit' for the transmission of private communications and ought to be able to provide services without
having a legal effect on the nature (or, in this case, the protection) of these communications.[74]

As noted, the case concerned intercept of text messages. While the
issue was not before the court, there is no principled basis to treat telecommunications in the form of text or content data differently from
telecommunications that comes in the form of metadata surrounding
that content. If the third-party intermediary rule does not apply to
one form of telecommunications, it should not apply to the other. The
Supreme Court's seeming indifference to third-party intermediary
rule in deciding privacy issues in the area of electronic communication is further affirmed by its *Spencer* decision, discussed below.

In sum, there are very compelling reasons to conclude that at
least some metadata created through communications over a third-
party conduit remain private communication.

4. Metadata May Meet the Geographic Requirements of "Private Communication"

Geography is a final consideration raised by definition of private
communication. A private communication is "made by an originator
who is in Canada or is intended by the originator to be received by a
person who is in Canada." It follows that only those communications
that have a beginning and end outside of the territory of Canada are
excluded from private communication.

Notably, the government may not "outsource" collection of a
private communication to a foreign allied agency to circumvent the
rules on private communication. As the Federal Court has observed,
"Canadian law cannot either authorize or prohibit the second parties [i.e., the foreign allies] from carrying out any investigation
they choose to initiate with respect to Canadian subjects outside
of Canada. That does not exempt Canadian officials from potential
liability for requesting the interception and receiving the intercepted
communication."[75]

In sum, if CSE acts on legal advice that denies metadata "private communication" status, it does so at considerable risk. The matter has not

yet been decided definitively. However, it is now more reasonable to assert that metadata are private communication than to assert that they are not. Because an incorrect conclusion about metadata's status as private communication opens the door to criminal culpability and civil liability for its unauthorized intercept, the government would be prudent to seek full private communication" authorization for metadata collection activities having a possible Canadian geographic nexus.

Metadata and the Charter

Private communications under Part VI of the *Criminal Code* is data in relation to which a person has a reasonable expectation of privacy, and to which Charter section 8 protections also apply.

While all private communications may be protected by section 8, it does not follow, however, that section 8 is limited to private communications. This is a banal statement, since the *Criminal Code* is replete with other warrant requirements above and beyond Part VI designed to meet section 8 standards in relation to other forms of search and seizure.

In what follows, therefore, I consider whether metadata are protected by section 8, regardless of how they might be treated by courts for purposes of Part VI and its concept of private communication. I begin with a brief overview of section 8 and its rules. I then apply those rules to the CSE metadata program.

1. Basics of Section 8

Section 8 guarantees the right to be free from unreasonable searches and seizures.[76] In practice, the section 8 analysis turns on "whether in a particular situation the public's interest in being left alone by government must give way to the government's interest in intruding on the individual's privacy in order to advance its goals, notably those of law enforcement."[77] In consequence, a section 8 analysis raises two questions: First, has there been a search or seizure? Second, if so, was that search or seizure reasonable?[78]

a) Reasonable expectation of privacy

A search or seizure is equated, in practice, with the existence of a "reasonable expectation of privacy,"[79] one that includes both a subjective and objective expectation.[80] The Supreme Court has spoken of three "zones" of privacy: "The territorial zone refers to places such as one's home. Personal or corporeal privacy is concerned with the human body (body, images such as photographs, voice or name)." Finally, a person has a right to informational privacy, or "the claim of individuals, groups, or institutions to determine for themselves when, how, and to what extent information about them is communicated to others."[81] Information attracting constitutional protection includes "information which tends to reveal intimate details of the lifestyle and personal choices of the individual."[82]

Electronic surveillance may transgress a reasonable expectation of privacy and constitute a search and seizure regulated by section 8 of the *Charter*.[83] The Supreme Court has described its jurisprudence in this area as "embrac[ing] all existing means by which the agencies of the state can electronically intrude on the privacy of the individual, and any means which technology places at the disposal of law enforcement authorities in the future."[84]

However, whether a particular electronic intercept activity amounts to a "search" remains highly fact-specific. In defining the scope of this "reasonable expectation" in individual instances, Canadian courts have focused on the "totality of circumstances"[85] and have spoken of the privacy expectation being "normative" and not "descriptive."[86] That is, "the impugned state conduct has reached the point at which the values underlying contemporary Canadian society dictate that the state must respect the personal privacy of individuals unless it is able to constitutionally justify any interference with that personal privacy."[87]

Relevant considerations in the "totality of circumstances" include, for example, the place where the search takes place, whether the subject matter of the search was in public view or abandoned, the intrusiveness of the search, and "whether the information was already in the hands of third parties" and if so whether it was "subject to an obligation of confidentiality."[88]

Notably, this last consideration is not definitive. In *Ward*, the Ontario Court of Appeal expressly recognized the concept of "public privacy":

> While the public nature of the forum in which an activity occurs will affect the degree of privacy reasonably expected, the public nature of the forum does not eliminate all privacy claims... If the state could unilaterally, and without restraint, gather information to identify individuals engaged in public

activities of interest to the state, individual freedom and with
it meaningful participation in the democratic process would be
curtailed. It is hardly surprising that constant unchecked state
surveillance of those engaged in public activities is a feature of
many dystopian novels.[89]

Nor does voluntary disclosure to third parties necessarily defeat a
reasonable expectation of privacy. Thus, voluntarily surrendering
information to a service provider does not definitively nullify a
person's privacy interests in relation to state actors. In the past, it has
been relevant to the reasonableness of any privacy expectation,[90] but
even that position now seems muted by the Supreme Court's *Spencer*
decision, discussed below.

b) Reasonableness of the search

Where a reasonable expectation of privacy exists, the interference
with that right must be "reasonable." The gold standard for a reasonable search is the existence of a judicial warrant.

Warrants are "a means of preventing unjustified searches before
they happen, not simply of determining, after the fact, whether they
ought to have occurred in the first place."[91] Thus, electronic surveillance is rendered constitutional by "subjecting the power of the state to
record our private communications to external restraint and requiring
it to be justified by application of an objective criterion."[92] A "detached
judicial officer" supplies this external restraint.[93] The Supreme Court
has held that "the importance of prior judicial authorization is even
greater for covert interceptions of private communications, which
constitute serious intrusions into the privacy rights of those affected."[94]

Warrantless searches "are presumptively unreasonable, absent
exigent circumstances."[95] Warrantless searches are *Charter*-compliant
only where the government proves that the law authorized the
searches, the law itself was reasonable, and the manner of the search
was also reasonable.[96]

In its past jurisprudence, the Supreme Court has found that law
sometimes does authorize warrantless searches in at least exigent
circumstances. In practice, these have usually involved police "safety
searches" — that is, searches "carried out in response to dangerous
situations created by individuals, to which the police must react
'on the sudden.'"[97] This common law rule is reasonable, given the
imminent threat to safety.[98]

The Supreme Court has also considered warrantless intercept of private communications under Part VI of the *Criminal Code*. The warrantless intercept provision, as it existed at the time, permitted warrantless electronic intercepts on an urgent basis to prevent serious and imminent harm.[99] In *Tse*, the Supreme Court concluded that this provision violated section 8, in large part because the person whose communications were intercepted was never given notice of the intercept. In consequence,

> Parliament has failed to provide adequate safeguards to address the issue of accountability… Unless a criminal prosecution results, the targets of the wiretapping may never learn of the interceptions and will be unable to challenge police use of this power… In its present form, the provision fails to meet the minimum constitutional standards of s. 8 of the Charter.[100]

This same failure to include a notification regime meant that the impact on the section 8 right was disproportionate to the government's objective of avoiding imminent harm. For this reason, the provision was not saved by section 1 of the *Charter*.[101]

2. *Metadata May Meet the Threshold of Reasonable Expectation of Privacy*

I turn now to the application of these principles to CSE metadata collection. As discussed in Part I, metadata may be enormously revealing of private information; that is, it may amount to what the Supreme Court has called "information which tends to reveal intimate details of the lifestyle and personal choices of the individual."[102] It is, therefore, a prime candidate for reasonable expectation of privacy treatment.

While there do not yet appear to be any decided court cases focusing on metadata and the application of section 8, some judgments have focused on related issues, not least so-called "subscriber information." Here, police in possession of an Internet IP address seek and obtain customer identity information associated with this IP from the Internet service provider (ISP) to whom the IP belongs. IP addresses can be regarded as a form of metadata associated with Internet use. The cases to date seem to have turned on the implications of these data being collected, not from the individual or his or her devices directly, but from third-party service providers.

Notably, under the *Personal Information Protection Electronic Documents Act (*PIPEDA*)* (and its provincial equivalents), a business such as an ISP may disclose personal information to a government institution for purposes of law enforcement or where the information may relate to national security, international affairs, or national defence.[103] Several lower court decisions have considered whether this disclosure of subscriber information to police by ISPs offends section 8 of the *Charter*.

The approach of these courts was mixed: at least one such decision suggested that section 8 is not violated, a decision then appealed to the Supreme Court and discussed below.[104] Two other cases offered much more nuanced views but did not decide the issue definitively.[105]

The matter now seems to have been laid to rest firmly and definitively by the Supreme Court's 2014 decision in *R. v. Spencer.*[106] *Spencer* was about Internet subscriber data in a police child pornography investigation. The information in question was the name, address, and telephone number of the customer associated with an IP address. It was, in other words, the most benign form of data attached to an IP address.

In a nutshell, the court nevertheless held that the *Charter*'s section 8 protections against unreasonable searches and seizures extends to this subscriber data. In key passages, the court wrote,

> the identity of a person linked to their use of the Internet must be recognized as giving rise to a privacy interest beyond that inherent in the person's name, address and telephone number found in the subscriber information… Subscriber information, by tending to link particular kinds of information to identifiable individuals, may implicate privacy interests relating not simply to the person's name or address but to his or her identity as the source, possessor or user of that information… The police request to link a given IP address to subscriber information was in effect a request to link a specific person (or a limited number of persons in the case of shared Internet services) to specific online activities. This sort of request engages the anonymity aspect of the informational privacy interest by attempting to link the suspect with anonymously undertaken online activities, activities which have been recognized by the Court in other circumstances as engaging significant privacy interests.[107]

The Supreme Court was unmoved by the fact that the information was in the possession of a third-party service provider or that there was a service contract that (ambiguously) suggested disclosure was a possibility. Nor did it read the *Personal Information Protection and Electronics Documents Act* as somehow vitiating the reasonable expectation of privacy. In the result, Mr. Spencer's section 8 rights were violated — the police had no warrant.

Spencer is clear authority that there is nothing magic about metadata, whether housed with a third-party service provider or not. Having reached such pointed and firmly voiced conclusions on ISP subscriber information, it seems inconceivable that the Supreme Court would find that section 8 does not protect other, even more intimate forms of metadata created by modern communication — geolocation, place called, call duration, website visited, and so on.

While the reasonable expectation of privacy will always depend on the totality of circumstances, it seems that the constitutional die is now cast when it comes to the sorts of metadata most contentious in the post-Snowden debates. Specifically, nothing in *Spencer* is confined to police searches and seizures. And there is no reason to conclude that intelligence surveillance of the sort potentially at issue in the CSE metadata project lies outside the zone of privacy protected by the *Charter*. Indeed, even before *Spencer*, the government itself appeared to accept that some metadata collected by CSE gives rise to a reasonable expectation of privacy.[108]

3. The Present Form of CSE Metadata Collection May Not Constitute a Reasonable "Search"

If metadata collected by CSE falls with the constitutional zone of privacy protected by section 8, then CSE acts unconstitutionally if it collects Canadian metadata unreasonably.

a) Ministerial authorization does not amount to the judicial warrant
The quintessential reasonable search requires judicial authorization. In comparison, the CSE statute relies on ministerial authorizations whenever private communications might be collected.

Past CSE commissioners have apparently considered this rule sufficient to meet *Charter* standards. In his 2002–03 report, then Commissioner Claude Bisson noted, "before December 2001, CSE would have been in violation of privacy related provisions of both the *Criminal Code* and the *Canadian Charter of Rights and Freedoms* had it intercepted communications without the certainty that, in doing so, it would not intercept private communications."[109] However, Antonio Lamer, in his 2004–05 report, took the view that the modern regime vitiated this concern: "I am of the opinion that [the post-2001 system for ministerial authorization of private communication intercepts] is both reasonable and consistent with other legislation that establishes an authority to engage in activities that would, in the absence of adequate justification, be judged an infringement on the rights of individuals as protected by the *Charter of Rights and Freedoms*."[110]

It is not clear to me that these commissioners were in a position to consider the sweep of data that is now apparently subject to CSE intercept. Moreover, Lamer, at least, seemed to believe the CSE regime necessary because of the extraterritorial nature of its intercepts — a warrant system could not reach extra-Canadian surveillance. I believe that, in a contemporary context, their views require careful reconsideration.

First, because the ministerial authorization regime is aimed at private communication, it applies, by definition, to a communication with a Canadian nexus. This is not a purely extraterritorial intercept; it is one that risks capturing Canadian communications. There is nothing inherently doubtful about instead asking a judge to authorize those intercepts that may capture Canadian-origin communications, even if the latter is embedded in a foreign intelligence collection operation.

Second, it should not be assumed that the categories of "private communications" and information in which a person has a "reasonable expectation of privacy" for *Charter* purposes overlap in full. Something may not be private communication but may still give rise to a reasonable expectation of privacy. The concepts do not move in lock step. Put another way, since the ministerial authorization regime is triggered only when information reaches the level of private communication, it risks being under-inclusive of the data that attract constitutional protection, even assuming it is a proper alternative to a judicial warrant.

Third, I do not believe that it is an adequate alternative. The section 8 jurisprudence focuses on advance authorization provided by an independent judicial officer, not a political minister. That minister's exact statutory duty under the *National Defence Act* is to manage and direct "all matters relating to national defence."[111] As such, he or she is hardly an independent and disinterested reviewer of government search and seizure requests, as required by the *Charter*. It is simply impossible to imagine a court honouring the section 8 jurisprudence and viewing an executive actor as a proxy for the impartial judge promised in it.

b) The CSE statute does not meet the standards for permissible
warrantless intercepts
At issue, therefore, is warrantless interference with privacy. The government's own recent legal position on CSE collection is that any search is, nevertheless, reasonable. According to the Government of Canada response, the intercepts are:

- "carried out in the context of foreign intelligence...(not law enforcement)";
- "authorized by the National Defence Act and, where applicable, through the Ministerial authorizations provided for in the National Defence Act";
- "in furtherance of government objectives of the utmost importance";
- "minimally intrusive in terms of the type of private information which may be acquired from telecommunications or their Metadata, as well as tailored in scope to the objectives of Part V.I of the National Defence Act and minimized as much as possible through a variety of privacy safeguards provided for in the National Defence Act, Ministerial directives, Ministerial authorizations and other applicable policies and procedures."[112]

These arguments do not, however, appear to dovetail with the current jurisprudence on warrantless searches. As of March 2015, the government has succeeded in justifying warrantless searches where the law authorizes those measures in *exigent* circumstances (with the proviso that the affected individual is then notified of the warrantless search).

Whatever the importance of foreign intelligence, there is nothing in CSE's law that limits CSE intercepts to exigent circumstances. Nor is there notification to the affected individual, although here the government might argue that *ex post facto* review by the commissioner serves the same purpose.

Boiled to its essence, defence of CSE's warrantless intercept activity rests on the view that declaring something of national security importance puts it on a different footing than all the other circumstances in which section 8 protects privacy. That is, warrant-less intercept is justified by the importance of the issue, and the various prudential measures listed in the government defence backstop a departure from the regular expectations of the *Charter*.

c) The national security imperative does not justify a departure from regular constitutional expectations

I do not, however, believe this to be a persuasive approach. Certainly, others have argued that national security places search rules on a different footing than in a conventional law enforcement context.[113] There is some dated and decontextualized judicial musing in support of this view.[114]

But setting aside the issue of whether this argument is best considered as part of the section 8 discussion or instead under section 1, it is not compelling for one simple reason: Canadian practice has already demonstrated unequivocally that national security surveil-lance need not be treated truly differently from regular police sur-veillance. The *CSIS Act*, which deals with sensitive national security issues, superimposes a full judicial warrant regime on CSIS surveil-lance activities, in which CSIS persuades a Federal Court judge on "reasonable and probable grounds established by sworn evidence, that a threat to the security of Canada exists and that a warrant is required to enable its investigation."[115]

There is, in other words, nothing foundational about CSE's national security functions that demand ministerial authorization over a judicial authorization. Nor is there any evident reason why the CSE approval regime could not draw on the CSIS precedent. Here, a judge would replace the minister in the CSE authorization process, and that authorization regime extends to the collection of any information in which there is a reasonable expectation of privacy. This would have the welcome effect of preserving the promise and integrity of section 8, while still meeting the government's pressing objectives in relation to foreign intelligence.

In sum, the current ministerial authorization regime under CSE's law looks much more like expediency than necessity. It is an awkward fix built on doubtful theories about the scope of Canadian privacy law. It deserves no special exemption from the regular con-stitutional law of the land. Interposing a judge in lieu of a minister to perform the latter's current functions in overseeing privacy issues would do no violence to CSE's operations, while, at the same time, it would honour the long-established requirements of the *Charter*.

Conclusion

In the final analysis, it is difficult to explain why the government has pursued the legal direction suggested by documents released under access law, and in its defence to the current BC Civil Liberties Association challenge to CSE's law. The prescription offered by this chapter is simple: always get ministerial authorizations for metadata collection, and amend CSE's law to task a judge (in addition to or instead of the minister) with authorizing any intercept that may raise reasonable expectations of privacy. Because, by its own admission, the government does not know when information with a Canadian nexus may be swept into its surveillance, prudence suggests that judicial authorization should be sought often.

It is hard to see how either of these suggestions bring real inconvenience on the government. Indeed, civil libertarian critics of these modest proposals might regard them as laughingly formalistic and inadequate. For my part, I believe that it matters both in principle and practice that judicial authorizations bless intercepts. I agree, however, that the intervention of a judge prior to collection is not alone sufficient protection in the world of Big Data. Other questions — not least, how long government may retain data that forms the Big Data haystack and how it may search that haystack — are now even more pressing. Those matters are, however, the topic of another article.[116]

The concluding point of this chapter is much simpler: the evolution of invasive search and Big Data analysis powers in the hands of the state's intelligence services should not change the existing scope of privacy protections, whether statutory or constitutional. This is a common-sense principle that Canadians should reasonably expect a government to honour by instinct, not resist at every turn.

Notes

1. Barton Gellman & Laura Poitras, "U.S., British intelligence Mining Data from Nine U.S. Internet Companies in Broad Secret Programs," *Washington Post*, 6 June 2013, <http://www.washingtonpost.com/investigations/us-intelligence-mining-data-from-nine-us-internet-companies-in-broad-secret-program/2013/06/06/3a0coda8-

cebf-11e2-8845-d970ccb04497_story.html>; Glenn Greenwald, "NSA Collecting Phone Records of Millions of Verizon Customers Daily," *The Guardian*, 6 June 2013, <http://www.theguardian.com/world/2013/jun/06/nsa-phone-records-verizon-court-order>.

2. James Bell, "NSA Stores Metadata of Millions of Web Users for up to a Year, Secret Files Show," *The Guardian*, 30 September 2013, <http://www.theguardian.com/world/2013/sep/30/nsa-americans-metadata-year-documents>; Greenwald, *supra* note 1.

3. "A Guardian Guide to Your Metadata," *The Guardian*, 12 June 2013, <http://www.theguardian.com/technology/interactive/2013/jun/12/what-is-metadata-nsa-surveillance#meta=0000000>.

4. See, e.g., Colin Freeze, "How Canada's Shadowy Metadata-Gathering Program Went Awry," *Globe and Mail*, 15 June 2013, <http://www.theglobeandmail.com/news/national/how-canadas-shadowy-metadata-gathering-program-went-awry/article12580225/?page=all#dashboard/follows/>.

5. Greg Weston, Glenn Greenwald & Ryan Gallagher, "CSEC Used Airport Wi-Fi to Track Canadian Travellers: Edward Snowden Documents," *CBC News*, 30 January 2014, <http://www.cbc.ca/news/politics/csec-used-airport-wi-fi-to-track-canadian-travellers-edward-snowden-documents-1.2517881>. The actual CSEC document is posted at <http://www.cbc.ca/news2/pdf/airports_redacted.pdf>.

6. See BCCLA, Notice of Civil Claim, Supreme Court of British Columbia, 2013, <http://bccla.org/wp-content/uploads/2013/10/2013-10-22-Notice-of-Civil-Claim.pdf>.

7. See the CSEC responses to Snowden disclosures at <http://www.cse-cst.gc.ca/home-accueil/media/media-2014-01-30-eng.html> and <http://www.cse-cst.gc.ca/home-accueil/media/media-2014-01-29-eng.html>. See also the CSEC chief's testimony in front of the Standing Senate Committee on National Security and Defence, 2nd Sess., 41st Parl., Issue 2, Evidence (3 February 2014), <http://www.parl.gc.ca/content/sen/committee/412/SECD/02EV-51162-E.HTM>.

8. See the reporting of CBC journalists Dave Seglins, Amber Hildebrandt, and Michael Pereira. For example, "CSE Tracks Millions of Downloads Daily: Snowden Documents," *CBC News*, 27 January 2015, <http://www.cbc.ca/news/canada/cse-tracks-millions-of-downloads-daily-snowden-documents-1.2930120>.

9. *IN THE MATTER OF an application by [X] for a warrant pursuant to Sections 12 and 21 of the Canadian Security Intelligence Service Act, R.S.C. 1985, c. C-23*, 2013 FC 1275, aff'd, 2014 FCA 249, leave to appeal to the Supreme Court of Canada, allowed.

10. Part I, *The Constitution Act, 1982*, being Schedule B to the *Canada Act 1982* (UK), 1982, c 11.

11. Ann Cavoukian, *A Primer on Metadata: Separating Fact from Fiction* (Information and Privacy Commissioner, Ontario, July 2013) at 3.

12. *Ibid.*

13. *Ibid.* at 4.

14. E. Nakashima, "Metadata Reveals the Secrets of Social Position, Company Hierarchy, Terrorist Cells," *Washington Post*, 15 June 2013, cited in Cavoukian, supra note 11 at 3.

15. An IP address "is a numerical identification and logical address that is assigned to devices participating in a computer network utilizing the Internet Protocol." Office of the Privacy Commissioner of Canada, *What an IP Address Can Reveal about You* (May 2013), <http://www.priv.gc.ca/information/research-recherche/2013/ip_201305_e.asp>.

16. *Ibid.*

17. "The Big Data Conundrum: How to Define It?" *MIT Technology Review* (3 October 2013), <http://www.technologyreview.com/view/519851/the-big-data-conundrum-how-to-define-it/>.

18. *National Defence Act (NDA)*, R.S.C., 1985 c. N-5, s. 273.64. CSEC also provides "advice, guidance and services to help ensure the protection of electronic information and of information infrastructures of importance to the Government of Canada." This Mandate "B" does not, however, figure in this article.

19. *Ibid.*, s. 273.61.

20. *Ibid.*, s. 273.64.

21. Government of Canada, Attorney General of Canada, *Response to Civil Claim, in BC Civil Liberties Association v. AG of Canada, Supreme Court of British Columbia*, No. S137827, 20 January 2014, at para. 5, on file with author (hereafter "GOC Response").

22. *Ibid.* at para. 5.

23. NDA, *supra* note 18, s. 273.65(1).

24. *Criminal Code*, R.S.C., 1985, c. C-46.

25. NDA, *supra* note 18, s. 273.69 ("Part VI of the *Criminal Code* does not apply in relation to an interception of a communication under the authority of an [ministerial] authorization issued under this Part or in relation to a communication so intercepted.")

26. *Crown Liability and Proceedings Act*, R.S.C. 1985, c. C-50, s. 17.

27. Commissioner of the Communications Security Establishment, *2011–2012 Annual Report*, <http://www.ocsec-bccst.gc.ca/ann-rpt/2011-2012/5_e.php>. See also GOC Response, *supra* note 21 at paras. 7 and 8.

28. GOC Response, *supra* note 21. at para. 14. These presumably included authorizations under CSEC's IT security mandate (Mandate B), not discussed in this article.

29. *Ibid.* at para. 16.

30. NDA, *supra* note 18, s. 273.64(3).

31. Hereafter, March 2004 Ministerial Directive (on file with the author). Except as otherwise noted, all documents referred to in this section were obtained by Colin Freeze of the *Globe and Mail* under access to information law. As described by the government, "Ministerial directives do not grant any authority that does not already exist in law and cannot enhance any existing authority. They serve as additional direction or guidance, setting out the Minister's expectations for, or imposing restrictions on, CSE. Where a Ministerial directive applies, CSE's activities must be consistent with that Ministerial directive." GOC Response, above note 21 at para. 17.

32. Hereafter, March 2005 Ministerial Directive (on file with the author).

33. The directive also points to CSEC's mandate to protect government cyber systems, a Mandate B issue not discussed further in this article.

34. NDA, *supra* note 18, s.273.63(2).

35. OCSEC Review of the Ministerial Directive, Communications Security Establishment, Collection and Use of Metadata, 9 March 2005 at 2 (on file with author).

36. *Ibid.* at 7.

37. *Ibid.* at 16.

38. *Ibid.* at 32.

39. *Ibid.* at 18. See also pages 22–24, raising the same doubts and suggesting that some metadata activities were properly something that should have been pursued under Mandate C.

40. *Ibid.* at 24.

41. Letter to Minister MacKay from CSEC Chief John Adams (n.d.), (on file with author).

42. Letter to Minister MacKay from Commissioner Gonthier (16 September 2008), (on file with author).

43. Advice to the Minister, CSEC Issues (19 December 2011), (on file with author), <http://www.theglobeandmail.com/news/national/raw-documents-canadas-top-secret-data-mining-program/article12446852/?from=12444909#dashboard/follows/>.

44. Scenario Note for Chief's Briefing to the National Security Advisor (10 January 2011), (on file with the author).

45. Ministerial Directive, Communications Security Establishment, Collection and Use of Metadata (21 November 2011), (on file with author), <http://www.theglobeandmail.com/news/national/raw-documents-canadas-top-secret-data-mining-program/article12446852/?from=12444909#dashboard/follows/>.

46. Memorandum for the Chief: Updated Collection and Use of Metadata Ministerial Directive (14 November 2011) at 18 (in file) and 14 (on document), (on file with the author), <http://www.theglobeandmail.com/news/national/raw-documents-canadas-top-secret-data-mining-program/article12446852/?from=12444909#dashboard/follows/>.

47. *Ibid.* at 20 (in file).
48. CSEC, OPS-1 *Protecting the Privacy of Canadians and Ensuring Legal Compliance in the Conduct of CSEC Activities* (Effective date: 1 December 2012) at 5, (on file with the author).
49. GOC Response, above note 21 at para 1.
50. *Ibid.* Div. 3, paras. 6–7. See discussion on **Metadata and the Law** in this chapter.
51. A third issue relates to the question of vires — that is, whether CSEC collects metadata pursuant to the correct mandate in its statute. This matter has obviously been the source of considerable discussion inside of government, and is not a question that can be plumbed in greater depth here, given the paucity of public documents that contextualize the debate. For the balance of this chapter, I assume that metadata is collected correctly under a Mandate A justification — that is, it relates to foreign intelligence and not assistance to law enforcement or CSIS. I do not address in this article a related issue: the precise sweep and contours of Mandate A.
52. *Criminal Code, supra* note 24, s.183.
53. See, e.g., *R. v. Telus*, 2013 SCC 16, at para. 26 (per Abella J).
54. *Interpretation Act*, R.S.C., c. I-21, s. 35.
55. *Telus, supra* note 53 at para. 26.
56. [2013] N.J. No. 395 at para. 22. That court seems to have in part been motivated by the immediacy of the exchanges between the participants. This immediacy concept reflects, in part, the notion that Part VI only applies to an "intercept." In Part VI "intercept" "includes listen to, record or acquire a communication or acquire the substance, meaning or purport thereof." Some courts have held that an "intercept" must be contemporaneous with the communication. Part VI does not apply, in other words, to search of stored communications. *R. v. Bahr*, 2006 ABPC 360 at para. 42; *R. v. Singh*, 2012 ONSC 3633. This approach was rejected by Abella J, for a plurality of the Supreme Court in *Telus, supra* note 53: "A technical approach to 'intercept' would essentially render Part VI irrelevant to the protection of the right to privacy in new, electronic and text-based communications technologies, which generate and store copies of private communications as part of the transmission process... A narrow or technical definition of 'intercept' that requires the act of interception to occur simultaneously with the making of the communication itself is therefore unhelpful in addressing new, text-based electronic communications." Abella J, for a plurality, at paras. 33 and 34. (The Abella position was been followed in *R. v. Croft*, 2013 ABQB 640.) For his part, Moldaver J, writing for himself and another, appears also to accept that the recording of a communication by the telecommunications company does not exonerate the police from obtaining a Part VI authorization.

Moldaver J. at para. 67 *et seq.* As Moldaver J. correctly notes, it would be artificial and unrealistic to distinguish (for the purposes of Part VI) privacy protection between a communication captured instantaneously and one captured on a time delay, however short or long.

57. *Telus, supra* note 53 (per Abella J.) at para. 25, emphasis added.
58. *Lyons v. The Queen,* [1984] 2 S.C.R. 633 at 664.
59. *R v. Vu,* 2013 SCC 60 at para. 42.
60. *Criminal Code, supra* note 24, s.492.2(4).
61. *Ibid.*
62. *R. v. Fegan* (1993), 80 C.C.C. (3d) 356 (On CA) at 366. See also *R. v. Beck,* [1993] B.C.J. No. 1141 (QL); *R. v. Samson* (1983), 45 Nfld. & P.E.I.R. 32 (Nfld. C.A.).
63. In *R. v. Skrepetz,* [1990] BCJ No. 1467 (BC Prov Ct), the Crown even argued that recourse to the *Interpretation Act* was improper and inconsistent with the Supreme Court's approach. This position, even if correct at the time, has obviously been completely superseded by *Telus, supra* note 53.
64. See, e.g., *R. v. Griffith* (1988), 44 C.C.C. (3d) 63 (Ont. Dist. Ct.); *R. v. Khiamal* (1990), 73 Alta. L.R. (2d) 359 (Q.B.); *R. v. Mikituk* (1993), 101 Sask R. 286 (Q.B.)
65. *R. v. Lee,* 2007 ABQB 767 at para. 282. See also *Croft, supra* note 56 at para. 22 (following *Lee* on this issue).
66. *Lee, supra* note 65, at para. 283.
67. *R. v. Duarte,* [1990] 1 SCR 30 at para. 47.
68. *R. v. Goldman,* (1979), 13 C.R. (3d) 228 at 248 *et seq.* (S.C.C.). Note that the Supreme Court did not equate "originator" with "person who made the call." Rather, the originator is the person who made the statement/communication that the police now wish to use.
69. *Ibid.*
70. *R. v. Tessling,* 2004 SCC 67 at para. 16.
71. *Duarte, supra* note 677 at para. 32.
72. See *R. v. Ward,* 2012 ONCA 660 at para. 87, and cases there cited.
73. *Tessling, supra* note 70 at para. 42.
74. *Telus, supra* note 53 at para. 41 per Abella J (for a plurality).
75. *In the MATTER OF an application for a warrant pursuant to Sections 12 and 21 of the Canadian Security Intelligence Service Act,* 2013 FC 1275 at para. 101.
76. *Constitution Act 1982, supra* note 10. See *Lavigne v. Canada (Commissioner of Official Languages),* [2002] 2 S.C.R. 773 at para. 25 (labelling this a privacy right).
77. *Hunter v. Southam Inc.,* [1984] 2 S.C.R. 145 at 159–60.
78. *Tessling, supra* note 70 at para. 18.
79. *Ibid.* at para. 18.

80. *Ibid.* at para. 19.
81. *Tessling, supra* note 70 at para. 23, citing A. F. Westin, Privacy and Freedom (1970) at 7.
82. *R. v. Plant,* [1993] 1 SCR 281 at 293.
83. *Duarte, supra* note 67 at paras. 18 & 19 ("as a general proposition, surreptitious electronic surveillance of the individual by an agency of the state constitutes an unreasonable search or seizure under s. 8 of the Charter… One can scarcely imagine a state activity more dangerous to individual privacy than electronic surveillance and to which, in consequence, the protection accorded by s. 8 should be more directly aimed").
84. *R. v. Wong,* [1990] 3 SCR 36 at 43–44 (per La Forest J. for majority).
85. *Tessling, supra* note 70 at para. 19.
86. *Ibid.* at para. 42.
87. *Ward, supra* note 72 at para. 82.
88. *Tessling, supra* note 70 at para. 32.
89. *Ward, supra* note 72 at paras. 73 and 74.
90. *Ibid.* at para. 76.
91. *Hunter, supra* note 77 at 160.
92. *Duarte, supra* note 67 at para. 25.
93. *Ibid.* at para. 25 (noting that "if privacy may be defined as the right of the individual to determine for himself when, how, and to what extent he will release personal information about himself, a reasonable expectation of privacy would seem to demand that an individual may proceed on the assumption that the state may only violate this right by recording private communications on a clandestine basis when it has established to the satisfaction of a *detached judicial officer* that an offence has been or is being committed and that interception of private communications stands to afford evidence of the offence." [emphasis added]).
94. *R. v. Tse,* 2012 SCC 16 at para. 17.
95. *Tessling, supra* note 70 at para. 33.
96. *R. v. Collins,* [1987] 1 S.C.R. 265 at para. 23; *R. v. MacDonald,* 2014 SCC 3 at para. 29.
97. *Ibid.* at para. 32.
98. *Ibid.* at para. 43.
99. *Criminal Code, supra* note 24, s.184.4, as interpreted by *R. v. Tse, supra* note 94 at para. 27.
100. *Tse, supra* note 94 at para. 85.
101. *Ibid.* at para. 98.
102. *Plant, supra* note 82 at 293.
103. *Personal Information Protection and Electronic Documents Act (PIPEDA),* S.C. 2000, c.5, s.7(3)(c.1).
104. *R. v. Spencer,* 2011 SKCA 144.

105. *Ward, supra* note 72; R. v. Trapp, 2011 SKCA 143.

106. *R. v. Spencer,* 2014 SCC 43.

107. *Spencer, supra* note 106 at paras. 47 and 50.

108. GOC Response, *supra* note 21, Div. 3 at para. 6.

109. Canada, Communications Security Establishment Commissioner, *Annual Report 2002–2003,* <http://www.ocsec-bccst.gc.ca/ann-rpt/2002-2003/role_e.php>, at 3, n1.

110. Canada, Communications Security Establishment Commissioner, *Annual Report 2004–2005,* <http://www.ocsec-bccst.gc.ca/ann-rpt/2004-2005/activit_e.php>, at 9.

111. NDA, *supra* note 18, s. 4.

112. GOC Response, *supra* note 21 at Div. 3, Pt. 2, para 7.

113. See, e.g., Stanley A. Cohen, *Privacy, Crime and Terror: Legal Rights and Security in a Time of Peril* (Markham: LexisNexis Butterworths, 2005) at 232.

114. *Hunter, supra* note 77 at 186 (suggesting, without actually deciding, that the search and seizure standard developed in that case might be different "where state security is involved").

115. *Atwal v. Canada,* [1988] 1 F.C. 107 at para. 36 (FCA), paraphrasing section 21 of the *Canadian Security Intelligence Service Act,* R.S.C., 1985, c. C-23. *Atwal* concluded that this system satisfied section 8.

116. For a preliminary discussion of these issues, see Craig Forcese, *The Limits of Reasonableness: The Failures of the Conventional Search and Seizure Paradigm in Information-Rich Environments* (Ottawa: Privacy Commissioner of Canada, July 2011) <http://www.priv.gc.ca/information/research-recherche/2011/forcese_201107_e.asp>.

PART III

REFORMS AND ACCOUNTABILITY

CHAPTER VI

Permanent Accountability Gaps and Partial Remedies

Kent Roach

Introction

Accountability gaps occur when those who review or oversee national security activities do not have the necessary legal powers or resources to keep pace with the enhanced and integrated nature of those activities. Both the Arar Commission in 2006 and the Air India Commission in 2010 sounded alarm bells that neither review or oversight was keeping up with whole-of-government-approaches to security. The Arar Commission,[1] in what was, until the early 2015 debates about Bill C-51,[2] a neglected six-hundred-page second report, recommended that review be extended to other security agencies and that the reviewers be able, like the security agencies themselves, to share information with each other and to conduct joint investigations. The Air India Commission recommended an enhanced role for the prime minister's national security advisor to oversee and resolve inevitable disputes between security agencies, especially the Canadian Security Intelligence Service (CSIS) and the RCMP.[3] The government rejected both these recommendations.

Now the accountability gap problem has come home to roost in the wake of the fallout from the October 2014 terrorist attacks in Saint-Jean-sur-Richelieu and Ottawa. The government has introduced Bill C-51, which will authorize whole-of-government information sharing for extremely broadly defined security reasons, but without enhanced whole-of-government review.[4] The new legislation will also give CSIS new surveillance and disruption powers, including the ability to break Canadian and foreign laws and to conduct surveillance and disruption outside of Canada.[5] In recognition of the *Charter* implications of such new powers and perhaps also in recognition of the outdated and shaky nature of Canada's review structures, the government has assigned the task of reviewing and overseeing many of these powers to Federal Court judges. The government has stressed the importance of judicial oversight in defending the new legislation, raising squarely the question of the strengths and weaknesses of judicial review and oversight of national security activities.

The first part of the chapter will define what is meant by review, oversight, accountability, and accountability gaps to clarify thinking about these matters. The second part will examine the dangers of the permanent accountability gaps that are emerging between enhanced and integrated national security activities and their review and oversight. A lack of accountability can shelter misconduct, including human rights and privacy violations. It can also hide governmental inefficiencies and failures in protecting national security. The Arar and the Air India Commissions both recommended means of improving accountability. The Arar Commission focused on the propriety of national security activities, while the Air India Commission focused on the efficacy of national security activities. Both commissions were agreed, however, that review and oversight of national security activities were manifestly inadequate. The Harper government, unfortunately, has rejected the major recommendations of both commissions. It has even characterized enhanced review as "needless red tape"[6] in response to concerns that new information sharing powers in Bill C-51 are not matched by increased and whole-of-government accountability. It has also characterized legislative review as foreign to Canadian traditions and has stressed the superiority of judicial oversight, especially with regards to new CSIS powers.[7]

The third part of the chapter will examine proposals for enhanced legislative review of national security activities. Opposition parties, especially the Liberals, have made the need for enhanced parliamentary review the focus of much of their opposition to Bill C-51. Canada, alone of its Five Eyes security partners, does not allow even a select group of parliamentarians have access to secret information. There cannot be meaningful detailed review of security matters without access to secret information. But, as is often the case, be careful what you wish for. Although enhanced parliamentary review might increase public knowledge and perhaps ministerial accountability, the record in other democracies and current proposals before Parliament do not provide grounds for optimism that legislative committees will be effective in promoting robust accountability.

What about judicial oversight? Judicial oversight is the main form of oversight offered in the expansion of CSIS powers in both Bills C-44[8] and C-51. Judicial oversight can have teeth in the right circumstances. Justice Mosley issued a scathing judgment when he learned that CSIS and Communications Security Establishment (CSE) had enlisted the help of Five Eyes foreign partners without statutory or judicial authorization. The government is appealing this decision to the Supreme Court.[9] Although the judiciary has been a more effective mechanism for propriety-based review than in the pre-9/11 past,[10] caution is in order when relying on judicial oversight. Justice Mosley was able to leverage his considerable expertise and his interest in reading reports of review agencies to discover that CSIS had gone beyond the terms of the warrant he issued, but this raises the question of whether judges will always be able to engage in similar monitoring. Federal Court judges will review the new CSIS powers in a warrant setting, where it is only the judge and the government lawyer in the room. Once a warrant is granted, there are unlikely to be appeals, and the national security context makes it unlikely the warrant will be reviewed when evidence is introduced in a criminal trial. Moreover, the new disruption warrants in Bill C-51 are based on the constitutionally radical premise that the judicial role is not to prevent *Charter* violations but to authorize them. Such authorizations, including judicial judgments about what limits on rights are proportionate and reasonable, are unlikely to be reviewed on appeal. Review bodies and parliamentary committees may be reluctant to question the ambit of judicial warrants, even if they have concerns that they have gone too far.

The fifth part of this chapter will suggest that the most important accountability mechanisms are located not in the legislature or the judiciary but in the executive itself. National security activities that are themselves dominated by the executive must be closely monitored from within the executive. This is consistent with the fundamental principle accepted by both the Arar Commission and President Obama's review committee[11] that review should mirror and match the activities being reviewed. In particular, effective review of national security activities will require the initiative and secrecy associated with the executive, as opposed to the more public and responsive nature of both legislative and judicial review. Executive review can take many forms. CSIS used to have an Inspector General, an internal watchdog who reported on the legality of its operations. The CSE commissioner is an independent retired judge who reviews the legality of the work of CSE. Legality is an important aspect of propriety, but it can be under-inclusive. The government has taken much comfort in the CSE commissioner's repeated assurances, after each Snowden revelation about Canada, that CSE's actions remain legal because they have been not directed at Canadians. Conclusions of legality are only as good as the underlying law. Former CSE commissioners themselves have raised concerns about the CSE's enabling legislation enacted hastily after 9/11 and some of the broad interpretations that Department of Justice lawyers have placed on the law.[12]

The time may have come for fundamental reform to Canada's accountability architecture. In my view, what is now necessary is the creation of a new independent committee or "super SIRC" (Security Intelligence Review Committee) with jurisdiction to review all national security activities within the federal government. This committee, like the Arar Commission itself, should have the ability to see all secret information and to challenge governmental redaction decisions in court. A larger committee might require a full-time chair, more staff who can specialize in working with different agencies, and a composition that includes a broader cross-section of the public. Although formerly classified in the executive, review bodies can be seen as hybrid institutions that combine elements of all three branches of government, especially if retired judges are used as reviewers.

The last part of this chapter will suggest that even if a "super SIRC" and a parliamentary committee with access to secret information were created, it would not be enough. There would still be a need for "whole of society" accountability. In other words, there is a need for multiple layers of accountability, including ad hoc inquiries, investigative media, civil society, consumer activism, privacy-sensitive telecommunications companies, and whistle-blowers. The President's Review Group was correct to conceive of accountability in risk management terms and to draw on all branches of government,[13] but its proposals to stop leaks could decrease accountability in the future. Those proposals, along with other proposed new legislation in the United States also rely on corporate and consumer resistance to surveillance in its proposals to allow the private sector, as opposed to government, to store metadata about communications. Social accountability will require greater consumer knowledge and activism in demanding that both governments and telecommunication companies respect privacy. My focus on social accountability reflects the need for democratic demands for reducing accountability gaps.[14] It also reflects the growing recognition of the importance of "civil society constitutionalism."[15]

The Need for Conceptual Clarity about Some Critical Distinctions and Definitions

Given the ongoing expansion of security powers and surveillance capabilities, it is understandable and healthy that many people are increasingly concerned about the adequacy of review and oversight of national security activities. Alas, much public discussion conflates the distinct meanings of review and oversight. Loose language and muddled thinking is a real danger. Without conceptual clarity at the start about the different ambitions of review and oversight, there will only be confusion and disappointment even if reforms are implemented.

Review and Oversight
Review refers to the ability of independent bodies retrospectively to evaluate security activities.[16] A reviewer does not have operational responsibility for what is being reviewed. This helps ensure that reviewers remain independent and are not complicit or seen to be complicit in what is being reviewed. SIRC, the CSE commissioner, and the Civilian Review and Complaints Commission for the RCMP are all examples of review bodies that conduct reviews after the fact. In addition to hearing complaints, they make findings and recommendations that attempt to foster accountability to the government and promote public trust and confidence.[17] They do not have the power to impose remedies on the agencies they review.

Oversight refers to a command and control process where those who practice oversight may be able to influence the conduct that they are examining.[18] The responsible minister is supposed to have an important oversight role in a parliamentary democracy. The minister of public safety is responsible for both the RCMP and CSIS. One manifestation of ministerial oversight is the issuance of guidelines and directives to the agencies. Ministerial oversight of the police is limited by the constitutional principle of police independence over law enforcement decisions such as investigations, arrests, and charges.[19] The Arar Commission did not recommend oversight of the RCMP in part because such a role could interfere with police independence. It also expressed concerns that an oversight role that intruded on the management of the agency could compromise the independence of the review body by implicating it in the decisions being reviewed.[20]

Propriety and Efficacy

Distinctions are often drawn between review of the propriety and the efficacy of national security activities. The Arar Commission noted that independent review is generally concerned with propriety, including but not limited to, compliance with law. Some propriety-based reviews, such as the review of the proportionality of a measure, may touch on matters of efficacy and competence, but they are not the focus of such reviews. The Arar Commission suggested that questions about "the efficacy of the intelligence community as a whole... may be an appropriate subject for the proposed Parliamentary Committee on National Security."[21] Those who practice oversight, such as ministers, would also be concerned about efficacy, in part because they may have to answer for security failures.

Accountability and Accountability Gaps

Accountability refers to processes in which officials and organizations provide explanations and justifications for their conduct. A body can demand an accounting even if it does not have the power to control or change the behaviour for which it is demanding an explanation.[22] In other words, a review body that is not in the chain of command can still demand accountability. So too can those in the chain of command, such as ministers who have oversight powers. Accountability, like review and oversight, can relate to the propriety and/or the efficacy of conduct.

Accountability gaps occur when reviewers or overseers do not have adequate powers or resources to match the conduct that is being reviewed. All democracies post-9/11 are struggling with accountability gaps in national security matters. These gaps have been created as governments move to more intense and more integrated "whole-of-government" national security activities, but without always ensuring that reviewers and overseers have corresponding enhanced whole-of-government powers and adequate resources to keep pace with what is being reviewed.[23] In other words, accountability gaps occur when reviewers and overseers remain stuck in twentieth-century silos, while security agencies escape silos in order to work with domestic and foreign partners.

Accountability gaps may have been created unwittingly at first, given the rapid response to 9/11, but their persistence many years later raises questions of whether it may be in the interest of governments to have them. Accountability gaps should be a matter of concern, because they create risks to both rights and security. The risks to rights are that whole-of-government activities may violate rights such as privacy, while the risks to security involve inefficient practices and security failures.

The Role of All Three Branches of Government and Hybrid Institutions
Matters are made even more complicated because all three branches of government can be engaged in review and oversight. Judges can review national security activities by means of judicial review and after the fact in the course of criminal or civil trials. They may be involved in oversight, for example, in ensuring that intelligence agencies properly execute warrants. Legislative committees generally are concerned with after the fact review, but in some extraordinary cases they can play a more hands-on oversight role. Finally, the executive in its many guises plays a variety of roles. Ministers are supposed to engage in oversight for both the efficacy and propriety of national security activities. In addition, watchdog executive bodies in the executive, such as SIRC and the CSE commissioner, engage in retrospective reviews of the propriety and legality of the conduct of CSIS and the CSE.

Although part of the executive, SIRC and the CSE commissioner are hybrid institutions. SIRC members are appointed by the prime minister, but in consultation with the leaders of major parties in the House of Commons.[24] Although SIRC members cannot be current members of Parliament, by convention, they often have had experience in the legislature and its political parties. More recently, they include retired judges and former civil servants. The CSE commissioner must be a supernumerary or retired judge.[25] This also brings a judicial element into the review process.

The Danger of Accountability Gaps for Propriety and Efficacy: The Rejected Arar and Air India Commission Recommendations

Accountability is often associated with the need to reveal and prevent improprieties such as possible complicity in torture and the massive privacy invasions revealed by the Snowden leaks. For example, the Commission of Inquiry into the Actions of Canadian Officials in Relation to Maher Arar's extraordinary rendition and torture crafted its recommendations with a focus on reviewing for propriety while also noting that, in some circumstances, "issues of efficacy and propriety are interwoven, and comments about competence or capacity related to propriety will be highly useful and desirable."[26]

In contrast, the Air India Commission evaluated "how effectively the government uses the resources available to it to deal with the terrorist threat"[27] with particular attention to the distribution of intelligence and its relation to evidence. It recommended that CSIS (and by implication CSE) should no longer have an unreviewable discretion not to share relevant intelligence with others in government. Instead, it recommended that intelligence should be shared and protected by a new legislated privilege from disclosure until a decision was made by the prime minister's national security advisor about whether the intelligence should be more broadly shared within government, even at the risk of possible leaks or legal demands for disclosure. In essence, the PM's national security advisor would decide in the public interest among the competing demands that intelligence be kept secret or that it be used for prosecutorial or other purposes that would risk its disclosure. The government has shown little interest in this recommendation that would have increased and focused oversight and accountability at the centre for the efficacy of national security decisions.[28]

Accountability and Secrecy

Accountability is impossible to achieve if relevant information is kept secret from those demanding accountability. For this reason, the Arar Commission stressed that those who review national security activities should have access to all relevant information regardless of its classification. In addition, the secrecy of national security activities meant that reviewers should be able to conduct self-initiated reviews and not simply respond to complaints. It concluded that while SIRC and the CSE commissioner had such powers, the commission reviewing the RCMP's national security activities lacked such powers. Subsequent legislation stopped short of the Arar Commission's recommendations because the RCMP's Civilian Review and Complaints Commission must go through an elaborate process involving an advisory opinion from a retired judge if the RCMP commissioner refuses to provide it with access to secret information.[29]

The Arar Commission also recommended that statutory gateways be created between the three review bodies for CSIS, CSE, and the RCMP so that the review bodies, like the security agencies themselves, could share secret information and if necessary conduct joint investigations. The government has refused to implement this recommendation, even while proposing in Bill C-51 to facilitate information sharing within government.

To be sure, the Arar Commission recognized that the government and reviewers may disagree over what information could be made public, but it stressed that these disputes should be resolved after review was conducted. Much of the work done by SIRC and the CSE commissioner remains secret and is submitted only to the minister. Given recent experiences of the government overclaiming secrecy, thought should be given to allowing review agencies to use section 38 of the *Canada Evidence Act*, as the Arar Commission did with some success,[30] to challenge the government's secrecy claims.

Given the time-sensitive nature of secrecy and the importance of publicity to accountability, some of the older but still secret review reports submitted by SIRC and the CSE commissioner to the minister of public safety should be considered for public disclosure. The United States has declassified much material in response to Snowden revelations, but Canada has not. SIRC lists close to two hundred secret reports submitted to the minister starting in 1986,[31] and the CSE commissioner lists over eighty classified reports since 1997.[32] Given the government's sustained practice of overclaiming secrecy, it is difficult to think that not one of these reports could be declassified.

The Values of Accountability

The lack of transparency and effective accountability for national security activities, including signals intelligence, creates dangers for both human rights and security. The immediate concern is often, as it has been in the wake of the Snowden revelations, on human rights abuses and invasions of privacy. At the same time, a lack of accountability can shelter inefficiencies or national security activities that are counterproductive or not properly authorized. Much of the criticism of CSE spying on Brazil revealed by the Snowden leaks has been about the efficacy of such measures. Similarly, the Air India Commission largely accepted allegations by former security official James Bartleman that the predecessor of CSE had access to signals intelligence about the threat to Air India planes before the 1985 bombings that killed 331 people in the world's most deadly act of aviation terrorism before 9/11. Efficacy concerns cannot be ignored, given that it may be difficult and sometimes impossible to find actionable intelligence in the Big Data collected by the NSA and CSE.

Although accountability proposals do not command nearly as much attention as the underlying impropriety or inefficiency that leads to them, we should all be concerned about permanent accountability gaps in which intelligence agencies remain one or more steps ahead of their political masters, their reviewers, civil society, and the citizenry. To be sure, past accountability failures and an increasing cynicism about government makes many skeptical about accountability reform. The former CSE commissioner has dismissed the Arar Commission's proposals for enhanced accountability as "an additional super-bureaucracy, with the associated burden and costs."[33] Such statements have likely encouraged the Canadian government aggressively to characterize additional review as "needless red tape,"[34] even as it dramatically increases security powers in Bill C-51.

The Consequences of Shortchanging Review

Equating review with red tape is short-sighted. It ignores the dramatic increase in resources, intensity, and integration of national security activities since 9/11. One result is that the resources devoted to the review of national security activities have been dwarfed by the expanded budgets of intelligence agencies. For example, the CSE commissioner has an annual budget of around $2 million and ten full-time equivalents to review CSE, which has a reported budget of $350 to $422 million and almost two thousand full-time equivalents.[35] SIRC, with an annual budget under $3 million and seventeen full-time equivalents (down from twenty in 2006, despite the abolition of the Inspector General), reviews CSIS, which has over 3,200 employees and a budget of over $500 million.[36] The government has in its April 2015 budget committed to almost doubling SIRC's budget, but not to alter its lack of power to share secret information and conduct joint reviews.

Accountability gaps have implications for public confidence in and social license for security activities. Bill C-51's broad definition of the ambit of information sharing has set off alarm bells within Canada's Muslim community and among a broad range of Aboriginal, environmental, and separatist groups that may be subject to security information sharing. The Canadian government could more credibly rebut these concerns as alarmist if it had an adequately resourced, whole-of-government review body that could review information sharing. The government has argued that the Privacy Commissioner provides such whole-of-government review. But the Privacy Commissioner, in a 2014 report, raised concerns that it is operating under out-of-date legislation that does not give it adequate powers to share information and conduct joint reviews or have access to the Federal Court with respect to collection and disclosure of personal information that is classified secret.[37] Nothing in Bill C-51 responds to these recent concerns articulated by the Privacy Commissioner.

The accountability gaps that have emerged between whole-of-government security responses and their review and oversight are very troubling, especially in an era when the government is embarking on a second round of post-9/11 increases in security powers to respond to the real foreign terrorist fighter threat. Such gaps can harm rights, including privacy. There are also concerns about chilling expression and protests and discriminatory profiling and guilt by association reasoning. This, in turn, affects public confidence and social licence for intelligence and other security activities. Finally, accountability gaps can hurt security if they prevent independent reviewers from being able to see the big picture to determine whether the appropriate amount of intelligence is being collected and shared with whom ever it needs to be shared with in a timely and useful manner. These oversight concerns are particularly pressing given the increases in CSIS's powers and privileges under Bills C-44 and C-51 and the possibility that the new privilege for CSIS human powers and its new powers of disruption may have the unintended effect of making terrorism prosecutions even more difficult.[38]

Legislative Accountability: Be Careful What You Wish For

Canada, unlike its Five Eyes security partners, does not give any parliamentarians regular access to secret information. The Afghan detainee affair, in which Parliament had to hold the government *prima facie* in contempt of Parliament to get any access to secret documents relating to whether former detainees were tortured after being transferred from the custody of Canadian Forces to Afghan officials, revealed this lack of access as a critical weakness. It resulted in struggles between the government and Parliament that saw Parliament prorogued in 2009 in the face of a motion demanding access. In addition, an ad hoc committee of retired judges and parliamentarians from all parties (except the NDP) was created to review secret documents in the wake of the Speaker's ruling on contempt. Despite this crisis, there has been very little interest in Canada in giving parliamentarians regular access to secret information. This may change after the opposition parties, especially the Liberals, make lack of parliamentary review the focus of their opposition to Bill C-51.

Current Reform Proposals

Most current proposals to give Parliamentarians access to secret information are quite modest and suggest that increased Parliamentary review will not cure Bill C-51's many ills. A private member's bill introduced by Liberal MP Wayne Easter was particularly anaemic. Not only would members of the proposed committee be permanently bound to secrecy by statute,[39] but the responsible minister would have final and non-reviewable power to decide how much, if any, secret information to provide the committee.[40] Such a deferential approach may be related to the novelty of giving Canadian parliamentarians any access to secret information. It may also reflect anxieties that Canada's oft-noted status as a net importer of intelligence renders it vulnerable to having the intelligence tap cut off by allies if secrets are leaked.[41] An often unspoken but real factor behind Canada's persistent fear of leaks is the concern that separatist or radical parliamentarians are less trustworthy. In any event, the Easter bill would do little more than give parliamentarians the most tentative toehold inside the secrecy tent.

Another private members' bill, sponsored by Liberal MP Joyce Murray, had more robust powers to access secret information, but it was defeated by the government in October 2014. This bill also took a multi-pronged approach to accountability and attempted to increase judicial and ministerial oversight of CSE as well as the oversight role of the CSE commissioner.[42] It will be suggested in the conclusion that such a multi-pronged approach is indeed necessary if we are to close accountability gaps.

Some commentators have criticized the Arar Commission for not including enhanced parliamentary reform within their proposals.[43] In my view, such criticisms are unfair, given the commission's mandate, which focused on review of the RCMP's national security activities. In any event, such criticisms overestimate what can be achieved through parliamentary review. The experience of other democracies with legislative review suggests the contributions of parliamentary review are likely to be modest. This is especially so given that Canadian committees are poorly staffed, the high turnover rate among parliamentarians and the haphazard nature of their knowledge and interest in security matters.

The Intelligence and Security Committee (ISC) in the UK is often held up as an example, but Canadian accounts of the ISC often discount UK criticisms of its performance on sensitive issues, including possible complicity in torture. The performance of legislative review in the United States has been, if anything, even less inspiring than in the UK. Various members of Congress were briefed on the activities of the NSA after 9/11 but it took the *New York Times* in 2005 to reveal President Bush's illegal orders for NSA domestic spying and then the Snowden leaks to reveal the NSA's more recent activities.

American legislative committees are much better staffed than Canadian ones, but there are still concerns that legislators in Congress often lack the expertise or the budgetary powers to conduct effective oversight.[44] Giving legislators access to secret information but no mechanism to disclose it may only allow the government to claim legitimacy for illegal and improper conduct because some legislators had been "briefed in" to the activities. Some American commentators have made interesting recommendations that would give opposition parties with access to secret information powers to push for the declassification of documents,[45] but there has been little uptake on such proposals. A committee with access to secret information could question ministers and officials *in camera*, but it could not make secret information public even if the information had been over-classified as secret.

What Do We Want from Enhanced Parliamentary Review?
More thought needs to be given to exactly what we want from enhanced legislative review. The Afghan detainee issue shows that parliamentarians may be concerned about propriety, albeit with a distinctly partisan edge. The opposition maintained interest in

whether Canadian Forces had been complicit with torture for an extended period of time, but interest in this issue eventually died down. Most other security matters will be considerably less dramatic. Parliamentary accountability may ultimately depend on the degree of interest and knowledge about security matters in the media and civil society, matters to be discussed in the last part of this chapter.

A parliamentary committee with access to the many confidential reports that review bodies provide to ministers could hold the ministers to account for their response to those reports. It must be understood that review bodies such as SIRC and the CSE commissioner only have powers to make non-binding recommendations to the minister and the agencies. A parliamentary committee would be able to demand explanations from the responsible ministers but would not have oversight or chain-of-command powers to force the minister or the agency to take remedial action.

A parliamentary committee could address efficacy issues that may be downplayed by other review bodies. For example, it could help ensure that ministers can be held accountable for controversial forms of surveillance such as CSE's spying in Brazil.[46]

A national security committee at present would have to require both the minister of public safety and the minister of defence responsible for CSE to explain their actions. There may be a case for making the minister of public safety responsible for all non-military aspects of intelligence so that ministerial accountability for intelligence is not diffuse.

Any proposals for increased parliamentary review must confront the fact that Canadian committees do not have the same research capacities as American or British committees. The Privacy Commissioner's recent proposal that parliamentarians conduct "a global study of Canada's intelligence oversight and review mechanisms"[47] ignores the limited resources of parliamentary committees even when assisted by the Library of Parliament. It also ignores that much of this work has already been done by the multimillion-dollar Arar Commission in its neglected second report.

Some claim that a parliamentary committee might make security issues less partisan, but there are no guarantees. Bill C-51 was introduced by Prime Minister Harper in an election style rally in January, 2015, and not in Parliament. The way the Afghan detainee affair was handled was also quite partisan on all sides. It is also not certain that parliamentary committees will increase public confidence in our security responses, especially because confidence in both elected members of Parliament and the unelected Senate seems at an all-time low. Rather than relying on its members, much of the legitimacy of a parliamentary committee might come from its engagement with civil society and the media. Any parliamentary committee will have to win public confidence through its work.

Increased parliamentary review might help increase parliamentary and public knowledge of security matters. At the same time, the challenges for parliamentarians, especially those in the Commons, of mastering security matters should not be underestimated. For example, Bill C-51 lists seventeen different departments and agencies that could receive security information. It will create two new security statutes on information sharing and the no-fly list, and it will amend fifteen other acts, including the *CSIS Act*, the *Criminal Code*, and the *Immigration and Refugee Protection Act*. Will parliamentarians be able to stay on top of this mass of laws, let alone understand how they are enforced? To be sure, we need enhanced parliamentary review with access to secret information, but it would be a serious mistake to expect too much of that process.

Judicial Accountability: Into the Breach or Creating the Breach?

The Arar Commission was not optimistic about relying on judicial review of national security activities because "the judiciary is a reactive institution" that can only respond to misconduct when it becomes the subject of litigation. It warned that, because of secrecy, "affected individuals may never know that they have been subject to a national security investigation. This reduced level of judicial oversight is a further reason for independent review."[48] Even if individuals do have such knowledge, they may not have the resources to bring a court challenge. And even if they do have the resources, they will face great secrecy barriers in their litigation. Finally, the comparative lack of prosecutions in the national security area means that the courts provide "less oversight" for national security investigations "than they do for other criminal investigations."[49]

There are, however, some virtues of involving the judiciary in review and oversight. The judiciary's traditional deference on national security matters has eroded in the wake of post-9/11 security abuses. Gone are the days when judges would not even look at secret information, and courts in Canada and elsewhere have pushed back on a number of fronts in the post-9/11 era. The judiciary has been at its strongest in insisting on greater transparency where secret information has been used. Particularly noteworthy are Supreme Court decisions insisting on retention of raw intelligence investigating specific individuals, adversarial challenge to such intelligence, and insistence on minimal disclosure in security certificate cases.[50] Another precedent that may be particularly relevant in the era of foreign terrorist fighters is a Federal Court decision upholding the right of a Canadian citizen to return to Canada even though he was at the time listed by the UN as affiliated with al-Qaeda.[51]

Justice Mosley's Decision on the Outsourcing of Surveillance to Five Eyes Partners

Judges can be tenacious in ensuring that security agencies do not go beyond the scope of what they have authorized. In 2009, Justice Mosley issued warrants to allow CSIS to intercept foreign communications of Canadian citizens. In August 2013, upon reading the annual public report of the CSE commissioner, he convened a new hearing on his own initiative. He was not happy.

Justice Mosley concluded that CSIS had misled him by not revealing its plans to draw on the assistance of CSE's Five Eyes signals intelligence partners in carrying out the surveillance. He called this a "deliberate decision to keep the Court in the dark about the scope and extent of the foreign collection efforts that would flow from the Court's issuance of a warrant."[52] He also concluded that the tasking of foreign agencies by Canadian officials to conduct the surveillance was unlawful. He was concerned that the warrants he'd granted had been used as "protective cover."[53]

What happened in this case was not an isolated occurrence. Drawing on a SIRC report, Justice Mosley noted that foreign assets had been used in as many as thirty-five warrants issued since 2009. Justice Mosley warned that Canada could lose control of intelligence it asked its foreign partners to collect. He underlined the grave risks when Canada loses control over its own intelligence with reference to the role that Canadian information and requests for foreign assistance had played in the torture of Maher Arar and other Canadians in Syria.[54]

Justice Mosley's extraordinary decision provides a rare glimpse into the Five Eyes relationship, normally one of Ottawa's most closely guarded secrets. Justice Mosley ruled that no reference should be

made by CSIS, CSE, or its legal advisors to the erroneous idea that
a CSIS warrant authorized the tasking of foreign agencies. He read
down Canadian laws so as to prevent a transnational accountability
gap that would occur if Canada tasked foreign agencies to conduct
surveillance of Canadian targets in a manner that effectively left
Canada without control of the intelligence produced by its own
targeting and tasking. Judicial attempts to plug and stop accountability gaps are welcome, but they will generally only occur when
states attempts to abuse judicial authority and engage in blatant
misconduct. Indeed, much of Justice Mosley's bold judgment was
premised on the assumption that Canadian tasking of surveillance
by its Five Eyes partners would violate international law.

Justice Mosley also recognized the need for continual review
by executive watchdog agencies, review that he had benefited from.
To this end, he required that a copy of his decision be provided to
both SIRC and the CSE commissioner. This judgment, like some of
the American Foreign Intelligence Surveillance Court (FISC) decisions declassified in the wake of the Snowden leaks, demonstrates
how judges can complement the review process but also how they
may depend on executive watchdog review.

The federal government might point to the Justice Mosley decision as exhibit A revealing the strength of the judicial oversight that
will be required when Federal Court judges consider CSIS warrant
requests for otherwise illegal conduct under Bills C-44 and C-51. One
problem with such an approach is that the government is appealing
Justice Mosley's decision all the way to the Supreme Court. If the
government wins in the Supreme Court, CSIS may not have to bother
with warrants with respect to investigations outside of Canada.

The Supreme Court's decision to hear the government's appeal
opens up the possibility that the court might say that warrants are
not required for some extraterritorial CSIS investigations. Such a
ruling would allow CSIS to act without warrants and without the
judicial oversight that the government has promised in its defence
of Bills C-44 and C-51. Conversely, the court might uphold Justice
Mosley's judgments in even more ringing and emphatic terms than
the Federal Court of Appeal. That would be good, but we should not
underestimate how much the judgment depended on heroic levels of
knowledge and initiative of one judge with a particularly long history
of expertise in national security matters.

Judges Being Asked to Approve and Oversee Breaches of the Law and the Charter

Federal Court judges will soon be able, under both Bills C-44 and C-51, to grant warrants "without regard to any other law, including that of a foreign state."[55] Under Bill C-51 as introduced in Parliament, judges will even be able to grant CSIS a warrant to contravene the *Charter* provided that the proposed measure is proportionate to the threat and the reasonable availability of other measures to reduce the threat[56] and provided it does not intentionally or negligently inflict death or bodily harm, invade sexual integrity, or obstruct justice.[57] Bill C-51 builds on the pattern in Bill C-44 of allowing Federal Court judges to authorize CSIS to break domestic and foreign laws, but it goes a step farther by providing that CSIS may also obtain a judicial warrant to reduce a threat to the security of Canada in a manner that will contravene *Charter* rights.

The government is defending Bill C-51 by stressing that the powers will be subject to judicial oversight. Minister of Defence Jason Kenny has even argued that Bill C-51 "doesn't give new powers to police or intelligence agencies but rather to judges, to courts."[58] This ignores that CSIS will execute the warrants and that Justice Mosley's decision provides some grounds to be concerned about whether CSIS will go beyond what is specifically authorized in the warrant. It downplays the radical implications of a single judge authorizing a violation of the *Charter* in a warrant context where the decision is not likely to be reviewed in subsequent trials or on appeal.

Bills C-44 and C-51 are silent on what, if any, accountability measures Federal Court judges will provide to ensure that security agencies do not go beyond the terms of new warrants. Justice Mosley's judgment suggests that judges may not tolerate activity beyond what they have authorized *if they find out about it*. It is not comforting, however, that it appears to have been Justice Mosley's extracurricular reading of the reports of review bodies that led to the discovery that CSIS had subcontracted surveillance to foreign allies.

The nature of CSIS warrants means that the appropriateness of the limits that they set will not be generally tested on appeal. Warrant proceedings are generally one-sided proceedings. Although a security cleared *amicus* was appointed on some of the legal issues before and after Justice Mosley's warrant, that is not the norm and it is not specifically provided for in either Bill C-44 or C-51. Moreover, as the Arar Commission stressed, national security activities are much less subject to judicial review than ordinary warrants. Indeed, the leading appeal decision on CSIS warrants dates back to 1987.[59] In the wake of the Snowden revelations, the Privacy and Civil Liberties Board in the United States recommended that the Foreign Intelligence Surveillance Court (FISC), which also grants warrants *ex parte*, should be assisted by security-cleared special advocates. It also recommended that efforts should be made to encourage both more appeals from the warrants and more declassification of FISC decisions.[60]

Craig Forcese and I have raised concerns about wording in Bill C-51 that allows Federal Court judges to authorize *Charter* violations in the course of issuing CSIS warrants to reduce security threats.[61] In our view, this would be an unprecedented grant of power to judges to authorize *Charter* violations, as opposed to attempting to avoid *Charter* violations.[62] The grant of search warrants is traditionally seen as a method to avoid a violation of the right against unreasonable search and seizure under section 8 of the *Charter*. In contrast, a judge under Bill C-51 could authorize CSIS to take steps that will contravene a person's *Charter* rights, such as the right of citizens under section 6 of the *Charter* to leave or return to Canada.

The reasoning of Federal Court judges in warrant applications may for valid operational reasons relating to national security, national defence and foreign relations be kept secret for a long time. If released, such judgments may be heavily redacted. The leaked and declassified FISC decisions in the United States reveal that some of the credibility and trust that the judiciary enjoys may be undermined by secret jurisprudence, especially if it authorizes illegal and rights invasive conduct by intelligence agencies.

Professor Forcese and I also raise concerns that judges will be forced to make these difficult decisions in closed *ex parte* proceedings with at most security-cleared *amici curaie* (who are not specifically contemplated in the new warrant regime but are under proposed American reforms) playing a challenge role. Judges trained in an adversarial system may also not have the information and resources they need to ensure CSIS and those who assist them such as the CSE act in the manner specified in the warrant. Bill C-51 does not even ensure that the judge will know who CSIS asks to assist them in executing a threat reduction warrant. Nothing stops CSIS, especially when it acts outside of Canada, from enlisting foreign individuals and agencies.

The new warrant regime could change the role of the Federal Court, especially if the judges require the security agencies regularly to report back to them about operations. The specially designated judges of the Federal Court may become something more akin to specialized investigating magistrates used in the French and other civilian systems. Such a "hands on" and potentially "dirty hands" role could compromise the impartiality and independence of judges who have authorized illegal activities that violate the *Charter*.[63] Even if the judges come down hard on CSIS misconduct, judicially supervised CSIS investigations may not have the disciplinary effects of criminal trials, in part because many judgments may remain secret for operational reasons.

The Federal Court is guided not by *Criminal Code* concepts based on guilt or innocence, but by the more expansive definition of threats to the security of Canada. It is noteworthy that the Supreme Court, when upholding investigative hearings, took care to insist that judges observe the normal rules of evidence and the presumption of open courts. Moreover, two judges dissented on the basis that it was alien to our system to have judges preside over police investigations.[64] It would be even more alien to have judges preside over CSIS illegalities and *Charter* violations committed at home and abroad.

Under Bills C-44 and C-51, Federal Court judges are being called into the breach with respect to devising accountability structures for CSIS. They are also being called to create breaches in the form of pre-authorized violations of Canadian and foreign laws and the *Charter*. They will be asked to create ad hoc accountability structures for CSIS to ensure that it respects the limits of judicial orders when violating laws and *Charter* rights both at home and abroad. To be sure, Bill C-51 places some categorical limits on what can be authorized: the measures must be reasonable and proportionate,[65] and they must never cause intentional or negligent bodily harm, violate sexual integrity, or wilfully obstruct justice.[66] At the same time, however, these limits will be observed in warrant decisions that may authorize violations of the *Charter* and other laws; that will be difficult to appeal and that may remain shrouded in secrecy.

The government seems happy to enlist judges under Bill C-51, but the result may strain the capacities of even the most able and dedicated judges. If things go wrong in the execution of one of these warrants at home or abroad, the result could tarnish the reputation of the judiciary while at the same time providing CSIS with protective cover. The government is defending Bill C-51 by stressing the role that judges will play, but the warrant process defies public expectations that judges will act in a transparent and appealable manner after having heard adversarial argument from both sides. Finally, it asks judges who are supposed to uphold the law and the *Charter* to authorize and take responsibility for their violation by an intelligence agency.

Enhanced Executive Watchdog Review: The Need To See and Review the Big Picture for Propriety and Efficacy

Although legislative and judicial accountability mechanisms are needed, the most important mechanisms for holding intelligence agencies to account are those found within the executive. In Canada, these mechanisms include the role of retired judges as commissioners for the CSE, with broad public inquiry powers, and the ability of SIRC to have access to all secret information, except Cabinet confidences, held by CSIS. Both review mechanisms are hybrids between the executive and other branches of government. In the case of the CSE commissioner, the review body borrows from the brand of the judiciary with respect to independence and impartiality, and in the case of SIRC they borrow on the brand of the legislature in ensuring representation from all major political parties. Like other parts of the executive, they can be tasked by and report to responsible ministers and their number of classified reports directed to ministers is much greater than their number of annual public reports.

The Arar Commission stressed that any credible review mechanism for propriety should have unrestricted access to secret information and the ability to initiate its own audits or investigations. It was not opposed to review bodies hearing complaints, but recognized the limits of such mechanisms given the secrecy of most national security activities. After much deliberation, the commission opted for a model that would see a significant expansion of SIRC's mandate to include the national security activities of Citizenship and Immigration Canada, Transport Canada, the Financial and Transaction Report Analysis, and the Department of Foreign Affairs. A revitalized RCMP complaints agency would have jurisdiction to review the national security work of the Canada Border Services Agency. It also recommended that statutory gateways be created between three review agencies, SIRC for CSIS, the commissioner for CSE, and the RCMP review body. Finally, a coordinating committee composed of the chairs of the three main review bodies with an independent chair would play a role in coordinating reviews and ensuring that there were not duplicative reviews of national security activities where the RCMP, CSIS, and CSE had overlapping responsibilities. All of these recommendations recognized the need for whole-of-government review to match whole-of-government security responses. At the same time, the commission ultimately opted for maintaining expertise by recommending that an expanded SIRC, the CSE commissioner, and a new RCMP review body all remain in place. It thus rejected proposals made to the commission for the creation of one big review committee or "super SIRC" that could review all national security activities.

The Changing Review Environment since the Arar Commission

The accountability gaps that the Arar Commission identified in 2006 have gotten worse since that time. The government reformed the RCMP review body but stopped short of giving that body full access to secret information by setting up a costly advisory process of retired judges mediating disputes about access to secret information. The government also rejected the recommendation that there be statutory gateways so the three review bodies could share secret information and conduct joint investigations. The government has not expanded review to cover the five other agencies with important national security responsibilities. Indeed, the government has even contradicted review by abolishing CSIS's Inspector General who served as the Minister's eyes and ears in CSIS and determined the legality of CSIS's actions.

In 2006, it was realistic to expect that the new Conservative government with its commitment to strengthening parliamentary review might adopt some version of Prime Minister Martin's 2005 proposals for a national security committee of parliamentarians. The Afghan detainee affair strengthened the case for a parliamentary committee with access to secret information, but the government was content to rely on a special ad hoc process. The government's largely successful obstruction of Parliament on that issue suggests that the prospect for parliamentary review has diminished. The government also refused to appoint a public inquiry as a means to make up for deficiencies in legislative and executive review as was done in the cases of Maher Arar and other Canadians tortured in Syria. The most recent indication that parliamentary review is not likely are attempts by the government in the Bill C-51 debate to paint it as American and foreign to parliamentary systems.[67] This may simply reflect common and erroneous conflation of retrospective review with chain of command oversight, but it does not bode well for increased parliamentary review.

SIRC's brand has been diminished by the exploits of Arthur Porter, who resigned in late 2011 after his ties to the government of Sierra Leone were revealed. In early 2014, the public learned that three members of SIRC had financial ties to pipelines. Chair Chuck Strahl eventually resigned over the controversy.[68] I do not wish to impugn in any way the integrity of Mr. Strahl or other members of SIRC. They serve part time and are paid at rates well below what they would receive in the private sector. Nevertheless, the fact that a majority of SIRC members in 2014 had ties to pipeline companies makes it difficult for SIRC to command public confidence when it reviews CSIS's surveillance of those who oppose the pipelines, including environmentalists and Aboriginal groups. At the same time, it should be noted that the latest SIRC annual report was particularly hard-hitting and raised concerns about difficulties in obtaining information from CSIS and that several new appointments have been made to SIRC, including a retired judge, an academic, and a former civil servant, all professions associated with independence.[69]

The office of the CSE commissioner has escaped the scandals that have plagued SIRC, but its performance in response to the Snowden leaks has been questionable. On 13 June 2013, just a week after the first Snowden leaks, then Commissioner Décary issued a statement explaining his role of independent review and assuring the public that CSE was acting legally. He verified "that CSEC [CSE] does not direct its foreign signals intelligence collection…at any person in Canada," that it is "prohibited from requesting an international partner to undertake activities that CSEC itself is legally prohibited from conducting," and "that CSEC complies with any limitations imposed by law on the agency to which CSEC is providing assistance, for example, any conditions imposed by a judge in a warrant."[70] This statement would prove controversial in light of Justice Mosley's decision, released in December 2013. Commissioner Décary's 13 June 2013 statement also provided that he had "reviewed CSEC metadata activities and have found them to be in compliance with the law and to be subject to comprehensive and satisfactory measures to protect the privacy of Canadians."[71] This statement would be relied upon and prove controversial in light of subsequent Snowden leaks about metadata.

In an annual report dated June 2013 but released on 21 August 2013, Commissioner Décary verified that he had examined CSE assistance to CSIS in carrying out the warrant and that "CSEC conducted its activities in accordance with the law and ministerial direction, and in a manner that included measures to protect the privacy of Canadians."[72] The commissioner did, however, recommend that "CSEC advise CSIS to provide the Federal Court of Canada with certain additional information about the nature and extent of the assistance CSEC may provide CSIS."[73] This opaque and carefully worded reference did not retract the commissioner's assurance made earlier that month and in the annual report that CSE had complied with legal limits on its authority. Although the commissioner's recommendation, as well as the SIRC report, played a role in triggering Justice Mosley's re-evaluation of the warrants he had granted, the CSE commissioner's approach stopped short of ringing alarm bells. The commissioner's public performance is not nearly as robust as Justice Mosley's subsequent judgment, which concluded that CSE's activities were not authorized by his warrant or any legislation. In other words, they were illegal.[74]

The tension, if not the inconsistency, between Commissioner Décary's conclusion and those of Justice Mosley about the legality of CSE conduct are troubling, especially because the commissioner is limited to reviewing the legality of CSE activities. Former CSE commissioners, former Chief Justice of Canada Antonio Lamer and former Supreme Court Justice Charles Gonthier, expressed concerns about the way CSE and their Department of Justice advisors interpreted CSE's enabling legislation.[75] Conclusions of legality can mask disputed and complex questions of law. It does not assist public confidence that many of these disputes about legality may be sheltered from public exposure, given claims of both national security confidentiality and solicitor-client privilege.

Within a day of the story breaking that CSE had collected metadata from people using Wi-Fi in a Canadian Airport, CSE Commissioner Plouffe issued a press release stating, "In light of the most recent unauthorized disclosure of classified information of the Communications Security Establishment Canada (CSEC), I can state that I am aware of the metadata activities referred to." He noted that past commissioners had "reviewed CSEC metadata activities and have found them to be in compliance with the law and to be subject to comprehensive and satisfactory measures to protect the privacy of Canadians."[76]

Although Commissioner Plouffe's statement stopped short of declaring the airport program lawful, the government used these conclusions to defend CSE and to argue that the program "only" collected metadata and that the collection was not directed at Canadians in violation of CSE's legal mandate. Others argued that the program exceeded CSE's mandate and stressed the harmful effects on privacy of collecting metadata.[77] The commissioner's focus on legality downplayed the concerns about the effect of such activities on privacy.[78] A few weeks later, on 12 February 2014, the CSE commissioner issued another press release. It concluded that "CSEC activity does not involve 'mass surveillance' or tracking of Canadians or persons in Canada; no CSEC activity was directed at Canadians or persons in Canada."[79] The former conclusion responded to media concerns about the Snowden leaks, while the later tracked the language of CSE's enabling legislation.

CSE's enabling legislation was hastily enacted after 9/11 and it only prohibits surveillance that is "directed at Canadians or any person in Canada."[80] This legislation is being challenged under the *Charter*,[81] and indeed it seems to be at odds with fundamental *Charter* principles that suggest that the government can violate the *Charter* if its actions have the effect, even the unintended effect, of violating rights, including privacy. In other words, the fact that government actions are not designed for the purpose of violating the *Charter* does not necessarily mean that they are consistent with the *Charter*.

The commissioner's response to the Snowden revelations was defensive of the review status quo, asserting that its resources were adequate to review CSE and consistent with those of other agencies. The commissioner also affirmed that he would not allow embarrassing information to be taken out of his report. This, however, avoided the question of whether embarrassing information could be classified as secret and the lack of transparency of the process used to determine how much of the Commissioner's reports is classified.

The Need for a Super SIRC with a Whole-of-Government National Security Mandate

Increased security powers under Bill C-51, especially broad information sharing powers under the proposed *Security of Information Sharing Act*, as well as mandates to CSIS to act abroad in violation of Canadian and foreign law, suggest that the time has come for fundamental reform of Canada's review structure. SIRC was a state-of-art institution that Canada could be proud of in 1984, but thirty-one years later it is showing its age. SIRC's powers of access to information are limited to the CSIS silo. The countervailing whole-of-government approach is epitomized in the proposed *Security of Canada Information Sharing Act*, which would allow any federal institution to share security information with seventeen different departments, many of which are subject to no independent review. The government has insisted that the existing review structures are up to the task.[82] Unfortunately, this ignores the stovepiped nature of existing reviews for CSIS, CSE, and the RCMP, and the limited mandate and powers of the Privacy Commissioner, underlined most recently in a 2014 report which found that its powers were not up to the task of reviewing information-sharing in the security context.[83]

All of these developments suggest that the time has come for more major reform than was recommended by the Arar Commission. There is also a need to respond to perceptions and at times reali-ties of duplicative reviews that are often only a symptom of archaic twentieth-century stovepiped review functions.[84] In other words, the time has come to replace SIRC, the CSE commissioner, and that part of the RCMP review agency that reviews its national security activi-ties, with one big committee or "super SIRC."[85] The new committee should ultimately have jurisdiction to review all of the government's national security activities, including security related information sharing.[86] Such an approach would have the virtue of allowing such a committee to follow the trail of intelligence, information sharing, and other national security activities throughout government without the need for statutory gateways.

A one-committee approach could also create possibilities for increased resources, full-time members, and broader representation of expertise and interests on the committee. One of the successful features of Canada's existing review mechanisms is that, while situ-ated in the executive, they are hybrid institutions, with both the CSE commissioner and public inquiries benefiting from the presence of retired or sitting judges and SIRC having the advantage of represent-ing former parliamentarians from all the major political parties. A new committee might include these elements,[87] but also include bet-ter representation from civil society in partial recognition that the existing parties do not command the same type of support from the public, and especially the young, as they once did. Thought should be given to creative ways to recruit and appoint members of such a committee. There may also be a case for term limits, to prevent any perception or reality of capture. At the same time, staged appointments and staged expansion of a super SIRC's mandate could help ensure necessary expertise and experience. Those who serve either permanently or part-time on such a committee should be prepared to cut ties that may lead to reasonable perceptions of conflict of interest. Such a diverse committee should ideally have resources to hold public hearings and contribute to public education in a way that existing review bodies are unable to do.

A larger, more diverse and better-resourced super SIRC could also open up room for expertise of various forms and could expand review to include not only questions of legality but broader questions of propriety and even efficacy. Even with respect to propriety, it would be important that any new committee, unlike the CSE commissioner, not be restricted to reviewing the legality of actions. Retired judges are well-suited to making conclusions about legality, but such conclusions are only as good as the underlying law. The CSE commissioner's conclusions about legality have understandably been couched in terms that mirror the language of its enabling statute quickly enacted after 9/11. As discussed above, the commissioner has often stressed that CSE activities are not "directed" at Canadians or persons in Canada and that the information it collects is used for the "purpose of foreign intelligence." To be sure, these phrases mirror those found in section 273.64 of the *National Defence Act* defining the mandate of CSE, but it is far from clear whether they are sufficient to maintain public confidence in the face of the staggering Snowden revelations.

Indeed, a case may be made that CSE's mandate may already be out of date and insufficient to ensure privacy. For example, its focus on CSE's purposes in obtaining foreign intelligence are at odds with fundamental *Charter* principles that stress that government's conduct may be unconstitutional because of its effects on persons even if the purposes animating the state are entirely proper. The tension between the purpose-based statutory framework and the effects-based *Charter* framework has only been increased by the Supreme Court's recent decision recognizing privacy and anonymity interests in metadata.[88] Conclusions of legality are only as good as the underlying law.[89] Review for propriety should not be limited to legality. Conclusions of legality also echo the unfortunate torture memo experience where security agencies took comfort in secret and unreasonable legal opinions to provide protective cover for problematic practices. Lawyers routinely disagree over matters of interpretation and some CSE commissioners have been unhappy with how Department of Justice lawyers have interpreted CSE's enabling statute.[90] Propriety issues including privacy are too important to be left to lawyerly sparring.

Although it focuses on propriety, the US Privacy and Civil Liberties Oversight Board has also been concerned about questions of efficacy and argues that the government should attempt to measure efficacy.[91] It has also held public hearings in a way that Canadian review bodies have not. It remains to be seen how the Privacy and Civil Liberties Board created under new British legislation will work,[92] but its creation is another sign that Canada is falling behind other democracies with respect to review of national security activities.

Any new watchdog and review body must have sufficient legal powers and resources to make progress on closing the accountability gaps that are increasing with increased legal powers and technological capacities for surveillance. A new review body requires a whole-of-government mandate and an ability to access the increasing amount of material that is classified as secret as government invests more in intelligence and secrecy. A new review body, like the Arar Commission, should not only have access to all relevant material regardless of its classification, but it should also be able to bring a court challenge to refusals by the government to allow it to publish part of its reports. Such challenges should be rare, but they would give the committee more power in dealing with the security agencies. Court challenges would provide a much more transparent process than that which governs the negotiations that apparently go on between SIRC and CSIS and the CSE commissioner and CSE over what material can be made public. Another alternative would be to allow a super SIRC to submit its classified reports to a parliamentary committee that could both the use the report in questioning ministers and officials and might be able to take steps to challenge the secrecy classification.

It is, of course, highly unlikely that a super SIRC will be adopted. The security establishment in Ottawa, as in other countries, has much leverage. In Canada, this leverage is increased by concerns that enhanced accountability may result in disclosures that could threaten intelligence-sharing relationships with foreign agencies. The time to fundamentally reform review structures was not in the quasi crisis that have followed the October 2014 attacks and the Paris and Copenhagen attacks in early 2015, but in the quieter years after the Arar Commission's 2006 report. The government has prioritized giving security agencies and especially CSIS more power in Bills C-44 and C-51. Once they are enacted, there may be little incentive or energy to revisit the neglected question of review.

Whole of Society Review and Whistle-Blowing

Even if a super SIRC with adequate powers and resources were created, it would not be enough. As Michael Geist suggests in his chapter in this collection, we cannot just focus on watching public surveillance agencies but must be concerned about their corporate partners.[93] In addition civil society, the media and even whistle blowers all have a role to play in narrowing accountability gaps.

Corporate Accountability
The President's Review Group helpfully recommended that corporations publish more data about the information they provide to government. Legislative proposals related to the *USA Freedom Act* contemplate that corporations will hold domestic metadata and be able to challenge governmental requests for various forms of information. This raises the question of whether corporations will resist giving the government data. Ultimately this may depend on whether consumers and citizens will demand increased privacy protection from corporations. To what extent is there a market demand for privacy? There are many reasons for Blackberry's decline, but it is an interesting question whether its decision to co-operate with the government of India to allow a backdoor into its once-secure devices is one of them.[94] The power of corporations should not be underestimated. In the end, corporations will be driven by consumer demand and much will depend on how much consumers value their privacy.

Social Accountability
Both security and review of security are complex matters. Polls suggest that a large amount of the Canadian public are supportive of increased security powers but also want to see enhanced review and oversight.[95] The Canadian government seems to be promoting the idea that courts can be relied upon to ensure propriety-based

review of CSIS's increased powers. They also point to SIRC, the CSE commissioner, the RCMP review and complaints body, the Privacy Commissioner, and the Auditor General as evidence that there is enough review. The impression and sometimes the reality of duplicative and overlapping review may create review fatigue. There was no pressure on the government to respond to the Arar Commission's 2006 findings that the present review structure was inadequate. The Bill C-51 debate in early 2015 fortunately placed more emphasis on review. An impressive list of former prime ministers, judges and reviewers all wrote a public letter that echoed the Arar Commission's conclusions that the present review structure is inadequate.[96] Unfortunately, however, the government has only responded by increasing SIRC's budget, but not its jurisdiction.

If public demands for effective propriety-based review are not effective, perhaps demands for efficacy-based review may be. The Air India Commission stressed the need for better oversight of security and especially a need to resolve both historical and contemporary tensions between the RCMP and CSIS. CSIS has from its inception insisted that it does not collect evidence and the RCMP has facilitated this approach by relying as little as possible on CSIS information. This was a damning indictment of the system, but most of the fundamental reforms that the Commission recommended to improve the transition from intelligence to evidence have been rejected. Even in the wake of the October 2014 attacks, the public seems to be placated with the government's assurances that giving the police and especially CSIS more powers and privileges will be sufficient.

Accountability for both the propriety and efficacy of security activities will depend on public knowledge and demands. There is a need for civil society, the media, parliamentarians, academics and ultimately citizens to engage on these issues. In the end, we will only get the level of accountability that we are prepared to demand.

Whistle-Blowing

There is a need for multiple and even potentially redundant accountability mechanisms. One such fail-safe, one that the President's Review Group appointed in the wake of the Snowden revelations seems determined to shut down, is whistle-blowing. To be sure, whistle-blowing is a delicate subject, especially given Canada's vulnerable status as a net importer of intelligence and the recent memory of Jeffrey Delisle's criminal leaks that put at risk much Five

Eyes information. Nevertheless, there is a need for a more credible whistle-blowing mechanism than section 15 of the *Security of
Information Act*.[97] This provision authorizes only a most limited form
of whistle-blowing when a person with access to secret information
has a reasonable belief that an offence has been committed. The
whistle-blower must inform his or her civil service boss first, thus
risking dismissal and prosecution. He or she can only inform SIRC
or the CSE commissioner if he or she has not received a reasonable
response from his or her boss. The CSE commissioner has never
reported receiving a complaint from a potential whistle-blower.

If legal whistle-blowing is to be a realistic option, legislative
reform is necessary. There needs to be real protection against prosecutions and perhaps a "single person and office"[98] such as a super
SIRC to hear from whistle-blowers. The President's Review Group
similarly recommended that an expanded civil liberties and privacy protection board have enhanced powers to hear from whistle-
blowers.[99] In Canada, however, there is no parliamentary interest
(even in Bills C-44 and C-51) in modernizing the *Security of Information
Act* on whistle-blowing or other subjects. For example, Parliament has
not even replaced an offence of the possession of secret information
that was found by a trial judge in Ontario to violate the *Charter*.[100]

The impact of the WikiLeaks and Snowden leaks raises the
uncomfortable question of the role of civil disobedience, or what
Reg Whitaker aptly calls "guerilla accountability."[101] Although the
Delisle leaks were embarrassingly low tech and done without good
motives, the very same technology that empowers surveillance also
empowers equally massive leaks. It took Daniel Ellsberg a year to
sneak the seven thousand pages of the Pentagon Papers out of the
Pentagon. Today, massive amounts of information can be downloaded
and leaked in a matter of minutes.[102] The President's Review Group
was well aware of this danger. It called for much tighter standards of
access to secret information, with little apparent thought to whether
its attack on the "need to share" could impede the quick flow of intelligence and the breaking down of walls that so many thought was
so important after 9/11.[103]

To be sure, the Snowden leaks were unlawful. The robust
debate about Mr. Snowden's fate is revealing. In some respects, it
invokes Oren Gross's controversial post-9/11 proposal of an extra-
legal approach to counterterrorism.[104] In other words, a failure to
prosecute Snowden or even a light sentence would amount to a

form of ratification of his conduct. Future leakers, however, would not know for sure whether their leaks would be prosecuted or not. The idea that illegal leaks can be considered as a legitimate part of a system of accountability is an uncomfortable thought, but it cannot be ignored.

The Role of the Investigative Media

There could be no Edward Snowden without reporters such as Glenn Greenwald. This raises the precarious state of the traditional media today. Leaks publicized by the *New York Times*, *The Guardian*, and *der Spiegel* have a legitimacy (and a sense of responsibility about endangering individuals) that may not be present when they come from "some guy" with a computer and a blog. But the media itself is becoming more fragmented. Some question whether there will even be a mainstream media in the future. If there is not, governments may be able to dismiss dissent to surveillance and the security state as simply the musings of an extremist, radical, and disenfranchised fringe. Once again, the theme that we will ultimately get the accountability we deserve emerges with some force.

Conclusion

There are accountability gaps in all democracies, but Canada's accountability gap is particularly pronounced. Alone out of our Five Eyes partners, Canada still does not give any parliamentarians access to secret information. SIRC was state-of-the-art when it was created in 1984, but comparable Australian and British reviewers now are much closer to a whole-of-government mandate that is fit to review whole-of-government security. American Inspectors General have had more success than Canadian review bodies in conducting joint investigations.[105] The government abolished CSIS's Inspector General in 2012. The US Privacy and Civil Liberties Board and a similar one created in 2015 in the UK have a whole-of-government mandate. These developments suggest that review in Canada is becoming increasingly out of date and out of step with attempts in other democracies to plug post–9/11 accountability gaps. Bill C-51 and especially its *Security of Canada Information Sharing Act* will significantly expand Canada's already large accountability gap by its failure to match whole-of-government information sharing with effective whole-of-government review.

At the same time, Bill C-51 has resulted in increased public and political attention to review and oversight. Increased interest in parliamentary review will not, however, plug fundamental accountability gaps. Proposals for enhanced parliamentary review have been mild proposals for a statutory committee of parliamentarians who will be bound by Canada's strict official secrets legislation. The experience of other democracies suggests that legislators can have their hands tied when they are briefed into alarming secret programs. Parliamentarians may have difficulties navigating the legal and bureaucratic complexities of complex whole-of-government approaches to security, especially without dedicated staff. They will also face temptations to use security issues for partisan advantage. Even if some parliamentarians, especially in the unelected Senate, can rise above the fray and master the complex security environment, they will still remain part-time amateurs. To be sure, they can make contributions, but they are likely to be modest ones.

Enter the professionals. Both Bill C-44 and Bill C-51 will give specially designated Federal Court judges new roles in authorizing CSIS to conduct surveillance and engage in disruption and threat reduction in violation of Canadian and foreign laws, including the *Charter*. Many will be comforted by the prospect of a judge being on the case and the government's defence of both bills stresses this feature. Moreover, Justice Mosley's expert calling-out of CSIS for subcontracting surveillance to Five Eyes partners demonstrates the power of a judge scorned. At the same time, however, heroic efforts of judges only go so far. The judicial oversight offered in these bills will typically be in the form of a closed proceeding with only the government's lawyer present. Although judges will expect their orders to be obeyed, there are no provisions in the new warrant provisions for adversarial challenges or appeals. Once a judge has determined the extent that CSIS must break laws and contravene the *Charter*, that one decision will generally be the final word. Indeed, even criticism of the judgment may not be possible if the judgment must for operational reasons remain secret or heavily redacted. Review bodies will hopefully be able to see the classified reasons, but they may also understandably be reluctant to question judicial decisions.

Full-time professional executive watchdogs are critical to closing accountability gaps. Here, matters have gotten worse since the Arar Commission concluded in 2006 that Canada's silo-based, twentieth-century review structure was manifestly inadequate for the post–9/11 whole-of-government approach to security. SIRC has struggled in the intervening years with personnel issues. After the Inspector General for CSIS was abolished in 2012, SIRC had to take on the important work of determining the legality of CSIS's conduct. The CSE commissioner has been quick but often defensive in responding to the Canadian aspects of the Snowden leaks. The proposed *Security of Canada Information Sharing Act* in Bill C-51 will considerably widen the accountability gap by allowing all government entities to share broadly defined security information with seventeen federal agencies and departments. When Bill C-51 is enacted, Canada's significant accountability gap will become an accountability chasm.

Although the government warns that increased review will be "needless red tape," the time has come to replace SIRC, the CSE commissioner, and others with a "super SIRC" that has jurisdiction to review all of the government's national security activities, including information sharing, under the proposed *Security of Canada Information Sharing Act*. A super SIRC should be creatively appointed and staffed. It could include elements of the quasi-judicial found in the CSE commissioner and elements of the tri-partisan found in SIRC. But more creativity will be required to command the confidence and engagement of a more diverse and fragmented public. A super SIRC needs not only a whole-of-government mandate but adequate resources, expertise, and staff to review the agencies and to engage with civil society.

Even if all of this happened, closing accountability gaps would remain an uphill battle. All branches of government and new and creative hybrid institutions must contribute, but so too must civil society, corporations (especially telecommunications companies), and the investigative media. A continued failure to close our growing accountability gap will leave both our rights and our security in increased jeopardy.

Acknowledgements

I thank Mel Cappe, Craig Forcese, and Wesley Wark for helpful and challenging comments on a much earlier draft of this chapter. I wish also to thank Mel Cappe for his enthusiastic support for increasing and enriching public debate about national security matters in Canada and his dedicated public service.

Notes

1. Canada, Commission of Inquiry into the Actions of Canadian Officials in Relation to Maher Arar, *A New Review Mechanism for the RCMP's National Security Activities* (Ottawa: Public Works, 2006) at 456–58. The author was part of a research advisory committee for this report.

2. Four former prime ministers, as well as former members of the Security Intelligence Review Commission (SIRC) and Privacy Commissioners, signed a joint letter in February 2015 that noted that the government had not acted on the recommendations of the Arar Commission and stressing the need for "cross agency reviews." Jean Chrétien, Joe Clark, Paul Martin, & John Turner, "A Close Eye on Security Makes Canadians Safer," *Globe and Mail*, 19 February 2015.

3. Commission of Inquiry into the Investigation of the Bombing of Air India Flight 182, *Air India Flight 182: A Canadian Tragedy* (Ottawa: Public Works and Government Services Canada, 2010). The author was the director of research (legal studies) for the commission.

4. Bill C-51, *Anti-Terrorism Act*, 2015 1st reading, 30 January 2015, Part I, *Security of Canada Information Sharing Act*. The government's back-grounder stresses that the Privacy Commissioner will conduct whole-of-government review, even though the Privacy Commissioner indicated in a 2014 report that the office requires more legal powers with respect to security information sharing, including joint investigations and access to the Federal Court with respect to collection and disclosure of personal information. See Canada, Office of the Privacy Commissioner of Canada, *Checks and Controls: Reinforcing Privacy Protection and Oversight for the Canadian Intelligence Community in an Era of Cyber-Surveillance* (Ottawa: Public Works and Government Services Canada, 2014). Bill C-51 does not contain the reforms suggested by the Privacy Commissioner.

5. Bill C-51 *Ibid.*, Part 4. See also *Protecting Canadians from Terrorism Act* S.C. 2015 c.,9 (Bill C-44)

6. David Pugliese, "Government Knows Best, Says Conservative MP, No Need for More Oversight on Spy and Security Agencies," *Ottawa Citizen*, 1 February 2015; Aaron Wherry, "The Heart of Our Democracy in a Time of Terror," *Maclean's*, 5 February 2015, <http://www.macleans.ca/politics/the-heart-of-our-democracy-in-time-terror/>.

7. Hansard, 19 February 2015, per Hon. Peter Van Loan; Tonda MacCharles & Bruce Campion-Smith, "Stephen Harper Rejects Calls for More Oversight of New Spy Powers," *Toronto Star*, 19 February 2015.

8. *Protecting Canadians from Terrorism Act, supra* note 5.

9. In the matter of an application by X for a warrant pursuant to sections 12 and 21 of the *Canadian Security Intelligence Service Act* [2013] FC 1275, aff'd [2014] FCA 249 leave to SCC granted 5 February 2015.

10. For an argument that judges as unelected amateurs should defer to the state on security matters, see Adrian Vermeule & Eric Posner, *Terror in the Balance* (New York: Oxford, 2007).

11. US, The Review Group on Intelligence and Communications Technologies, *Liberty and Security in a Changing World* (Washington, DC, 2013).

12. See, for example, Office of the Communications Security Establishment Commissioner [CSEC Commissioner], *Annual Report 2005–2006* at 9–10 (Ottawa: Public Works and Government Services Canada, 2006); CSEC Commissioner, *Annual Report 2006–2007* at 2–3 (Ottawa: Public Works and Government Services Canada, 2007).

13. *Supra* note 11.

14. For my earlier conceptualization of social accountability, see Kent Roach, "Public Inquiries and Three Processes of Accountability," in *Accountability for Criminal Justice*, ed. Philip Stenning (Toronto: University of Toronto Press, 1995), 268–293.

15. David Cole, "Where Liberty Lies: Society and Individual Rights," (2011) 57 Wayne L. Rev. 1203.

16. For additional analysis of the distinction between efficacy and propriety based review, see Reg Whitaker & Stuart Farson, "Accountability in and for National Security," (2009) 15:9 IRPP Choices 1.

17. *Supra* note 1 at 499–503.

18. *Ibid.* at 456–58.

19. *Ibid.* at 458–63.

20. *Ibid.* at 500.

21. *Ibid.* at 467.

22. See generally Phillip Stenning, ed. *Accountability for Criminal Justice* (Toronto: University of Toronto Press, 1995).

23. For discussion of accountability gaps, including how public inquiries have had to be appointed with extraordinary jurisdiction to review the activities of all government officials in particular security areas, see Kent Roach, *The 9/11 Effect: Comparative Counter-Terrorism* (Cambridge: Cambridge University Press, 2011) at 455–59; Kent Roach, "Public Inquiries as an Attempt to Fill Accountability Gaps Left by Judicial and Legislative Review," in *Critical Debates on Counter-Terrorism Judicial Review*, eds. Davis & de Londras (Cambridge: Cambridge University Press, 2014) at 183ff.

24. *CSIS Act*, s. 34.

25. *National Defence Act*, s. 273.63.

26. *Supra* note 17 at 468.

27. Canada, Commission of Inquiry into the Investigation of the Bombing of Air India Flight 182, *Air India Flight 182: A Canadian Tragedy* (Ottawa: Public Works and Government Services Canada, 2010) vol. 3 at 1.

28. The government has provided a formal response to the report and issued a progress report but both documents are silent with respect to this critical recommendation about the enhanced role of the PM's national security advisor.

29. *Act to amend the RCMP Act* S.C. 2013, c. 18, ss. 45.4–45.43.

30. *Attorney General of Canada v. Commission of Inquiry into the Actions of Canadian Officials in Relation to Maher Arar*, 2007, FC 766.

31. List of SIRC reviews under section 54 of the *CSIS Act*, 10 November 2014, <http://www.sirc-csars.gc.ca/opbapb/lsrlse-eng.html>.

32. Classified reports, 20 August 2014, <http://www.ocsec-bccst.gc.ca/ann-rpt/cr-rc_e.php>.

33. Justice Décary made this statement while at the same time correctly noting that "where CSEC and CSIS cooperate and conduct joint activities, my office and SIRC do not have an equivalent authority to conduct joint reviews." Canada, CSEC, *Annual Report 2012–2013* (Ottawa: Minister of Public Works and Government Services, 2012) at 5.

34. Pugliese, *supra* note 6.

35. *Ibid.*

36. Chris Hall, "CSIS Watchdog Agency Starved of Staff, Resources," *CBC News*, 20 February 2015, <http://www.cbc.ca/news/politics/csis-watchdog-agency-starved-of-staff-resources-1.2965276>.

37. Canada, Office of the Privacy Commissioner of Canada, *supra* note 4.

38. Kent Roach, "The Problems with the New CSIS Human Source Privilege in Bill C-44," (2014) 61 C.L.Q. 451.

39. *An Act to Establish the National Security Committee of Parliamentarians*, 2nd Sess., 41st Parl., 2013, cls. 10–11 (first reading 7 November 2013) Bill C-551.

40. *Ibid.* cl. 14.

41. Section 14(4) (c) of the bill encourages the minister not to disclose information to the committee if it was obtained from foreign states without even asking, as courts increasingly require, whether the foreign state would be prepared to amend any caveat restricting further disclosure of shared intelligence.

42. Bill C-622, 2nd Sess., 41st Parl., defeated on second reading, 5 November 2014.

43. *Supra* note 16 at 35.

44. Amy Zegart, *Eyes on Spies* (Stanford: Hoover Institution Press, 2011).

45. Bruce Ackerman, *Before the Next Attack* (New Haven, CT: Yale University Press, 2005); Stephen Schulhofer, "Oversight of National Security Activities in the United States," in *Secrecy, National Security and the Vindication of Constitutional Law*, eds. David Cole et al. (Cheltenham: Elgar, 2013) at 42.

46. Phillipe Lagassé, "Accountability for National Defence," (2010) 4 IRPP Study at 8-12. Lagassé conflates accountability and control when he

asserts that a stronger parliamentary committee could undermine the responsibility of the minister and the Cabinet for defence.

47. Canada, Office of the Privacy Commissioner of Canada, *supra* note 4 at 12.

48. *Supra* note 1 at 491.

49. *Ibid.* at 439.

50. *Charkaoui v. Canada*, [2007] 1 S.C.R. 350; *Charkaoui v. Canada* [2008] 2 S.C.R. 326; *Harkat v. Canada* 2014 SCC 37.

51. *Abdelrazik v. Canada*, [2009], F.C. 580.

52. [2013] FC 1275 at para. 117.

53. *Ibid.* at para. 110.

54. *Ibid.* at para. 115.

55. *Protecting Canadians from Terrorism Act* S.C. 2015 c. 9 adding s. 21(3.1) to the *CSIS Act*; Bill C-51, adding s. 21.1(4) to the *CSIS Act*.

56. Bill C-51, adding ss. 12.1(3) and 21.1 to the *CSIS Act*.

57. Bill C-51, adding s. 12.2 to the *CSIS Act*.

58. Laura Payton, "C-51 Confusion Abounds as Tories Rush Bill C-51 to Committee," *CBC News*, 20 February 2015, <http://www.cbc.ca/news/politics/c-51-confusion-abounds-as-tories-rush-anti-terrorism-bill-to-committee-1.2963569>.

59. *Atwal v. Canada*, (1987), 36 C.C.C. (3d) 16 (Fed.C.A.).

60. Privacy and Civil Liberties Oversight Board, R*eport on the Telephone Records Program Conducted under Section 215 of the USA Patriot Act and on the Operations of the Foreign Intelligence Surveillance Court*, 23 January 2014, <https://www.pclob.gov/library/215-Report_on_the_Telephone_Records_Program.pdf>.

61. Craig Forcese & Kent Roach, "Bill C-51 Backgrounder # 2: The Canadian Security Intelligence Service's Power to 'Reduce' Security Threats Through Conduct that May Violate the Law and Charter," *Social Science Research Network*, 12 February 2015, <http://papers.ssrn.com/sol3/papers.cfm?abstract_id=2564272>. See also Kent Roach & Craig Forcese, "Legislating in Fearful and Politicized Times: The Limits of Bill C-51's Disruption Powers in Making Us Safer" in Edward Iacobucci and Stephen Toope, eds. *After the Paris Attacks: Responses in Canada, Europe and Around the Globe* (Toronto: University of Toronto Press, 2015).

62. Bill C-51, adding ss. 21.1 to the *CSIS Act*.

63. Human Rights Watch, *Preempting Justice: Counter-Terrorism Laws and Procedure in France* (New York: Human Rights Watch, 2008) at 14–18.

64. Application under s. 83.28 of the *Criminal Code*, [2004] 2 S.C.R. 248; Re *Vancouver Sun*, [2004] 2 S.C.R. 332.

65. Bill C-51, adding s. 12.1(2) to the *CSIS Act*.

66. Bill C-51, adding s. 12.2 to the *CSIS Act*.

67. MacCharles & Campion-Smith, *supra* note 7.

68. Greg Weston, "Other Spy Watchdogs Have Ties to the Oil Business," *CBC News*, 10 January 2014, <http://www.cbc.ca/news/politics/other-spy-watchdogs-have-ties-to-oil-business-1.2491093>.

69. SIRC, *Lifting the Shroud of Secrecy: Thirty Years of Security Intelligence Accountability, Annual Report 2013–2014* (Ottawa: Public Works and Government Services Canada, 2014), <http://www.sirc-csars.gc.ca/pdfs/ar_2013-2014-eng.pdf>.

70. "Statement by CSE Commissioner the Honourable Robert Décary," *Office of the Communications Security Establishment Commissioner*, 13 June 2013, <http://www.ocsec-bccst.gc.ca/media/pr/2013-06-14_e.php>.

71. *Ibid.*

72. *Supra* note 33 at 25.

73. *Ibid.*

74. Commissioner Décary announced, "It is well understood that Canadian federal law enforcement and security agencies may lawfully investigate Canadians. When these organizations request the assistance of CSEC, I verify that CSEC complies with any limitations imposed by law on the agency to which CSEC is providing assistance, for example, any conditions imposed by a judge in a warrant." *Supra* note 70. As discussed above, Justice Mosley's subsequent decision released in December 2013 found that the enlistment of Five Eyes partners to assist in the surveillance of Canadian citizens outside of Canada exceeded both the scope of his warrant and the limitations imposed in law on both CSIS and CSEC.

75. See, for example, CSEC Commissioner, *Annual Report 2005–2006* at 9–10; CSEC Commissioner, *Annual Report 2006–2007* at 2–3.

76. "Statement by CSE Commissioner the Honourable Jean-Pierre Plouffe re: January 30 CBC Story," *Office of the Communications Security Establishment Commissioner*, 31 January 2014, <http://ocsec-bccst.gc.ca/media/pr/2014-01-31_e.php>.

77. Greg Weston, "CSEC Used Airport Wi-Fi to Track Canadian Travellers: Edward Snowden Documents," *CBC News*, 31 January 2014, <http://www.cbc.ca/news/politics/csec-used-airport-wi-fi-to-track-canadian-travellers-edward-snowden-documents-1.2517881>, quoting security experts Ron Deibert and Wesley Wark that the activities were outside CSEC's legal mandate.

78. The commissioner's mandate under section 273.63 is to review the legality of CSEC's activities and inform the minister of defence and the attorney general of Canada of activities that are not in compliance with the law.

79. Office of the Communications Security Establishment Commissioner, "Current Issues: Questions and Answers," n.d., <http://www.ocsec-bccst.gc.ca/new-neuf/faq_e.php>.

80. *National Defence Act*, RSC, 1985, c N-5, s. 273.64(2)(a).

81. For details on this ongoing litigation, see British Columbia Civil Liberties Association, "Stop Illegal Spying: Case Details," <https://bccla.org/stop-illegal-spying/protect-our-privacy-case-details/>.

82. Canada, Public Safety Canada, "Backgrounder on the Security of Canada Information Sharing Act," 30 January 2015, <http://news.gc.ca/web/article-en.do?nid=926879>.

83. Canada, Office of the Privacy Commissioner of Canada, *supra* note 4.

84. Kent Roach, "Illusory Accountability but Real Accountability Gaps," in *Putting the State on Trial*, eds. M. Beare et al. (Vancouver: University of British Columbia Press, 2015).

85. For more detail, see Craig Forcese & Kent Roach with Leah Sherriff, Bill C-51 Backgrounder #5, "Oversight and Review: Turning Accountability Gaps into Canyons?" *Social Science Research Network*, 27 February 2015, <http://papers.ssrn.com/sol3/papers.cfm?abstract_id=2571245>.

86. This would greatly expand SIRC's mandate in part because of the breadth of the government's proposed security predicate for the *Security of Canada Information Sharing Act*. For criticism of this broad category of activities that undermine the security of Canada, see Roach & Forcese "Backgrounder #3: Sharing of Information and Lost Lessons from the Maher Arar Experience," 16 February 2015, <http://antiterrorlaw.ca>.

87. The need to include former parliamentarians on a super SIRC, with the potential for conflicts of interest, might be less if a parliamentary committee with access to secret information was also created. Indeed, there seems to be a trend away from appointing former parliamentarians to serve on SIRC with none of the members as of April 2015 having served in elective office.

88. *R. v. Spencer*, 2014, SCC 43.

89. Canada, Office of the Privacy Commissioner of Canada, *supra* note 4 at 11, calling for better definition of terms in the CSEC enabling legislation.

90. See, for example, CSEC Commissioner, *Annual Report 2005–2006* at 9-10; CSEC Commissioner, *Annual Report 2006–2007* at 2–3.

91. Privacy and Civil Liberties Oversight Board, *Report on the Surveillance Program Operated under s. 702 of the Foreign Intelligence Surveillance Act*, July 2014 at 146.

92. *Counter Terrorism and Security Act*, 2015, c. 6, ss. 42–43.

93. See Michael Geist, Chapter VIII.

94. Ronald Diebert, "Shutting the Backdoor: The Perils of National Security and Digital Surveillance Programs," Strategic Working Group Papers (October 2013): 8, <http://opencanada.org/wp-content/uploads/SL13CIC018-SSWGP-Deibert-v3.pdf>.

95. Campbell Clark, "New Poll Finds Terrorism Bill a Political Juggernaut," *The Globe and Mail*, 19 February 2015, <http://www.theglobeandmail.com/news/politics/new-poll-finds-harpers-anti-terror-

bill-is-a-political-juggernaut/article23067983/>. Since that poll, public support for Bill C-51 seems to have declined, but the government has proceeded with the legislation.

96. Jean Chrétien, Joe Clark, Paul Martin & John Turner, "A Close Eye on Security Makes Canadians Safer," *Globe and Mail*, 19 February 2015, <http://www.theglobeandmail.com/globe-debate/a-close-eye-on-security-makes-canadians-safer/article23069152/>.

97. R.S.C., 1985 c. O-5. CSE and CSIS but not other agencies that use secret intelligence are exempted from general whistle-blower protection in the *Public Servants Disclosure Protection Act*, S.C. 2005, c. 46 that might otherwise apply in cases where illegal conduct, such as intelligence including metadata, was used in a way to pose a risk to a person's life.

98. Wesley Wark, "Intelligence Requirements and Anti-Terrorism Legislation," in *The Security of Freedom: Essays on Canada's Anti-Terrorism Bill*, eds. Ronald Daniels et al. (Toronto: University of Toronto Press, 2001) at 291.

99. *Supra* note 11 at 198. The report, however, only devotes one paragraph to this proposal. In contrast, the report devotes twenty-five pages of detailed analysis and recommendations to the stopping of leaks. *Ibid.* at 233–58.

100. *O'Neill et al. v. The Attorney General of Canada*, (2006) 82 O.R.(3d) 241 (Sup Ct.).

101. See Reg Whitaker, Chapter VII.

102. Jesse Kline, "Knowledge, Power And Accountability: The Democratic Significance of WikiLeaks in the Digital Age," *National Post*, 30 September 2013, <http://news.nationalpost.com/2013/09/30/knowledge-power-and-accountability-the-democractic-significance-of-wikileaks-in-the-digital-age/>.

103. *Supra* note 11 at ch. 8.

104. Oren Gross, "Chaos and Rules," (2003) 112 *Yale Law Journal* 1011.

105. More on these comparative review mechanisms can be found in Forcese and Roach with Sherriff, *supra* note 85.

CHAPTER VII

The Failure of Official Accountability and the Rise of Guerrilla Accountability

Reg Whitaker

Introduction

When Edward Snowden fled his job as National Security Agency (NSA) contractor to exile in Russia, bringing with him millions of pages of secret documents that soon began appearing in media outlets around the world, the effect was that of a serially detonating bombshell.[1] There has been a great deal of debate about the meaning and significance of Snowden's revelations.[2] Much debate has turned on an apparent binary opposition between accountability and whistle-blowing.

Some would, of course, deny the very validity of the term "whistle-blower," calling Snowden simply a traitor deserving dire punishment, but this obfuscates the crucial distinction between spying and whistle-blowing. Espionage involves the transmission of state secrets to other states or hostile non-state actors to provide them with competitive advantage; whistle-blowers reveal state secrets to the public at large according to some (self-defined) concept of serving the public interest and/or following their own conscience. Whistle-blowing is inherently an illegal activity, yet its potential for serving the public interest has led to special whistle-blower protection laws in many jurisdictions.[3] Conventional spies may be fairly termed traitors for betraying their nation to another state or to violent non-state actors. The moral culpability of whistle-blowers must be unwrapped from the context of their illegal actions. Motive is crucial. Even if one rejects, in part or in whole, the self-justifying rationale the whistle-blower offers for his or her acts, the fact remains that a disinterested motive distinguishes the whistle-blower from the spy. While legal sanctions may be appropriately applied to the law-breaking whistle-blower, the consequences of his or her unauthorized disclosures will be very different from the consequences of espionage. They may even be positive.

Snowden the whistle-blower, it is widely conceded, has raised questions to which the existing accountability mechanisms have failed to provide satisfactory answers, or in many cases any answers at all. Although the United States continues to demand Snowden's return from Russia to face legal charges, the President has in effect responded to Snowden's whistle-blowing message with a wide-ranging package of reforms circumscribing NSA activities and enhancing external controls over the agency's operations. The US Appeals Court dealt a potentially even more damaging blow when, in May 2015, it ruled the NSA bulk collection program illegal.[4] *Pro forma* denials that these changes have been prompted solely by the Snowden leaks are believed by no one. In other words, Snowden the whistle-blower has paradoxically prompted both legal action against himself and a policy response that recognizes the *de facto* legitimacy of the rationale that lay behind his illegal actions.

This is a very troubling observation, especially for those with a stake in the existing national security institutions. Stakeholders in a sense include all the citizenry that wishes to be protected from terrorist acts, but it applies particularly to those officials who them-selves have access to secret information, who are thus implicated in a system the shortcomings and dangers of which have been exposed by Snowden's leaks — and recognized as being well-founded at the highest levels of the American government.

Improved Official Accountability

A way out of this moral dilemma has been posed as improved offi-cial accountability. Snowden's leaks may have revealed problems, but his methods cannot be condoned. Therefore the answer must be found in responsible legitimate accountability replacing irre-sponsible, self-elected, self-justifying leakers. That was the core of President Obama's message on NSA reform. In Canada, the Harper government, as well as its national security agencies and their review bodies, have been blithely dismissive of concerns about the Canadian NSA equivalent, the Communications Security Establishment (CSE).[5] Unofficial calls for reform from lawyers and academics to privacy commissioners — although differing in detail — have all echoed the same broad policy prescription: strengthened official accountability mechanisms must be put in place that will reduce or obviate the need for more Snowden-like leaks.

As someone who has long advocated improved accountability in national security matters, I have no inclination to challenge the overall thrust of these calls for reform. Strengthened accountability mechanisms and stronger leadership of the review and oversight bodies should, if properly conceived and managed, contribute both to strengthening civil liberties, privacy rights and the rule of law, as well as contributing to effective national security and public safety. I do, however, think that the problems revealed by the Snowden revelations point to difficulties more complex and unsettling than are encompassed in the formula "Better accountability is the answer to whistle-blowers."

I would argue that the very need for, and existence of, whistle-blowers is rooted in the inherent limitations and inadequacies of existing mechanisms of accountability. Snowden, and leakers such as Bradley (now Chelsea) Manning, arise because of, not in spite of, existing accountability. Indeed, what Snowden has done can be understood as a form of "guerrilla accountability" that arises in the absence of effective official or orthodox forms of accountability.[6] I will further argue that there is good reason to believe that these inherent limitations in official accountability almost guarantee future whistle-blowers, even with reformed institutions. Accountability and whistle-blowing may thus be ensnared in a struggle with one another that may have no resolution in the foreseeable future.

Snowden, it must be said, is hardly a one-off (even when his actions are grouped with the earlier Manning WikiLeaks disclosures). It is historically striking how much critical information about the abuse of national security secrecy has been revealed by deliberate unauthorized disclosure, and how very little by official accountability. There is the celebrated precedent of Daniel Ellsberg's Pentagon Papers leaks in 1971, which blew the lid off the US government's secret wars in Southeast Asia, and which revealed publicly that the government had systematically lied about its activities, not only to the public but also to Congress, rendering ineffective legislative oversight of American covert activities abroad.

The now notorious COINTELPRO program, comprising often illegal projects conducted by J. Edgar Hoover's FBI aimed at infiltrating, discrediting, and disrupting domestic political activities, was revealed only when a group styling itself the "Citizens' Commission to Investigate the FBI" broke into an FBI field office in Pennsylvania, stealing documents that exposed the program when passed to media outlets. Facing a storm of public opprobrium, Hoover declared within a year that the once super-secret program — which had entirely escaped Congressional notice — was to be shut down.

Why are official accountability channels relatively ineffective in catching the really big problems in national security? There are multiple answers to this question, but a major one is regulatory capture, a phenomenon well known and amply described in public policy literature.[7] This explains how the gamekeeper turns poacher, the process by which a regulatory agency, formed to act in the public's interest, ends by serving the interests of the industry it is supposed to be regulating, rather than the public.

Among factors contributing to the prevalence of regulatory capture, one stands out for our purposes: *control over information*. Even in areas remote from national security concerns, the capacity of a regulated industry to control or influence the flow of information, which the regulatory body requires to perform its functions, is an important part of the regulated industry's ability to capture or tame its regulator. In national security, the greatly enhanced, indeed sometimes exclusive control by the agencies of national security information imposes a double bind on review or oversight bodies. Secrecy is a crucial bureaucratic resource that can yield power and relative autonomy to the bureaucratic actors with privileged access to secret information, both within the executive and in relation to the legislature and the public. National security review bodies require unrestricted access to the agencies' secrets in order to perform their oversight functions. But this is rarely granted in full, for a variety of more or less plausible reasons, such as the understandable reluctance of agencies to permit real-time intrusive surveillance of their ongoing operations. Sympathetic to this concern, review bodies generally refrain from attempting to scrutinize ongoing operations, concentrating instead on *post hoc review*.[8] This restraint however leaves open-ended the question of how the term "operational" is defined, and leaves the definition in the hands of the agencies.

Varying from jurisdiction to jurisdiction, in practice there are a number of constraints on access to information crucial to carrying out the review function (I will refer to more specifics below). While not necessarily fatal — except in the cases of particularly dysfunctional or toothless bodies such as the RCMP Public Complaints Commission — these constraints do impede the capacity of review bodies to escape some degree of regulatory capture.

It is the second part of the double bind on secrecy that is especially telling for the weakness of official review/oversight. Let us assume for a moment that a review body does have almost total command over pertinent information, including more or less unrestricted access to as wide a range of secret intelligence as allows it to make definitive judgment on the performance and behaviour of the agency in question. At this point a paradox emerges: the greater the access to secrets the review body has gained, the less it will be able to provide a substantive degree of transparency to Parliament and public.

Access to secrets places the review body inside the loop of national security confidentiality. But this is an enchanted circle from which the "external" review body can never fully return. In the ancient Greek myth Persephone, daughter of Demeter, goddess of the sunlit fields, was obliged to remain for part of every year in the dark Underworld with her abductor Hades because she had eaten seven seeds of a pomegranate from the land of the dead. So too review bodies, having tasted the secrets, must remain forever partially in the shadows. When they return to tell their stories, the public tends to see their narratives as thin, opaque, and dull. Which in truth they often are, once shorn of the secret information that would provide substance and credibility.

When the US Director of National Intelligence (DNI) James Clapper told a Congressional committee in March 2013 that the NSA does not collect any type of data at all on Americans, there were members of the House and Senate intelligence committees who knew this to be untrue but were unable (or unwilling) to break their commitment to secrecy. One senator's aides have claimed that they privately alerted Clapper's office to his error and unsuccessfully requested a correction of the public record.[9] It took the leaks of the whistle-blower Snowden, in safe refuge in Russia, to reveal publicly that the DNI had in fact lied to Congress and the American people. Faced with this embarrassment, Clapper initially said that he had provided the "least untruthful" answer he could in a public setting. Finally, with calls for perjury charges on the horizon, Clapper blurted out:

> I probably shouldn't say this, but I will. Had we been transparent about this from the outset right after 9/11 — which is the genesis of the 215 program [bulk data collection] — and said both to the American people and to their elected representatives, we need to cover this gap, we need to make sure this never happens to us again, so here is what we are going to set up, here is how it's going to work, and why we have to do it, and here are the safeguards... We wouldn't have had the problem we had.[10]

That transparency would have whisked away problems with an inherently problematic program is doubtful, but if so, Clapper's second (or third) thoughts actually constitute an indictment of the existing system: the agencies initiate in secret a legally dubious program; official accountability fails to bring the agencies to account and even contributes to a cover-up; an illegal leaker breaks the cover, revealing official deception; in the face of which the official ultimately responsible admits that the program should never have been carried out in secret in the first place. Of course, without the illegal leak, none of this would have been revealed and the apology would never have happened. And no reform of this deeply flawed system would ever have been contemplated.

The Three Basic Rules of Secrecy
The Clapper incident represents in microcosm the accountability/whistle-blowing conundrum. Official accountability failed to work because the oversight body — in this case Congress — was trapped by the same rules against disclosure of secrets that govern the agencies. It is worth paying close attention to these rules and how they are enforced to gain some appreciation of the difficulties that face even honest attempts at accountability reform.

If we briefly review the specific arguments that have been made in favour of secrecy in security and intelligence, we come upon an obvious and, in a way, unassailable, objection to any critical attack on privileged access to secrecy. The arguments for secrecy are reasonable and logical. Broadly speaking, they break down into three broad categories of information that cannot be publicly disclosed. These may be referred to as the three basic rules of secrecy:

1. No disclosure of the identification of secret sources of intelligence.
2. No disclosure of methods and techniques of covert operations.
3. No disclosure of information received in confidence from foreign governments or agencies.

Clearly these are all perfectly reasonable grounds for non-disclosure. No agency could operate covertly if its secret sources were publicly identified. No covert agency could operate effectively, or at all, if its methods were transparent to the very targets of its operations. And failure to secure information received in confidence from abroad would quickly lead to the damaging loss of access to such information. These three rules are, I believe, the core rationale for the exercise of secrecy in security and intelligence, and can stand alone without the cloak of particular legal sanction, and outside the peculiarities of different political systems, whether parliamentary or presidential. I do not intend to challenge these grounds, in themselves, although their interpretation in specific cases is quite another matter.

If we grant that these are all reasonable qualifications for secrecy, and that a serious breach in any one of these would fail an appropriate injury test, are we further contending that legitimate requirements for secrecy undermine or make impossible democratic responsibility in national security matters? Not quite. First, the claims for secrecy advanced by those within the national security loop cannot be taken at face value, and always require critical scrutiny from outside the loop. We start with a brief look at possible limitations on the three rules of secrecy.

On Rule 1: The core rationale for the rule is valid, but it is too often interpreted in a manner so expansive as to lose much of its legitimate force. Example: information is withheld that is purely contextual, rather than directly contributing to the identification of a secret source. The justification for this is that any smart journalist or, worse, the targeted organization or network, could deduce from contextual information the identity of a source. While this could be the case, sometimes so much non-specific contextual information is withheld that effective *public* accountability regarding the efficacy and/or propriety of intelligence sources is impossible. In such cases, too much trust must be accorded review/oversight agencies reporting in secret to the very governments they are reviewing. "Trust us" becomes a motto that has to be extended from the watchers to those who watch the watchers, something not always possible in all cases for a rightly sceptical media, political opposition, and public.

On Rule 2: Anyone who has been involved in declassification requests whether for scholarship, journalism, or in court proceedings or quasi-judicial hearings, will be aware of the so-called mosaic argument for non-disclosure. To critics on the outside of classification decisions, this is often seen as a ruse whereby virtually any and all information about the secret agencies is denied. The argument goes like this: small bits of information, however innocuous in themselves, could be put together by hostile forces to form a mosaic picture of methods and techniques of operation, and of targets. While this had some validity during the Cold War, when Soviet intelligence, for instance, could be assumed to seize with loving attention every tidbit that might deepen their knowledge of their professional adversary, it seems less compelling in the era of the war on terror, when networks or even nodes of non-state actors spring up, form, and reform more or less spontaneously with or without a great deal of continuity, and certainly without close central direction.

In any event, the mosaic effect is stretched beyond all reasonable bounds again and again. A recent example is afforded by Mr. Justice O'Connor's inquiry into the Maher Arar affair.[11] When early in its investigation, the Commission tried to make public a suitably sanitized summary of *in camera* Canadian Security Intelligence Service (CSIS) testimony, the government demanded major cuts and signalled its intention to contest the matter before the Federal Court, if necessary. Among the bits the government insisted should be excised was a reference to the startling fact that CSIS keeps files on suspected terrorists: surely *a reductio ad absurdum* of the mosaic effect![12] O'Connor chose at this stage of his inquiry not to contest the censorship, but when his final report was published, a number of excisions insisted upon by the government were later contested in the Federal Court and many, although not all, were ordered disclosed.[13] Threat of recourse to the courts forced additional disclosure of material published by another post-9/11 inquiry, Mr. Justice Iacobucci's inquiry into Messrs. Almalki, Elmaati, and Nureddin.[14]

It should be made clear that the additional information disclosed by court order in these two Canadian cases did not radically transform public understanding of the facts — in some instances it merely illustrated how inane some of the non-disclosure decisions were in the first place (that leading US intelligence agencies are called the "CIA" and the "FBI" was apparently judged a state secret!). More telling is that the commissions had already exercised prior self-censorship of the public report in anticipation of redactions to be applied. Even more to the point, public inquiries are one-off events. Official review bodies, always concerned about their ongoing working relationship with the agencies they review and deeply concerned to maintain their own legitimacy as players in the national security world, rarely contest the application of the government's expansive interpretation of non-disclosure in public reports of information deemed to fall under national security confidentiality. Judges are not brought into this process, unless the entire system has fallen into serious crisis (this has not yet happened anywhere to my knowledge). Thus interpretations of non-disclosure are normally subject to no third-party review beyond the agencies and the review bodies acting in concert. Until, that is, someone blows a whistle.

Whatever concerns are raised by close attention to the actual application of the first two rules, the Snowden revelations unequivocally point to the misuse and abuse of Rule 3 as crucial in understanding the failure of official accountability and the necessity of guerrilla accountability.

On Rule 3: The longer I have watched the operation of official secrecy in the name of national security, the more I have become convinced that the foreign confidence argument might better be called the foreign confidence trick. Of course, intelligence received in confidence from foreign sources cannot be splashed about without consequences. Yet the question that should be addressed, but almost never can be, is this: what criteria are being applied when caveats and restrictions are stamped on intelligence exchanged between allies? How do we know that this process is not part of a "you scratch my back, I'll scratch yours" operation of mutual convenience whereby allied governments and sister agencies simply cover for each other and prevent disclosure in each country by mutual consent — call it "information laundering." Conspiratorial suspicion should be resisted, but it is hard when the very bodies that are supposed to review and hold the agencies accountable may themselves be prevented from seeing information that is so laundered by international agreement.

Let me provide an example of this latter problem drawn from the experience of the strongest of Canadian review bodies, the Security Intelligence Review Committee (SIRC). In 1988, while still under the aggressive leadership of its first Chair, Ron Atkey, who never shrank from public tangles with CSIS, SIRC entered into a "third-party access protocol" with CSIS whereby the latter agency undertook, to the best of its ability, to gain the consent of foreign entities to disclose to SIRC documents originating from those entities that SIRC believed necessary for its investigations of CSIS activity.[15] There were, however, no guarantees provided, despite SIRC's clear mandate to "have access to any information under the control of the Service."[16] It is not known publicly how much, if any, foreign-origin documentation has actually been withheld from SIRC over the years, because such information itself cannot, of course, be disclosed under national security confidentiality. In the mid-1990s SIRC did publicly complain that a document it had sought was instead returned by CSIS to its foreign donor.[17]

A crucial fact about the Snowden revelations is that they disclose surveillance activities primarily by the NSA, but also by the NSA's main foreign counterparts in the so-called Five Eyes signals intelligence alliance — the "Anglosphere" of intelligence exchange and cooperation —, the United Kingdom (senior partner) and three junior partners: Canada, Australia, and New Zealand.[18] Intelligence collected is shared community-wide; targets of Five Eyes surveillance are global in scope. While the lead agencies operating within the alliance (NSA, Britain's Government Communications Headquarters [GCHQ], CSE) are national in origin and under national legal jurisdiction in the first instance, their operations as allies are enthusiastically *sans frontières*. Their respective review/oversight bodies, on the other hand, are anchored — one might cynically suggest, imprisoned — within their national jurisdictions. None of the review bodies have the capacity to track a trail of accountability past their own national agencies. Even in the name of public interest accountability they have no right and no means to compel the production of information of foreign origin.

A Call for Guerrilla Accountability

This has serious implications for their capacity to fulfill even their statutory requirements to review domestic operations. It has been widely conjectured that the Five Eyes partners may have organized end runs around their own publicly professed attestations that they never spy on their citizens, only on foreigners. This reportedly involves doing each other's intelligence laundry: GCHQ might do some spying on Canadians in exchange for CSE undertaking some surveillance in Britain, in which case, no domestic laws are broken, and no one is the wiser. All the allies have always denied this charge, but following the Snowden revelations, public trust in Clapper-like official assurances of legality and propriety has been eroded. The point is that official accountability mechanisms will not, and indeed, cannot provide any reassurance that information laundering is not taking place since none of the existing mechanisms can follow the trail across national boundaries. There is a clear call here for guerrilla accountability to do what official accountability cannot.

Another example: CSIS was granted permission by the Federal Court in 2009 to spy on Canadians abroad, but the judge who gave that permission, Richard Mosley, later discovered that CSIS had over-stepped legality by asking CSE to task their foreign partners with this assignment. CSIS and its lawyers had in effect lied to the court "about their intention to seek the assistance of the foreign partners," raising questions of exposing Canadians to human rights abuses.[19] "This would," he went on, "involve the breach of international law by the requested second parties."[20] A CSE official "candidly" admitted that his evidence in support of the original warrant application had been "crafted" with legal counsel to exclude any reference to plans to use second parties. Worse yet, Mosley indicated that the Deputy Attorney General of Canada had argued "that the Court should be kept in the dark about matters it may have reason to be concerned about if it was made aware of them."[21] Ironically, Mosley, an unusually vigilant and sceptical judge, was alerted to the problem by close reading of information in reports from SIRC and the CSE Commissioner. Yet these same review bodies had not flagged any suspicions. It was fortuitous that Mosley alone, from his uniquely strategic position in this case, could compel testimony that revealed deception of the court. On their own, the review bodies had neither the will nor the means to raise a finger of protest. A justice of the

Federal Court was, in a curious sense, providing the necessary guerrilla accountability to blow the whistle.

The government's response was to appeal Mosley's decision. This failed at the Federal Court of Appeal, but undeterred, the government has taken its appeal to the Supreme Court.[22] Whatever the outcome at the highest court, in late 2014 the government passed Bill C-44, amending the *Canadian Security Intelligence Service Act*, through the House of Commons. C-44 specifically authorizes CSIS under warrant to outsource its intelligence collection abroad.[23] This will effectively place its external intelligence collection out of the reach of any Canadian oversight, precluding for instance any critical notice of the use of intelligence derived from torture or other methods abusive of human rights against Canadian citizens.

O'Connor, in the second part of his Arar Report, made extensive recommendations for strengthening accountability in the light of what had happened to the unfortunate Mr. Arar at the hands of the American extraordinary rendition program and outsourced Syrian torturers. Central to his reform plan was the observation that in the face of a globalized terrorist threat post–9/11, counterterrorism operations were being integrated, across institutional stovepipes like CSIS and the RCMP, across federal-provincial jurisdictional boundaries and, most importantly, across national boundaries between allies and cooperating states.[24] Accountability should also be better integrated to match the growing integration of counterterrorism efforts; otherwise accountability would fall far behind the greatly increased legal and operational power of the agencies. A number of government agencies with national security responsibilities have inadequate oversight, and in some cases, such as the Canada Border Services Agency, no external accountability whatsoever. O'Connor recommended bringing them all together under integrated mechanisms of external scrutiny. Almost eight years later, the government response has been zero. Actually, less than zero. They have abolished one of the two main oversight bodies for CSIS, the Inspector General.[25] SIRC is in the midst of a leadership crisis, with the former Harper-appointed chair, Arthur Porter, facing extradition from Panama on multi-million dollar fraud charges, while his successor was forced to step down for possible conflict of interest.[26] While still the potentially most effective review body in Ottawa, SIRC has seen its resources flatlined over the past decade, and its staff resources diminished while CSIS has been expanding steadily in size and resources.[27] Nor have there been any official moves to create a parliamentary national security and intelligence committee.

In any event, not even O'Connor's recommendations for more integrated accountability mechanisms would touch on the international dimension. Indeed, even though Arar was a victim of counter-terrorism across borders, the inquiry into his case was strictly limited to the complicity of Canadian officials with the behaviour of a foreign government that was itself beyond the jurisdiction of a Canadian inquiry. American officials, the real authors of Arar's kidnapping and detention abroad, could be neither the object of the inquiry nor compelled to appear as witnesses. Even if greater integration of accountability were to be achieved in Canada, there is no legal or political basis at present for the extension of that integration across national boundaries. In this era of borderless terrorist networks and borderless counterterrorism operations, this is tantamount to say-ing that much, if not most, of what goes on in the world of security and intelligence is effectively beyond the reach of nationally based official accountability to bring transparency — leaving an important opening for guerrilla forms.

It is precisely this international dimension that has been dra-matically opened up by the Snowden revelations. As indicated earlier, Snowden's disclosures have shed light not only on the impact of the operations of the NSA on American citizens, but on the impact of NSA surveillance on governments and people across the world, and on the global reach of the Five Eyes alliance. Snowden's disclosures have had particular impact on Canada, revealing not only that Canada spies on other countries, like Brazil (perhaps out of alliance obligations, perhaps for its own economic espionage purposes); but more pointedly, revealing hard evidence of CSE intelligence collection on Canadian citizens, which it has always denied.[28] CSE has admitted that it does collect metadata on Canadian communications, although the Prime Minister has denied it.[29] The former CSE chief tried to square the circle by arguing before a parliamentary committee that metadata did not constitute "communication" under the law.[30] Claims that metadata do not constitute "real" data, "just the address on the envelope, not the letter inside," are deeply misleading. The Privacy Commissioner has suggested that "metadata can sometimes be more revealing than content itself."[31] The revelation that metadata is being collected on Canadians under unspecified parameters has led the British Columbia Civil Liberties Association to launch a lawsuit against CSE claiming that its "secret and unchecked surveillance of Canadians is unconstitutional,"[32] a lawsuit that at the very least is designed to open CSE's collection practices to greater transparency, and has won widespread approval.[33] Even the former CSE chief suggested that the agency should be put under the scrutiny of a parliamentary committee "to make Canadians more knowledgeable about what the intelligence agencies are trying to do on their behalf."[34]

Of course, the very knowledge that CSE *might* be violating the rights of Canadians would never have come to light without the guerrilla accountability of Edward Snowden.

That a serious official accountability deficit exists in Canada was spotlighted in early 2015 when the government introduced sweeping revisions to its anti-terrorism powers in Bill C-51, *The Anti-Terrorism Act, 2015*.[35] Among other things, this legislation hugely widens the definition of what might be encompassed under the category of "terrorist" activity; greatly expands the information-sharing capacity of the federal government; expands the boundaries of the no-fly list; extends the length of preventive detention while lowering the threshold conditions; creates new criminal offences for promoting or advocating terrorism (including "terrorism in general"); and enables CSIS to apply secretly for judicial "disruption" warrants that would permit CSIS agents to break Canadian law and violate *Charter* rights with impunity. This dramatic proposed expansion of intrusive state powers into civil society would be accompanied by not one improvement on the already failing and grossly inadequate accountability system. In its defence, government spokespersons stretched credulity by claiming that SIRC already provides "robust" accountability. It also made the odd claim that greater "judicial oversight" arises out of C-51, even though the disruption warrants actually constitute secret judicial enabling of law-breaking, making judges agents of the executive rather than overseers of the legal propriety of government actions.

C-51 has roused a storm of criticism,[36] much of it focussing on the lack of oversight over the newly empowered security agencies. The NDP and Green parties opposed and vowed to repeal C-51, and while the Liberals voted in favour of what they termed a flawed bill, this was with the caveat that if elected they would add effective oversight. Most strikingly, an open letter, signed by four former prime ministers, five retired Supreme Court justices, three former Ministers of Justice, four former Solicitors General, three former members of

SIRC, and former privacy and RCMP complaints commissioners, called for "independent oversight and effective review mechanisms [to] help ensure that resources devoted to national security activities are being utilized effectively and efficiently," as well as to prevent abuses of human rights.[37]

Given the government's majority in both houses of Parliament, and its consistent refusal to consider enhanced accountability, C-51 is likely to become law, more or less in its initial form. However much it might be improved by strengthened parliamentary and other forms of oversight and review, the limitations of formal accountability must be kept in mind. C-51 actually poses new limits on any external review. For instance, disruption warrants would be issued in such secrecy that they could very likely never come to the attention even of the intended targets and would equip CSIS in advance with judicially mandated "get out of jail free" cards that obviate any external scrutiny: it is unclear what oversight could oversee in such cases. Finally there is the all-too familiar problem already experienced in Canada and elsewhere, as described earlier, that oversight in secrecy is, in so many ways, oversight denied.

Nor should we look only to potential impropriety in the actions of the empowered national security agencies. Serious questions have been raised about the potential for renewed turf wars between the RCMP and CSIS, and the potential for CSIS actions impeding the capacity of the RCMP as a law enforcement agency to bring successful criminal cases.[38] The ballooning definitions of "terrorism" risk expanding the scope of surveillance and, now, disruption to groups such as First Nations and environmentalists protesting pipeline projects. This could potentially lead to the loss of social licence for CSIS and the RCMP, which would be counterproductive for fighting terrorism. Official accountability will be severely stretched to deal with these challenges, and particularly severely stretched to deal *publicly* with these challenges. Hence, the continued need for guerrilla accountability.

If Snowden guerrilla accountability alone exposed possible CSE excesses, how much greater will the need be for guerrilla accountability in a Canadian national security world governed by C-51. The Privacy Commissioner, Daniel Therrien, has weighed into the debate over C-51 with a strong warning about the almost unrestricted information sharing envisaged in the proposed legislation, which he terms "excessive," along with privacy safeguards that he finds "seriously deficient." "History," he points out, "has shown us that serious rights abuses can occur in the name of national security." He goes on to explain that "revelations by US whistle-blower Edward Snowden have shown how pervasive government surveillance programs can become."[39]

It is thus with some irony that Edward Snowden himself, via video link from his exile in Moscow, should warn Canadians that their country has one of the "weakest oversight" frameworks for intelligence gathering in the Western world. He called C-51 "an emulation of the *USA PATRIOT Act*" (not a complement) and went on to point out the critical importance of real accountability in protecting liberal freedoms when under pressure from the national security state.[40]

There has never been a Canadian Snowden. There have been rare examples of disgruntled ex-employees or ex-agents seeking journalistic outreach to make their concerns known,[41] but never whistle-blowers in place. Whether this will remain true in the future is a matter of conjecture.

Conclusion

Observers seeking to strike a reasonable balance between the need for effective security on the one hand and concern for the rule of law, privacy rights and the protection of liberal democracy on the other, will be uncomfortable with the idea of promoting illegal leakers as an answer to ineffective official accountability. While Snowden has provided moderate and reasonable arguments to support his actions, and his journalistic partners — *The Guardian*, *The Washington Post* and Glenn Greenwald — have been responsible in what they have released, there are of course no grounds for assuming that the next Snowden will have appropriate motives for breaking the law, and breaking the trust placed in him to access secret information. Leakers aspiring to the title of whistle-blower may be moved by private resentments; they may be on ego trips; they may be under extreme ideological direction; they may be just plain deranged. Yet unless truly radical revisions in how official accountability is allowed to operate are implemented — most importantly including the expansion of its scope to the international dimension —it is certain that if the powerful spy agencies are to be held to account and to operate under the rule of law, guerrilla accountability will remain a necessary part of the process.

Notes

1. For background on the Snowden affair, see Luke Harding, *The Snowden Files: The Inside Story of the World's Most Wanted Man* (London: Guardian Books, 2014).

2. The case for Snowden is made by his journalistic collaborator, Glenn Greenwald, *No Place to Hide: Edward Snowden, the NSA, and the U.S. Surveillance State* (Toronto: McClelland & Stewart, 2014). Alarmist claims by officials about profound damage to national security — even lives lost — are assessed by Shane Harris, "The Snowden Aftermath (Revised): Intelligence Leaks May Have Caused Damage but It's Not Irreparable" *Foreign Policy* (11 July 2014).

3. Rahul Sagar, *Secrets and Leaks: The Dilemma of State Secrecy* (Princeton, NJ: Princeton University Press, 2013) points to an intermediate category of leaker who discloses classified information under the cloak of anonymity. A whistle-blower is a leaker whose identity is made known to his or her employer. When Snowden chose to make his identity public he moved from leaker to whistle-blower.

4. "President Obama's Speech on NSA Surveillance Reforms — Full Text," *Guardian*, 17 January 2014, <http://www.theguardian.com/world/2014/jan/17/obama-speech-nsa-surveillance-reforms-full-text>. United States Court Of Appeals for the Second Circuit, August Term, 2014, Docket No. 14-42-cv, American Civil Liberties Union et al v. James R. Clapper & Michael S. Rogers.

5. See denials by CSE Chief John Foster in testimony to the Standing Senate Committee on National Security And Defence (3 February 2014), "Stephen Harper Says Canadians' Metadata Not Collected," Toronto Star, 26 February 2014, <http://www.thestar.com/news/canada/2014/09/26/stephen_harper_says_canadians_metadata_not_collected.html>. See also Stewart Bell, "Stephen Harper's Top Security Advisor Denies Reports of Illegal Spying on Canadians Using Airport Wi-Fi," *National Post*, 3 February 2014, <http://news.nationalpost.com/news/canada/harpers-top-security-advisor-denies-illegal-eavesdropping-of-canadian-travelers-using-airport-wi-fi>.

6. See *Brazil*, DVD (1985; Universal City, CA: Universal Studios, 1998), Terry Gilliam's British dystopian film, a reworking of Orwell's *1984*, where Robert De Niro plays a self-described "guerrilla repairman" who quits the incompetent if not malevolent official repair agency and now intercepts distress calls to his former agency and makes repairs properly before government agents arrive to wreak havoc. This captures something of the self-image of Snowden-style guerrilla accountability.

7. Michael E Levine & Jennifer L Forrence, "Regulatory Capture, Public Interest, and the Public Agenda: Toward a Synthesis" (1990) 6:1 *Journal of Law, Economics & Organization* 167.

8. "Oversight" is often used as denoting scrutiny of operations in real time, while "review" is defined as only after the fact. I have used both terms here interchangeably as review is an element of oversight.

9. Aaron Blake, "Sen. Wyden: Clapper Didn't Give 'Straight Answer' on NSA Programs," *Washington Post*, 11 June 2013, <http://www.washingtonpost.com/blogs/post-politics/wp/2013/06/11/sen-wyden-clapper-didnt-give-straight-answer-on-nsa-programs/>; David Cole, "The Three Leakers and What to Do About Them," *New York Review of Books*, 6 February 2014, <http://www.nybooks.com/articles/archives/2014/feb/06/three-leakers-and-what-do-about-them/>.

10. Spencer Ackerman, "US Intelligence Chief: NSA Should Have Been More Open About Data Collection," *The Guardian*, 18 February 2014, <http://www.theguardian.com/world/2014/feb/18/us-intelligence-chief-nsa-open-bulk-phone-collection>.

11. Commission of Inquiry into the Actions of Canadian Officials in Relation to Maher Arar, *Report of the Events Relating to Maher Arar* (Ottawa: Public Works and Government Services Canada, 2006), <http://www.sirc-csars.gc.ca/pdfs/cm_arar_bgv1-eng.pdf>.

12. I am drawing here on my experience as an adviser to O'Connor at the Arar inquiry. See Reg Whitaker, "Arar: the Affair, the Inquiry, the Aftermath," Institute for Research on Public Policy, *Policy Matters* (May 2008) 9:1.

13. Federal Court of Canada DES-4-06, Attorney General of Canada and the Commission of Inquiry (24 July 2007).

14. The Honourable Frank Iacobucci, *Internal Inquiry into the Actions of Canadian Officials in Relation to Abdullah Almalki, Ahmad Abou-Elmati and Muayyed Nureddin* (Ottawa: Public Works and Government Services, 2008) and "Supplement to the Public Report" (2010).

15. Memorandum from Ron Atkey, Chair of Security Intelligence Review Committee to J Reid Morden, Canadian Security Intelligence Service Director (25 May 1988) with Annex of same date, disclosed under Access to Information Request to SIRC, 23 January 1995.

16. *Canadian Security Intelligence Service Act*, R.S.C. 1985, c. C-23, s. 39(2). S. 39(3) indicates that apart from Cabinet confidences, "No information described in subsection (2)... may be withheld from the Committee on any grounds."

17. Canada, Security Intelligence Review Committee, *Annual Report 1995-1996* (Ottawa: Public Works and Government Services Canada, 1996) at 5–6.

18. A quick introduction to the Five Eyes is Paul Farrell, "History of 5-Eyes — Explainer," *The Guardian*, 2 December 2013, <http://www.theguardian.com/world/2013/dec/02/history-of-5-eyes-explainer>.

19. X *(Re)* 2013 FC 1275, 69 DLR (4th) 157 at para. 90.

20. *Ibid.* at para. 105.

21. *Ibid.* at para. 89.

22. Jim Bronskill, "Overseas CSIS Terror Tracking Case to be Heard by Supreme Court," *The Canadian Press*, 5 February 2015, <http://www.cbc.ca/news/politics/overseas-csis-terror-tracking-case-to-be-heard-by-supreme-court-1.2946162>.

23. Bill C-44, *An Act to amend the Canadian Security Intelligence Service Act and other Acts*, 2d Sess, 41st Parl, 2014, s. 8(1).

24. Canada, *A New Review Mechanism for the RCMP's National Security Activities* (Ottawa: Public Works and Government Services Canada, 2006).

25. Jim Bronskill, "Axing CSIS Watchdog 'Huge Loss,' Says Former Inspector General," *The Canadian Press*, 9 August 2012, <http://www.cbc.ca/news/politics/axing-csis-watchdog-huge-loss-says-former-inspector-general-1.1143212>.

26. "Arthur Porter, ex-McGill Hospital Director, to be Extradited from Panama," CBC News, 17 January 2015, <http://www.cbc.ca/news/canada/montreal/arthur-porter-ex-mcgill-hospital-director-to-be-extradited-from-panama-1.2916610>. His successor, former cabinet minister Chuck Strahl, felt compelled to step down in the face of criticism of his connections with the Enbridge pipeline corporation at a time when anti-pipeline protestors were complaining of CSIS surveillance of their activities. Chris Plecash & Mark Burgess, "Tougher Conflict of Interest Act Needed Following SIRC Controversy Say Experts," *Hill Times*, 2 March 2014, <http://www.hilltimes.com/news/news/2014/02/03/tougher-conflict-of-interest-act-needed-following-sirc-controversy-say-experts/37318>.

27. Chris Hall, "CSIS Watchdog Agency Starved of Staff, Resources," *CBC News*, 20 February 2015, <http://www.cbc.ca/news/politics/csis-watchdog-agency-starved-of-staff-resources-1.2965276>.

28. A useful summary of Snowden's impact on Canada can be found in Michael Geist's blog, "Citizen Four and the Canadian Surveillance Story," 23 February 2015, <http://www.michaelgeist.ca/>.

29. *Supra* note 5.

30. *Proceedings of the Standing Senate Committee on National Security and Defence*, Issue 15: Evidence (30 April 2007). Semantic hair-splitting over distinctions between data and metadata bring to mind the notorious "Clinton defence" ("I did not have sex with that woman").

31. Office of the Information and Privacy Commissioner of Canada, *Metadata and Privacy: A Technical and Legal Overview*, October 2014, <https://www.priv.gc.ca/information/research-recherche/2014/md_201410_e.asp>.

32. British Columbia Civil Liberties Association, "Stop Illegal Spying — Case Details" <https://bccla.org/stop-illegal-spying/protect-our-privacy-case-details/>.

33. "Too much information going in...," *Globe and Mail*, Editorial 26 October 2013, <http://www.theglobeandmail.com/globe-debate/editorials/too-much-information-going-in/article15092678/>.

34. Greg Weston, "Spy agency CSE Needs MPs' Oversight ex-Director Says," *CBC News*, 7 October 2013, <http://www.cbc.ca/news/politics/spy-agency-csec-needs-mps-oversight-ex-director-says-1.1928983>.

35. Bill C-51, *The Anti-Terrorism Act*, 2d Sess, 41st Parl, 2015, C-51.

36. See for instance the open letter to parliamentarians from over 100 academics, mainly from law faculties across the country: "Open letter to Parliament: Amend C-51 or kill it," *National Post*, 27 February 2015, <http://news.nationalpost.com/full-comment/open-letter-to-parliament-amend-c-51-or-kill-it>. Disclosure: I am one of the signatories.

37. Jean Chrétien, Joe Clark, Paul Martin & John Turner, "A Close Eye on Security Makes Canadians Safer," *Globe and Mail*, 19 February 2015, <http://www.theglobeandmail.com/globe-debate/a-close-eye-on-security-makes-canadians-safer/article23069152/>.

38. Craig Forcese & Kent Roach, *Bill C-51 Backgrounder #2: The Canadian Security Intelligence Service's Proposed Power to "Reduce" Security Threats Through Conduct that May Violate the Law and Charter* (February 12, 2015), <http://ssrn.com/abstract=2564272> or <http://dx.doi.org/10.2139/ssrn.2564272>.

39. Daniel Therrien, "Without Big Changes Bill C-51 Means Big Data," *Globe and Mail*, 6 March 2015, <http://www.theglobeandmail.com/globe-debate/without-big-changes-bill-c-51-means-big-data/article23320329/>.

40. "Edward Snowden Says Canadian Spying Has Weakest Oversight in Western World," *CBC News*, 4 March 2015, <http://www.cbc.ca/news/canada/edward-snowden-says-canadian-spying-has-weakest-oversight-in-western-world-1.2981051>.

41. Mike Frost as told to Michel Gratton, *Spyworld: Inside the Canadian & American Intelligence Establishments* (Toronto: Doubleday, 1994); Andrew Mitrovica, *Covert Entry: Spies, Lies and Crimes Inside Canada's Secret Service* (Toronto: Random House Canada, 2002).

CHAPTER VIII

Why Watching the Watchers Isn't Enough: Canadian Surveillance Law in the Post-Snowden Era

Michael Geist

Introduction

Months of surveillance-related leaks from US whistle-blower Edward Snowden have fuelled an international debate over privacy, spying, and Internet surveillance. The leaks have painted a picture of ubiquitous surveillance that captures "all the signals all the time," sweeping up billions of phone calls, texts, e-mails, and Internet activity with dragnet-style efficiency.

In the United States, the issue has emerged as a political concern, leading to promises from US President Barack Obama to more carefully circumscribe the scope of US surveillance programs.[1] Moreover, US telecom and Internet companies have also responded to political and customer pressure. Verizon[2] and AT&T,[3] two US telecom giants, have begun issuing regular transparency reports on the number of law enforcement requests they receive for customer information. The telecom transparency reports come following a similar trend from leading Internet companies such as Google, Twitter, Microsoft, and Facebook.

While the United States gradually grapples with the Snowden fallout, the Canadian response has been muted at best. Canadian government officials have said little about Canadian surveillance activities, despite revelations of spying activities in Brazil, capturing millions of Internet downloads daily, surveillance of airport wireless networks, cooperation with foreign intelligence agencies,[4] a federal court decision that criticized Canada's intelligence agencies for misleading the court, and a domestic metadata program that remains largely shrouded in secrecy. Canadian telecom companies such as Rogers and Telus[5] reluctantly followed their US counterparts in issuing transparency reports in 2014,[6] though Bell (the largest provider) remains a holdout and reports indicate that government officials expressed concern about any public reporting.[7] In fact, the Canadian government seems to have moved in the opposite direction, by adopting a lower threshold for warrants seeking metadata than is required for standard warrants in Bill C-13, a cyberbullying and lawful access bill that passed the House of Commons in October 2014.[8] Further, in January 2015, the government introduced Bill C-51, the *Anti-Terrorism Act, 2015*, which greatly expands information sharing between Communications Security Establishment (CSE), Canadian Security Intelligence Service (CSIS), and fifteen other government departments and agencies.[9]

As the leaks continue — journalist Glenn Greenwald has indicated that there is more Canadian-related information forth-coming[10] — Canadians are likely to demand greater transparency and accountability about government surveillance activities.[11] Should the issue emerge as a political liability, the question that this chapter examines is where the emphasis should lie. It argues that while the instinctive response may be to focus on improved oversight and accountability mechanisms,[12] the bigger challenge will be to address the substantive shortcomings of the current Canadian legal frame-work. Indeed, improved oversight without addressing the limitations within current law threatens to leave many of the core problems in place. In short, watching the watchers is not enough.

Background

The US role in global surveillance has unsurprisingly captured the lion's share of attention, yet Canada's participation — both as a member of the "Five Eyes" group of countries that includes the United States, the United Kingdom, Australia, and New Zealand, and as a country with an an active domestic and international surveillance program — merits closer examination.[13] Several statutes govern the scope of Canadian activities.

The *National Defence Act* governs the Canadian Security Establishment (CSE), which operates Canada's signals intelligence activities.[14] It limits the CSE mandate to the following three activities:

(a) to acquire and use information from the global informa-
     tion infrastructure for the purpose of providing foreign
     intelligence, in accordance with Government of Canada
     intelligence priorities;
(b) to provide advice, guidance and services to help ensure
     the protection of electronic information and of informa-
     tion infrastructures of importance to the Government of
     Canada; and
(c) to provide technical and operational assistance to federal
     law enforcement and security agencies in the performance
     of their lawful duties.[15]

This mandate was developed in the aftermath of the 11 September
2001 attacks in the United States. The Act further restricts the activities carried out under parts (a) and (b) by stating that they

(a) shall not be directed at Canadians or any person in Canada;
     and
(b) shall be subject to measures to protect the privacy of
     Canadians in the use and retention of intercepted
     information.[16]

The CSE commissioner has characterized the limitations on parts (a)
and (b) of the CSE mandate in the following manner:

> CSEC [CSE] is prohibited from directing its foreign signals
> intelligence collection and IT security activities at Canadians,
> regardless of their location anywhere in the world, or at any
> person in Canada, regardless of their nationality;
> In conducting these activities, CSEC may unintentionally inter-
> cept a communication that originates or terminates in Canada
> in which the originator has a reasonable expectation of pri-
> vacy, which is a "private communication" as defined by the
> *Criminal Code*. CSEC may use and retain a private commu-
> nication obtained this way but only if it is essential to either
> international affairs, defence or security, or to identify, isolate
> or prevent harm to Government of Canada computer systems
> or networks; and
> To provide a formal framework for the unintentional intercep-
> tion of private communications while conducting foreign signals

intelligence collection or IT security activities, the *National Defence Act* requires express authorization by the Minister of National Defence. These are known as ministerial authorizations. The Minister may authorize the activities once he or she is satisfied that specific conditions provided for in the Act have been met, which includes assurances of how such unintentional interceptions of private communications would be handled should they arise.[17]

The government has unsurprisingly defended CSE and consistently claimed that its activities are compliant with the law. In seeking to assure Canadians that there are appropriate safeguards, Justice Minister Peter MacKay told the House of Commons in 2013, "This program is specifically prohibited from looking at the information of Canadians. This program is very much directed at activities outside the country, foreign threats, in fact. There is rigorous oversight. There is legislation in place that specifically dictates what can and cannot be examined."[18]

When asked specifically about the Snowden leaks and the revelations of US surveillance programs, MacKay responded

I would point him, again, to the fact that CSE does not target the communications of Canadians. This is foreign intelligence. This is something that has been happening for years. In fact, as I said, the commissioner highlighted that the "activities were authorized and carried out in accordance with the law, ministerial requirements, and CSEC's policies and procedures.[19]

Notwithstanding the minister's assurances, there have been mounting calls for greater oversight and accountability in response to the Snowden revelations and Canada's participation in global surveillance activities. Those calls increased following the introduction of Bill C-51, which expanded CSIS powers without enhancing related oversight.[20] There is a CSE commissioner who issues annual reports and has been increasingly vocal about his oversight role.[21] Yet, despite the existence of an independent commissioner, many believe that more is needed. For example, University of Toronto professor Ron Deibert has argued that "The Canadian checks and balances just aren't there. We have no parliamentary oversight of CSEC, no adequate independent entity to watch the watchers and act as a constraint on misbehaviour. It just doesn't exist now."[22] Deibert's view is widely shared, with many experts (including some in this volume) pointing to the need for more robust review and oversight to provide Canadians with better assurances that the operation of surveillance programs are compliant with the law.

In fact, there have been repeated attempts at improving oversight, with particular attention paid to the role of parliamentarians.[23] In 2005, Bill C-81, *An Act to Establish the National Security Committee of Parliamentarians*, was introduced in the House of Commons.[24] The bill, which did not proceed past first reading, would have established new oversight powers for a committee comprised of members of Parliament. More recently, Liberal MP Wayne Easter sought to revive the bill in Bill C-551, a private members' bill.[25] In June 2014, Liberal MP Joyce Murray introduced Bill C-622, a CSE accountability and transparency bill.[26]

Oversight and accountability are certainly crucial issues and efforts to enhance the current model, which relies heavily on the CSE commissioner, should be pursued vigorously. However, the danger with focusing chiefly on stronger oversight is that the statutory framework governing CSE necessarily limits the review. In other words, reviews of agencies governed by laws that may permit privacy-invasive activities or that fail to establish a suitable level of oversight in order to engage in certain activities is doomed from the start.

Even if the CSE commissioner were fully empowered to review and publicly document concerns associated with CSE (which some critics doubt), substantive concerns within the legal framework might still go unaddressed. Therefore, this chapter argues that improved oversight without legal reforms is unlikely to address the broader public concerns about lawful surveillance activities that may extend beyond public expectations about the privacy of network communications.

Substantive Concerns With the Current Legal Framework

Metadata

The legality of surveillance programs that capture metadata sits at the heart of much of the legal debate in both the United States and Canada. Metadata — data about data — is information that is automatically generated by the use of communications devices and services such as cellphones, Internet browsing, and text messaging. The metadata may include information on the time of the communication, the parties to the communication, the devices used to communicate, and the location of the communication.[27]

In the United States, the NSA inspector general under the Clinton administration concluded in 1999 that searching telephone metadata constituted unauthorized surveillance:

> NSA proposed that it would perform contact chaining on metadata it had collected. Analysts would chain through masked U.S. telephone numbers to discover foreign connections to those numbers, without specifying, even for analysts, the U.S. number involved. In December 1999, the Department of Justice (DoJ), Office of intelligence Policy Review (OIPR) told NSA that the proposal fell within one of the FISA definitions of electronic surveillance and, therefore, was not permissible when applied to metadata associated with presumed U.S. persons (i.e., U.S. telephone numbers not approved for targeting by the FISC).[28]

Yet, in the aftermath of the September 11 attacks, the US approach to the question changed.[29] The United States began to collect metadata, with the Foreign Intelligence Surveillance Court (FISC) ordering telecom companies in 2006 to provide the NSA with "comprehensive communications routing information, including but not limited to session identifying information (e.g., originating and terminating telephone number, communications device identifier, and so forth), trunk identifier, and time and duration of call."[30] The legality of the US program has been the subject of conflicting court decisions and seems likely to be headed to the US Supreme Court.

While details on the Canadian metadata programs remain secret, there is little doubt that Canadian intelligence agencies are engaged in capturing metadata, much like their US counterparts.[31] The *Globe and Mail* reported in 2013 that a secret Canadian metadata surveillance program was first launched in 2005 under then-Prime Minister Paul Martin by Defence Minister Bill Graham, only to be stopped in 2008 amid privacy concerns. The program was restarted in 2011 with new rules.[32] The details of the program have never been publicly disclosed and the legal questions about the privacy protections granted to metadata collection remain unanswered.

There is reason to believe that CSE believes that metadata is not subject to the privacy protections accorded to content. In 2007, then-CSE chief John Adams told the Standing Senate Committee on National Security and Defence, "What is your interpretation of intercept, if I were to ask? If you asked me, it would be if I heard someone talking to someone else or if I read someone's writing. An intercept would not be to look on the outside of the envelope. That is not an intercept to me."[33] The reference to "outside of the envelope" would appear to be a reference to metadata.

Assurances that metadata surveillance is less invasive than tracking the content of telephone calls or Internet usage also ring hollow. Metadata can include geolocation information, call duration, call participants, and Internet protocol addresses. While officials suggest that this information is not sensitive, there are many studies that have concluded otherwise. These studies have found that metadata alone can be used to identify specific persons, reveal locational data, or even disclose important medical and business information.

For example, a Stanford study found that researchers could predict romantic relationships automatically using only phone metadata, while an MIT study that examined months of anonymized cellphone data and found that only four data points were needed to identify a specific person 95 per cent of the time.[34] Other studies have found that sexual identity can be guessed based on Facebook metadata.[35]

Canadian privacy commissioners have also highlighted the privacy implications of metadata and information that is not typically classified as "content." The Privacy Commissioner of Canada released a report on the privacy value of IP addresses in 2012, noting that one data point could lead to information on website habits that includes sites on sexual preferences.[36] Former Ontario Privacy Commissioner Ann Cavoukian has issued a primer on metadata that finds that it may be more revealing than content.[37]

The Supreme Court of Canada echoed similar concerns with privacy and metadata in *R. v. Vu*. The court specifically discussed the privacy importance of computer-generated metadata, noting that

> most browsers used to surf the Internet are programmed to automatically retain information about the websites the user has visited in recent weeks and the search terms that were employed to access those websites. Ordinarily, this information can help a user retrace his or her cybernetic steps. In the context of a criminal investigation, however, it can also enable investigators to access intimate details about a user's interests, habits, and

identity, drawing on a record that the user created unwittingly: O. S. Kerr, "Searches and Seizures in a Digital World" (2005), 119 Harv. L. Rev. 531, at pp. 542–43. This kind of information has no analogue in the physical world in which other types of receptacles are found.[38]

In fact, even CSE apparently acknowledged in 2008 that "bulk, unselected metadata presents too high a risk to share with second parties at this time, because of the requirement to ensure that the identities of Canadians or persons in Canada are minimised, but re-evaluation of this stance is ongoing."[39]

This position is consistent with US expert positions on the value of metadata. General Michael Hayden, former director of the NSA and the CIA has stated, "we kill people based on metadata."[40] Stewart Baker, former NSA general counsel, has said, "metadata absolutely tells you everything about somebody's life. If you have enough metadata, you don't really need content."[41]

A recent US court brief signed by some of the world's leading computer experts notes

Telephony metadata reveals private and sensitive information about people.

It can reveal political affiliation, religious practices, and people's most intimate associations. It reveals who calls a suicide prevention hotline and who calls their elected official; who calls the local Tea Party office and who calls Planned Parenthood. The aggregation of telephony metadata — about a single person over time, about groups of people, or with other datasets — only intensifies the sensitivity of the information.[42]

Despite the studies on the implications of metadata, the Canadian legal framework downplays the privacy import of such information.[43] As noted above, government officials have dismissed metadata collection as relatively insignificant when questioned about the practice.

In fact, the government recently created a specific warrant for law enforcement designed to obtain metadata with a lower threshold than that used for other sensitive information, such as content. Bill C-13, the lawful access/cyberbullying bill which took effect in March 2015, establishes a definition for transmission data as data that:

(a) relates to the telecommunication functions of dialling, routing, addressing or signalling; (b) is transmitted to identify,
activate or configure a device, including a computer program
as defined in subsection 342.1(2), in order to establish or maintain access to a telecommunication service for the purpose of
enabling a communication, or is generated during the creation,
transmission or reception of a communication and identifies or
purports to identify the type, direction, date, time, duration,
size, origin, destination or termination of the communication; (c) does not reveal the substance, meaning or purpose of
the communication.[44]

The bill created a new warrant that allows a judge to order the disclosure of transmission data where there are reasonable grounds to
suspect that an offence has been or will be committed, the identification of a device or person involved in the transmission will assist
in an investigation, or will help identify a person. The government
relied on the fact that this is a warrant with court oversight to support the claim that Canadians should not be concerned by this
provision. Yet the reality is that there is reason for concern, as the
implications of treating metadata as having a low privacy value is
enormously troubling. Given the level of privacy interest with metadata, many argued that the higher, "reasonable grounds to believe"
standard should have been adopted in the Bill C-13 transmission data
warrant provision.[45] The government rejected those submissions and
passed the bill in the House of Commons in October 2014.

Without addressing the privacy implications of metadata,
reforms to the accountability mechanisms built into Canada's surveillance frameworks are destined to fall short. The Canadian approach
to metadata reflects an outdated perspective that minimizes its privacy importance. Those views have played a crucial role in increasing the collection of metadata, while simultaneously adopting lower
standards of legal safeguards over its collection and use. With a
broad-based ministerial authorization on metadata collection seemingly establishing few limits, the metadata program now represents
one of the most significant privacy-related concerns with Canadian
surveillance practices.

The solution must therefore lie in developing policies that better reflect the privacy implications of metadata collection. A public
review of the metadata authorization is long overdue, accompanied

by a closer examination of potential limitations and oversight that can be adopted as part of any bulk metadata collection program. Moreover, the use of lower warrant thresholds for metadata collection (referred to in the legislation as transmission data) should be revisited with standards adopted that recognize the privacy equivalency of the metadata of a communication and the content of the communication itself. Absent a significant overhaul of the Canadian approach to metadata collection, improved oversight of surveillance activities will only guarantee that reviews are unable to fully address the privacy implications of the Canadian legal framework.

The Blurring of Jurisdiction

One of the most important distinctions within the current CSE legal framework is the stipulation that foreign intelligence activities "shall not be directed at Canadians or any person in Canada." The distinction between foreign collection of information (which is permitted by the statute) and domestic collection (which is not) is regularly cited as a clear line of demarcation between legal and illegal surveillance activities.[46] Indeed, CSE's own explanation of its activities states

> CSE's mandate involves the collection of foreign signals intelligence and the protection of the computer systems and networks of the Government of Canada from mischief, unauthorized use and interference. When fulfilling either of these mandates, CSE does not direct its activities at Canadians, Canadians abroad or any persons in Canada. In fact, CSE is prohibited by law from directing its activities at Canadians anywhere or at anyone in Canada.[47]

Yet, despite the repeated assurances, the commingling of data through integrated communications networks and "borderless" Internet services residing on servers around the world suggests that distinguishing between Canadian and foreign data seems like an outdated and increasingly impossible task. In the current communications environment, tracking Canadians seems inevitable and makes claims that such domestic surveillance is "inadvertent" increasingly implausible.

The extensive US surveillance programs appear to capture just about all communications: everything that enters or exits the United States, anything involving a non-US participant, and anything that travels through undersea cables. This would seem to leave Canadian cellphone and Internet users at a similar risk of surveillance regardless of the nationality of the carrier and suggests that Canadian companies may be facilitating surveillance of their customers by failing to adopt safeguards that render it more difficult for foreign agencies to access data.

For example, both Bell and Rogers link their e-mail systems for residential customers to US giants: Bell is linked to Microsoft and Rogers is linked to Yahoo. In both cases, the inclusion of a US e-mail service provider may allow for US surveillance of Canadian e-mail activity. While the Canadian privacy commissioner previously dismissed concerns associated with using US e-mail providers on the grounds that Canada had similar security laws,[48] the new surveillance revelations suggest that a re-examination of that conclusion may be warranted.

As further analyzed in Clement and Obar's chapter, the issue of avoiding US routing is particularly important, since even Canadian domestic communications that travel from one Canadian location to another may still transit through the United States and thus be captured by US surveillance. Despite these risks, Bell requires other Canadian Internet providers to exchange Internet traffic outside the country at US exchange points, ensuring that the data is potentially subject to US surveillance. In fact, some estimate that 90 per cent of Canadian communications traffic transits through the United States.[49] Moreover, with the regular surveillance demands for the e-mail traffic that passes through Blackberry's Waterloo-based servers and the likely interception of communications traffic through several undersea cables that enter Canada, there is little doubt that Canadian Internet and phone use is subject to significant US surveillance activity.[50]

While the current surveillance statutes may have been developed in a world where geography mattered, the communications borders have been largely blurred, leaving a North American communications network that has little regard for national boundaries. Canadian law is therefore increasingly unable to provide credible assurances about the limits of domestic collection.

Given the global nature of the surveillance activities and the likely commingling of Canadian data (even in instances where CSE activities are not directed toward the country or Canadians), revisiting the jurisdictional issues associated with CSE is essential. As with the need for a review of metadata collection that better reflects current technologies, an examination of the jurisdictional limits of CSE activities premised on modern communications networks is needed. The Canadian government may determine that the jurisdictional limits on CSE should be revisited and expanded. In such a case, the statute should better reflect those limits, rather than maintaining the fiction that CSE surveillance can be neatly divided between domestic and foreign-based activities.

Data and Intelligence Information Sharing

Data and intelligence information sharing is an important part of modern intelligence activities. Indeed, the prospect that US surveillance becomes a key source for Canadian agencies, while Canadian surveillance supports US agencies, does not strike anyone as particularly far-fetched. Wayne Easter, a former government minister with responsibility for CSIS, has said that such sharing is common.[51] In other words, relying on the domestic–foreign distinction is necessary for legal compliance, but does not provide much assurance to Canadians that they are not being tracked.

In fact, Bill C-51 would greatly expand potential information sharing practices. The bill includes the *Security of Canada Information Sharing Act* (SCISA), a bill within the bill, that permits information sharing across government for an incredibly wide range of purposes, most of which have nothing to do with terrorism. The government has tried to justify the provisions on the grounds that Canadians would support sharing information for national security purposes, but the bill allows sharing for reasons that would surprise and disturb most Canadians.[52] Moreover, the scope of sharing is exceptionally broad, covering seventeen government institutions, with government granting itself the right to expand sharing to other departments.[53] In fact, the bill notes that further use and disclosure may occur in accordance with the law."[54]

Canadian Laws That Harmonize Information Sharing

Law enforcement agencies in Canada and the United States currently employ a harmonized approach to sharing information related to cross-border crime, terrorist activity, and immigration matters. For example, a post-9/11 agreement between Canada and the United States established a thirty-point action plan for creating a secure border.[55] Moreover, integrated intelligence is one of eight objectives oriented towards joint data sharing and intelligence coordination. Canada has also established Integrated National Security Enforcement Teams (INSETs) to fight terrorist threats.[56] INSETs include representatives from federal enforcement and intelligence agencies, as well as US law enforcement agencies on a case-by-case basis. The federal government has identified increased joint antiterrorism efforts as a priority.[57]

Information-sharing instruments are also used to obtain information relating to financial investigations. For example, the US Securities and Exchange Commission (SEC) has Memorandums of Understanding (MOUs) with foreign securities regulators to cooperate and share information on the regulation of the financial industry.

Several Canadian statutes specifically authorize cross-border information transfers. The *Proceeds of Crime (Money Laundering) and Terrorist Financing Act* authorizes the Financial Transactions and Reports Analysis Centre of Canada to share financial information related to the goal of preventing money laundering and terrorist financing.[58] The *Department of Immigration and Citizenship Act* includes a provision that allows the minister to implement agreements with foreign governments in order to facilitate the coordination of policies for which he or she is responsible.[59]

The active connection between Canadian and US officials moved to the forefront with reports that Canadian officials may have played a starring role in facilitating US efforts to create a "backdoor" to widely used encryption standards. The Canadian role in these developments is linked to how the NSA managed to gain control over the standard setting process. In 2006, CSE ran the global standard setting process for the International Organization for Standardization. The NSA convinced CSE to allow it to rewrite an earlier draft and ultimately become the sole editor of the standard.

CSE claims that its relationship with the NSA during the standard setting process was merely designed to support the Canadian government's effort to secure its technological infrastructure. However, it is now clear that Canada worked with the United States to ensure that the backdoor was inserted into the encryption standard and that it may have gained access to decryption information in the process.

Given common threats, few doubt the importance of information sharing. Yet differing privacy laws raise serious concerns about whether personal information collected in Canada receives the same level of protection once it is provided to foreign intelligence agencies. Conducting effective reviews of data protection and policies that are outside of the physical control of Canadian agencies represents a significant challenge. Moreover, oversight and accountability mechanisms are largely limited to domestic reviews. Without an oversight mechanism capable to assessing the status of Canadians subject to information sharing practices, providing appropriate protection relies upon broader legal and contractual structures that govern the use of shared data. A review of those structures in an environment where data may flow freely between agencies is needed.

Federal Court Concerns

The Federal Court of Canada has also expressed concern about inappropriate data sharing activities. In 2013, Justice Richard Mosley, a federal court judge, issued a stinging rebuke to Canada's intelligence agencies and the Justice Department, ruling that they misled the court when they applied for warrants to permit the interception of electronic communications.[60] While the government has steadfastly defended its surveillance activities by maintaining that it operates within the law, Justice Mosley, a former official with the Justice Department who was involved with the creation of the *Anti-Terrorism Act*, found a particularly troubling example where this was not the case. Mosley's concern stemmed from warrants involving two individuals that were issued in 2009 permitting the interception of communications both in Canada and abroad using Canadian equipment. At the time, the Canadian intelligence agencies did not disclose that they might ask their foreign counterparts to intercept the foreign communications.

In June 2013, the CSE commissioner issued his annual report, which included a cryptic recommendation that the agency "provide the Federal Court of Canada with certain additional evidence about the nature and extent of the assistance CSE may provide to CSIS."[61] That recommendation caught Mosley's attention, and he ordered the CSE and CSIS to appear in court to disclose if the recommendation was linked to the warrants he had issued and discuss whether the additional evidence might have had an impact on the decision to grant the warrants in the first place.

It turned out that the additional evidence — which involved several warrants, including those issued by Mosley — was indeed the fact that CSE was tasking foreign agencies to conduct interceptions on its behalf. Based on the new submissions, Mosley concluded that Canadian intelligence agencies strategically omitted disclosing the information as they admitted that the evidence provided to the court "was 'crafted' with legal counsel to exclude any reference to the role of the second parties."[62]

The failure of Canada's intelligence agencies to meet their legal obligations of full and frank disclosure raises serious questions about the adequacy of oversight over Canada's surveillance activities. When concerns were raised in 2013 about the activities, then-Defence Minister Peter MacKay assured the public that there is "rigorous" oversight and that all aspects of the programs were carried out in compliance with the law.

The federal court ruling raised real doubt about the validity of those assurances. Indeed, there are lingering questions about both the impartiality of Justice lawyers who provided advice to "craft evidence" and the ability of the federal court to serve as a key oversight mechanism for Canadian surveillance, particularly when some programs do not require court approval and reports from the CSE commissioner have faced lengthy delays.

Rather than addressing these concerns directly, in October 2014, days after an attack on Parliament Hill, the government introduced Bill C-44, the *Protection of Canada from Terrorists Act*.[63] The bill seeks to address the Mosley decision by removing territorial restrictions on CSIS. The bill includes clauses that state that CSIS may conduct investigations within or outside Canada and seek a warrant to allow foreign investigations. Moreover, it opens the door to warrants that apply outside the country regardless of the law in Canada or elsewhere. It provides, "Without regard to any other law, including that of any foreign state, a judge may, in a warrant issued under subsection (3), authorize activities outside Canada to enable the Service to investigate a threat to the security of Canada."[64]

This is a remarkably broad provision, as it allows the federal court to issue warrants that violate the laws of other countries, including foreign privacy laws. The bill was passed through committee review within a matter of weeks. Bill C-44 may reverse the Mosley decision, but what it does not do is address ongoing concerns regarding the accountability and transparency of Canada's security intelligence agencies.[65] Indeed, the Mosley case in particular raised troubling questions about the adequacy of oversight over Canada's surveillance activities. Rather than address those concerns, the government has instead simply reversed the court rulings through legislative reform, leaving the current inadequate oversight system untouched.

European Union Concerns

The likelihood of Canadian data sharing has also attracted the attention of foreign governments, most notably the European Parliament. In December 2013, the European Parliament's Committee on Civil Liberties, Justice and Home Affairs has issued a draft report on US surveillance activities and its implications for European fundamental rights. The report brought Canada into the discussion, noting Canada's participation in the Five Eyes consortium and expressing concern about the implications for trust in the Canadian legal system. The report states

> whereas according to the information revealed and to the findings of the inquiry conducted by the LIBE Committee, the national security agencies of New Zealand and Canada have been involved on a large scale in mass surveillance of electronic communications and have actively cooperated with the US under the so called "Five eyes" programme, and may have exchanged with each other personal data of EU citizens transferred from the EU;
>
> whereas Commission Decisions 2013/651 and 2/2002 of 20 December 2001 have declared the adequate level of protection ensured by the New Zealand and the Canadian Personal Information Protection and Electronic Documents Act; whereas the aforementioned revelations also seriously affect trust in the legal systems of these countries as regards the continuity of protection afforded to EU citizens; whereas the Commission has not examined this aspect.[66]

As a result of the concerns with Canadian surveillance, the report recommends a re-examination of the adequacy finding of Canadian privacy law:

> Calls on the Commission and the Member States to assess without delay whether the adequate level of protection of the New

Zealand and of the Canadian Personal Information Protection and Electronic Documents Act, as declared by Commission Decisions 2013/651 and 2/2002 of 20 December 2001, have been affected by the involvement of their national intelligence agencies in the mass surveillance of EU citizens and, if necessary, to take appropriate measures to suspend or reverse the adequacy decisions; expects the Commission to report to the European Parliament on its findings on the above mentioned countries by December 2014 at the latest;[67]

European concerns with Canadian privacy practices arose again in November 2014 as the European Parliament voted to send a Canada–European Union data-sharing agreement on airline passenger name records to the European Court of Justice for further review. The review, which may not be completed for several years, seeks to ensure that the agreement is compliant with European Union treaties and with the *EU Charter of Fundamental Rights*.[68]

The recent revelations and court cases point to the need for a comprehensive review of Canada's role within Five Eyes and a greater understanding of data sharing and intelligence-gathering activities between intelligence agencies. Without such a review and potential reforms, claims that Canadian agencies operate within the law will provide only limited comfort to those concerned with surveillance that falls outside the current statutory framework.

The European responses to Canadian surveillance and privacy practices point to the risks associated with the current activities, since failure to adequately address the privacy implications of Canadian surveillance activities could hamper Canada's ability to conclude data sharing agreements with other governments or create restrictions on data transfers between Canada and other jurisdictions.

Limited Privacy Protections under Canadian Law

While Canadians often point to the existence of private sector privacy legislation as evidence that there are protections that do not exist under US law (which has not implemented a broadly applicable privacy statute for the private sector), the reality is that Canadian law currently affords limited protections as part of law enforcement or national security investigations. The exceptions within the law become particularly problematic given the increasingly important role of private sector companies such as telecom and Internet companies in the collection and disclosure of their communications activities.

The *Personal Information Protection and Electronic Documents Act* (PIPEDA) establishes the obligations of private organizations with regard to the data they collect in the course of commercial activity.[69] Unless subject to a substantially similar provincial law, the Act applies to every private-sector organization in Canada that collects, uses, or discloses personal information.[70]

PIPEDA includes several exceptions for disclosure of personal information without knowledge or consent. Section 7(3)(c) enables an organization to disclose personal information where it is required "to comply with a subpoena or warrant issued or an order made by a court, person or body with jurisdiction to compel the production of information."[71]

Domestic Disclosures

For many years, government, law enforcement, and telecom providers pointed to PIPEDA and the perceived limited privacy import of subscriber information to argue that it could be disclosed without a warrant. In 2014, the issue began to attract increasing attention, leading to disclosures that placed the spotlight on widespread warrantless access to subscriber information.

In 2011, the Privacy Commissioner of Canada sent letters to the twelve biggest Canadian telecom and Internet providers seeking information on their disclosure practices. Rogers, Bell, and RIM proposed aggregating the information to keep the data from individual companies secret. The response dragged on for months, with Bell admitting at one point that only four providers had provided data and expressing concern about whether it could submit even the aggregated response since it would be unable to maintain anonymity. The companies ultimately provided aggregated information revealing that, in 2011, there were 1,193,630 requests, the majority of which were not accompanied by a warrant or court order. The data indicates that telecom and Internet providers gave the government what it wanted: three providers alone disclosed information from 785,000 customer accounts.[72]

Those revelations, which only came to light in 2014, were preceded by NDP MP Charmaine Borg's effort to obtain information on government agencies' requests for subscriber data. While many agencies refused to disclose the relevant information, Canada Border Services Agency (CBSA) revealed that it had made 18,849 requests in one year for subscriber information including geolocation data and call records. The CBSA obtained a warrant in 52 instances with all other cases involving a simple request without court oversight. The telecom and Internet providers fulfilled the requests virtually every time — 18,824 of 18,849 — and the CBSA paid a fee of between one dollar and three dollars for each request.[73]

In fact, the CBSA revelations follow earlier information obtained under the *Access to Information Act* that in 2010 the RCMP alone made over 28,000 requests for subscriber information without a warrant. These requests go unreported — subscribers do not know their information has been disclosed and the Internet providers and telecom companies aren't talking either. In fact, according to a 2014 Privacy Commissioner of Canada audit, the RCMP itself maintains incomplete and inaccurate records of its requests.[74]

The disclosures also revealed that the telecom companies have established law enforcement databases that provide ready access to subscriber information in a more efficient manner. For example, the Competition Bureau reports that it "accessed the Bell Canada Law Enforcement Database" twenty times in 2012–2013.

The absence of court oversight may surprise many Canadians, but the government has long actively supported the warrantless disclosure model. In 2007, it told the Privacy Commissioner of Canada that an exception found in the private sector privacy law to allow for warrantless disclosure was designed "to allow organizations to collaborate with law enforcement and national security agencies without a subpoena, warrant or court order."[75]

While the massive disclosure of subscriber information without court oversight garnered considerable attention, the practices may change due to the Supreme Court of Canada *R. v. Spencer* decision, released in June 2014.[76] The *Spencer* decision, which examined the legality of voluntary warrantless disclosure of basic subscriber information to law enforcement, called into question long-standing practices and forced law enforcement and other agencies to re-examine their approach.

In a unanimous decision written by Justice Thomas Cromwell, the court issued a strong endorsement of Internet privacy, emphasizing the privacy importance of subscriber information, the right to anonymity, and the need for police to obtain a warrant for subscriber information except in exigent circumstances or under a reasonable law.

The court recognizes that there is a privacy interest in subscriber information. While the government has consistently sought to downplay that interest, the court finds that the information is much more than a simple name and address, particular in the context of the Internet. As the court states,

> the Internet has exponentially increased both the quality and quantity of information that is stored about Internet users. Browsing logs, for example, may provide detailed information about users' interests. Search engines may gather records of users' search terms. Advertisers may track their users across networks of websites, gathering an overview of their interests and concerns. Cookies may be used to track consumer habits and may provide information about the options selected within a website, which web pages were visited before and after the visit to the host website and any other personal information provided. The user cannot fully control or even necessarily be aware of who may observe a pattern of online activity, but by remaining anonymous — by guarding the link between the information and the identity of the person to whom it relates – the user can in large measure be assured that the activity remains private.[77]

Given all of this information, the privacy interest is about much more than just name and address.

Second, the court expands our understanding of informational privacy, concluding that there are three conceptually distinct issues: privacy as secrecy, privacy as control, and privacy as anonymity. It is anonymity that is particularly notable as the court recognizes its importance within the context of Internet usage. Given the importance of the information and the ability to link anonymous Internet activities with an identifiable person, a high level of informational privacy is at stake.

Third, not only is there a significant privacy interest, but there is also a reasonable expectation of privacy by the user. The court examined both PIPEDA and the Shaw terms of use (the ISP in the *Spencer* case) and concluded that PIPEDA must surely be understood within the context of protecting privacy (not opening the door to greater disclosures) and that the ISP agreement was confusing at best and may support the expectation of privacy. With those findings in mind,

> in the totality of the circumstances of this case, there is a reasonable expectation of privacy in the subscriber information. The disclosure of this information will often amount to the identification of a user with intimate or sensitive activities being carried out online, usually on the understanding that these activities would be anonymous. A request by a police officer that an ISP voluntarily disclose such information amounts to a search.[78]

Fourth, having concluded that obtaining subscriber information was a search with a reasonable expectation of privacy, the information was unconstitutionally obtained, therefore led to an unlawful search. Addressing the impact of the PIPEDA voluntary disclosure clause, the court noted,

> Since in the circumstances of this case the police do not have the power to conduct a search for subscriber information in the absence of exigent circumstances or a reasonable law, I do not see how they could gain a new search power through the combination of a declaratory provision and a provision enacted to promote the protection of personal information.[79]

The *Spencer* decision placed the spotlight on longstanding, albeit but legally questionable, law enforcement and government agencies subscriber information request practices that were actively supported by Canadian telecom providers. While the decision may result in significant practice reforms, the uncertainty confirms that Canadian domestic privacy law does not provide strong safeguards against warrantless disclosures of subscriber information.

Foreign Disclosures

In addition to PIPEDA's weakness on domestic warrantless disclosures, the statute does not address whether foreign orders, such as those made by a Foreign Intelligence Surveillance Court (FISC) or a grand jury can be considered as made by "a court, person or body with jurisdiction to compel" so as to fall within another PIPEDA consent exception. The statute is silent on the jurisdictional distinction making it possible that US orders validly made under US personal jurisdiction can be considered an exception.

Section 7(3)(c.1) permits disclosure without consent where the disclosure is made to a government institution where "(ii) the disclosure is requested for the purpose of enforcing any law of Canada, a province or a foreign jurisdiction, carrying out an investigation relating to the enforcement of any such law or gathering intelligence for the purpose of enforcing any such law."[80] The inclusion of foreign laws within this exception indicates that disclosure for US counterterrorism investigations through national security letters or section 215 orders might qualify under the act's exceptions. The related issue is whether "government institution" is limited to a Canadian government institution or whether a foreign government institution could suffice. If the exception is limited to Canadian government institutions, US authorities would likely need to tender their requests for disclosure through CSIS or the Canadian Department of Justice to qualify.

The Privacy Commissioner of Canada has addressed these issues in a series of complaints involving the Canadian Imperial Bank of Commerce and the outsourcing of credit card processing to the United States.[81] While each complainant raised slightly different issues, all complainants primarily objected to the possible scrutiny of their personal information by US authorities within the context of foreign intelligence gathering.

With regard to the risk of disclosure to US authorities, the Commissioner noted,

> The possibility of U.S. authorities accessing Canadians' personal information has been raised frequently since the passage of the Uniting and Strengthening America by Providing Appropriate Tools Required to Intercept and Obstruct Terrorism Act, 2001 (USA PATRIOT Act). Prior to the passage of this Act, U.S. authorities were able to access records held by U.S.-based firms relating to foreign intelligence gathering in a number of ways. What has changed with the passage of USA PATRIOT Act is that certain U.S. intelligence and police surveillance and information collection tools have been expanded, and procedural hurdles for U.S. law enforcement agencies have been minimized. Under section 215 of the USA PATRIOT Act, the Federal Bureau of Investigation (FBI) can access records held in the United States by applying for an order of the Foreign Intelligence Surveillance

Act Court. A company subject to a section 215 order cannot reveal that the FBI has sought or obtained information from it. The risk of personal information being disclosed to government authorities is not a risk unique to U.S. organizations. In the national security and anti-terrorism context, Canadian organizations are subject to similar types of orders to disclose personal information held in Canada to Canadian authorities.[82]

The Commissioner ruled that the complaints were not well-founded, acknowledging that "many Canadians are concerned about the flow of their personal information outside of our country's borders and its accessibility by foreign governments. In order to determine whether these complaints are founded or not, however, it is the obligations imposed by the Act on Canadian-based organizations, and how well CIBC met them, that are the primary considerations."[83]

In reaching her determination, the Commissioner stated that "there is a comparable legal risk that the personal information of Canadians held by any organization and its service provider — be it Canadian or American — can be obtained by government agencies, whether through the provisions of U.S. law or Canadian law."[84] The comparable legal risk in both jurisdictions points to the relative weakness of both systems. Given the weak protections (as identified by the Supreme Court in *Spencer*), more robust reviews or accountability mechanisms within the Canadian surveillance framework may not address the foundational concern regarding the need for stronger privacy protections as part of any private sector disclosures of sensitive subscriber information.

Limited Privacy Protections Under US Law

Inadequate privacy laws are not limited to Canada. Indeed, ensuring adequate privacy protections for Canadians also requires pressuring our Five Eyes partners, particularly the United States, to grant universal privacy protections that apply equally to US and non-US persons. This is particularly true given the realities of the current cloud computing environment, where Canadians rely heavily on US-based services that store data in the United States and are subject to US law.

Unlike US persons, who enjoy legal protections through a variety of mechanisms aimed at respecting their constitutional privacy rights and freedom of expression, non-US persons are granted limited protections through the definition of "foreign intelligence information." This includes information "with respect to a foreign power or foreign territory that relates to…the conduct of the foreign affairs of the United States."

Given this broad definition, non-US persons have practically no privacy protections. For example, the 2008 US *FISA Amendments Act* permits US authorities to seek broad certification to collect categories of foreign intelligence information for up to one year.[85] With such a certification in hand, authorities can then issue directives to US-based Internet companies such as Google or Facebook to compel them to disclose and decrypt information that falls within the broad terms of this certification. It should be noted certifications are not the equivalent of court orders and require a far lower evidentiary standard. Indeed, the US legislative approach grants authorities the power to engage in sweeping surveillance of both content and metadata of non-US persons whose data is stored within the United States.

This issue, which is canvassed more exhaustively in Lisa Austin's contribution in this volume,[86] suggests that the concerns for the Canadian privacy protections are not limited to the activities of Canadian security intelligence agencies and Canadian law. Indeed, with Canadian data regularly transiting across US communications networks, the absence of privacy protections for Canadians (i.e., non-US citizens) in the United States is a particular cause for concern. The issue is also one of the most difficult to address since improvements within domestic frameworks — whether on substantive provisions or oversight and accountability mechanisms — do not solve the lack of protection under US law. Indeed, the issue must be escalated between the countries, with Canadian officials seeking stronger protections in recognition of the increasingly integrated communications networks and surveillance agency activities.

Conclusion

As Canadians learn more about the current state of surveillance activities and technologies (including the ability to data mine massive amounts of information), there is a budding recognition that current surveillance and privacy laws were crafted for a much different world. The geographic or content limitations placed on surveillance activities by organizations such as CSE may have been effective years ago when such activities were largely confined to specific locations and the computing power needed to mine metadata was not readily available.

That is clearly no longer the case. The law seeks to differentiate surveillance based on geography, but there is often no real difference with today's technology. Moreover, the value of metadata is sometimes greater than the actual content of telephone conversations. The current law provides few privacy protections and ineffective oversight in the face of intelligence agencies investing billions of dollars in surveillance technologies and telecommunications and Internet companies providing assistance that remains subject to court-imposed gag orders.

The legal framework leaves Canadians with twentieth-century protections in a world of twenty-first-century surveillance. The recent call for improved oversight and accountability of Canada's surveillance agencies is both understandable and long overdue. However, the bigger challenge will be to address the substantive shortcomings of the current Canadian legal framework as well as the limitations found in foreign frameworks that have a direct impact on the privacy of Canadians. Indeed, improved oversight without addressing the limitations within current law threatens to leave many of the core problems in place. For Canadians concerned with the privacy implications of seemingly ubiquitous surveillance and a legal framework that does not reflect current technologies or network practices, doing a better job of watching the watchers is not enough.

Acknowledgements

My thanks to several anonymous reviewers for their helpful comments on earlier versions of this chapter and to Emily Murray for her research and citation assistance. Any errors or omissions are the sole responsibility of the author.

Notes

1. Chris Strome & Margaret Talev, "Obama Unveiling NSA Changes in Response to Snowden Leaks," *Bloomberg News*, 17 January 2014, <http://www.bloomberg.com/news/articles/2014-01-17/obama-unveiling-nsa-changes-in-response-to-snowden-leaks>.

2. See, e.g., Randal Milch, "Verizon Releases Transparency Report for First Half 2014," 8 July 2014, *Verizon Policy Blog*, <publicpolicy.verizon.com/blog/entry/verizon-releases-transparency-report-for-first-half-2014>.

3. See, e.g., "Transparency Report," (2014) ATT, <about.att.com/content/csr/home/frequently-requested-info/governance/transparencyreport.html>.

4. Greg Weston, "Snowden Document Shows Canada Set up Spy Posts for NSA," *CBC News*, 9 December 2013, <www.cbc.ca/news/politics/snowden-document-shows-canada-set-up-spy-posts-for-nsa-1.2456886>.

5. David Patton, "Telus Issues First 'Transparency Report' on Requests for Customer Information," *Toronto Star*, 18 September 2014, <www.thestar.com/business/2014/09/18/telus_issues_first_transparency_report_on_requests_for_customer_information.html>.

6. Colin Freeze et al, "TekSavvy, Rogers Break Silence Over Government Requests for Data," *Globe and Mail*, 5 June 2014,<http://www.theglobeandmail.com/technology/tech-news/teksavvy-opens-books-on-government-data-requests/article18999107/>.

7. Canadian Press, "Disclosure of 'Sensitive' Telecom Surveillance Details Worried Feds: Memo," *Maclean's*, 30 November 2014, <www.macleans.ca/news/canada/disclosure-of-sensitive-telecom-surveillance-details-worried-feds-memo/>.

8. Bill C-13, *An Act to amend the Criminal Code, the Canada Evidence Act, the Competition Act and the Mutual Legal Assistance in Criminal Matters Act*, 2nd Sess, 41st Parl, 2015 (as passed by the House of Commons 20 October 2014) [Bill C-13].

9. Bill C-51, *An Act to enact the Security of Canada Information Sharing Act and the Secure Air Travel Act, to amend the Criminal Code, the Canadian Security Intelligence Service Act and the Immigration and Refugee Protection Act and to make related and consequential amendments to other Acts*, 2nd Sess., 41st Parl., 2015 (first reading 30 January 2015), [Bill C-51].

10. "NSA Leaks on Canadian Surveillance Coming, Greenwald Says," *CBC News*, 9 November 2013, <www.cbc.ca>.

11. On Canadian concerns with surveillance, see Colin J. Bennett et al, eds., *Transparent Lives: Surveillance in Canada* (Edmonton: Athabasca University Press, 2014).

12. "NDP Wants Parliamentary Oversight of Government's Intelligence and Security Activities," 29 October 2013, *New Democratic Party of Canada*, <www.ndp.ca/news/ndp-wants-parliamentary-oversight-governments-intelligence-and-security-activities>. See also Craig Forcese, "Faith-Based Accountability: Metadata and CSEC Review," 13 February 2014, *National Security Law* (blog), <craigforcese.squarespace.com/national-security-law-blog/2014/2/13/faith-based-accountability-metadata-and-csec-review.html>.

13. James Cox, "Canada and Five Eyes Intelligence Community," (2012) Canada International Council, Working paper, <www.cdfai.org/PDF/Canada%20and%20the%20Five%20Eyes%20Intelligence%20Community.pdf>. See also Colin Freeze, "'Five Eyes' Intelligence Sharing Program Threatens Canadians Abroad, Watchdog Warns," *Globe and Mail*, 31 October 2013, <http://www.theglobeandmail.com/news/politics/five-eyes-intelligence-sharing-program-threatens-canadians-abroad-watchdog-warns/article15199925/>.

14. See generally Kevin Walby & Seantel Anaïs, "Communications Security Establishment Canada (CSEC): Structures of Secrecy, and Ministerial Authorization after September 11," (2012) 27:3 *Canadian Journal of Law and Society* 363; Martin Rudner, "Canada's Communications Security Establishment from Cold War to Globalization," (2001) 16:1 *Intelligence and National Security* 97; Martin Rudner, "Canada's Communications Security Establishment, Signals Intelligence and Counter Terrorism," (2007) 22:4 *Intelligence and National Security* 473; and Stéphane Lefebvre, "Canada's Legal Framework for Intelligence," (2010) 23:2 *International Journal of Intelligence and Counterintelligence* 247.

15. *National Defence Act*, RSC 1985, c N-5, s. 273.64.

16. *Ibid.*

17. Canada, Office of the Communications Security Establishment Commissioner, *2011–2012 Annual Report* (Ottawa: Public Works and Government Services Canada, 2012).

18. *House of Commons Debates*, 41st Parl., 1st Sess., No. 266 (10 June 2013), (Hon. Andrew Scheer).

19. *Ibid.*

20. *Bill C-51, supra* note 9.

21. Canada, Office of the Communications Security Establishment Commissioner, *2012–2013 Annual Report* (Ottawa: Public Works and Government Services Canada, 2013).

22. Mitch Potter & Michelle Shephard, "Canada's Electronic Watchers Enjoy Secrecy Second to None," *Toronto Star*, 9 November 2013, <http://www.thestar.com/news/world/2013/11/09/canadas_electronic_watchers_enjoy_secrecy_second_to_none.html>.

23. See generally Roy Rempel, "Canada's Parliamentary Oversight of Security and Intelligence," (2004) 17:4 *International Journal of Intelligence and CounterIntelligence* 634.

24. Bill C-81, *An Act to establish the National Security Committee of Parliamentarians*, 1st Sess., 38th Parl., 2005 (first reading 25 November 2005).

25. Bill C-551, *An Act to establish the National Security Committee of Parliamentarians*, 2nd Sess., 41st Parl., 2013 (first reading 7 November 2013).

26. Bill C-622, *An Act to amend the National Defence Act (transparency and accountability, to enact the Intelligence and Security Committee of Parliament*

Act and to make consequential amendments to other Acts, 2nd Sess., 41st Parl., 2014 (first reading 18 June 2014).

27. National Information Standards Organization, "Understanding Metadata," (2004) *NISO Press*, <www.niso.org/publications/press/UnderstandingMetadata.pdf>.

28. "ST-09-9002 Working Draft: Office of the Inspector General," (24 March 2009), National Security Agency, Central Security Service, Working paper ST-09-0002, <www.aclu.org/files/natsec/nsa/20130816/NSA%20IG%20Report.pdf>.

29. Ryan Lizza, "The Metadata Program in Eleven Documents," *New Yorker*, 13 December 2013, <http://www.newyorker.com/news/daily-comment/the-metadata-program-in-eleven-documents>.

30. *Ibid*.

31. Stephane Couture & Catherine Pappas, "Surveillance and Metadata Collection in Canada," (2014) GISWatch, <giswatch.org/en/country-report/communications-surveillance/canada>.

32. Colin Freeze, "Data-Collection Program Got Green Light from MacKay in 2011," *Globe and Mail*, 10 June 2013, <http://www.theglobeandmail.com/news/politics/data-collection-program-got-green-light-from-mackay-in-2011/article12444909/>.

33. Senate of Canada, Proceedings of the Standing Committee on National Security and Defence, 1st Sess., 39th Parl., No. 15 (30 April 2007), online: <www.parl.gc.ca/Content/SEN/Committee/391/defe/15evb-e.htm?comm_id=76&Language=E&Parl=39&Ses=1>.).

34. Ron Deibert, "Spy Agencies Have Turned Our Digital Lives Inside Out. We Need to Watch Them," *Globe and Mail*, 10 June 2013, <http://www.theglobeandmail.com/globe-debate/spy-agencies-have-turned-our-digital-lives-inside-out-we-need-to-watch-them/article12455029/>.

35. Jay Stanley & Ben Wizner, "Why The Government Wants Your Metadata," *Reuters*, 7 June 2013, <http://blogs.reuters.com/great-debate/2013/06/06/why-the-government-wants-your-metadata/>.

36. Canada, Office of the Privacy Commissioner of Canada, *What an IP Address Can Reveal About You: A Report Prepared by the Technology Analysis Branch of the Office of the Privacy Commissioner of Canada*, by Technology Analysis Branch, May 2013, <www.priv.gc.ca/information/research-recherche/2013/ip_201305_e.asp>.

37. Ontario, Information and Privacy Commissioner, *A Primer on Metadata: Separating Fact from Fiction*, July 2013, <www.privacybydesign.ca/content/uploads/2013/07/Metadata.pdf>.

38. *R. v. Vu*, 2013 SCC 60 at para. 42, [2013] 3 SCR 657.

39. Bill Robinson, "Metadata and Second Parties," (2 December 2013, *Lux Ex Umbra* (blog), <www.luxexumbra.blogspot.ca/2013/12/metadata-and-second-parties.html>.

40. David Cole, "'We Kill People Based on Metadata,'" 10 May 2014, *New York Review of Books Blog*, <www.nybooks.com/blogs/nyrblog/2014/may/10/we-kill-people-based-metadata/>.

41. Alan Rusbrigder, "The Snowden Leaks and the Public," (2013) 60:18 *New York Review of Books*, <www.nybooks.com/articles/archives/2013/nov/21/snowden-leaks-and-public/>.

42. *American Civil Liberties Union v. United States (National Security Agency & Federal Bureau of Investigation, 959 F Supp (2d) 724 (SD NY 2013) lead to appeal to 2nd Cir granted, (Amici Curiae* Brief of Experts in Computer and Data Science in Support of Appellants and Reversal), <*www.eff.org/document/computer-scientists-amicus-aclu-v-clapper*>.

43. See generally Nicholas Koutros & Julien Demers, "Big Brother's Shadow: Decline in Reported Use of Electronic Surveillance by Canadian Federal Law Enforcement," (2013) 11 CJLT 79 (WL Can).

44. Section 20, *Bill C-13, supra* note 8.

45. *Ibid.*

46. Tonda MacCharles, "Tories Deny Canadian Spy Agencies Are Targeting Canadians," *Toronto Star*, 10 June 2013, <www.thestar.com/news/canada/2013/06/10/tories_deny_canadian_spy_agencies_are_targeting_canadians.html>.

47. "Frequently Asked Questions," 8 August 2014, *Communications Security Establishment*, <www.cse-cst.gc.ca/en/about-apropos/faq>.

48. Office of the Privacy Commissioner of Canada, "Outsourcing of canada.com E-mail Services to U.S.-Based Firm Raises Questions for Subscribers," Findings under the *Personal Information Protection and Electronic Documents Act* Case Summary #2008-394, <www.priv.gc.ca/cf-dc/2008/394_20080807_e.asp>.

49. Mitch Potter & Michele Shephard, "Canadians Not Safe From U.S. Online Surveillance, Expert Says," *Toronto Star*, 7 June 2013, <www.thestar.com/news/world/2013/06/07/canadians_not_safe_from_us_online_surveillance_expert_says.html>.

50. For an expert discussion on Canadian surveillance technologies and the likely activities of Research in Motion, see Ron Deibert, *Black Code: Inside the Battle for Cyberspace* (Toronto: Signal, 2013).

51. Asad Ismi, "Massive Secret Surveillance in Canada," 1 November 2013, *The Monitor*, <https://www.policyalternatives.ca/publications/monitor>.

52. Section 2, *Bill C-51, supra* note 9.

53. *Ibid.*, Schedule 3.

54. *Ibid.*, s. 6.

55. Canada Border Services Agency, "North American Partnerships," 12 January 2007, *CBSA*, <www.cbsa-asfc.gc.ca/agency-agence/partner-partenaire-eng.html>.

56. Royal Canadian Mounted Police, "Integrated National Security Enforcement Teams," 18 July 2014, *RCMP*, <www.rcmp-grc.gc.ca/secur/insets-eisn-eng.htm>.

57. Canada's Economic Action Plan, "Perimeter Security & Economic Competitiveness," *Canada's EAP*, <actionplan.gc.ca/en/page/bbg-tpf/canada-us-border-cooperation>.

58. *Proceeds of Crime (Money Laundering) and Terrorist Financing Act*, SC 2000, c. 17.

59. *Department of Citizenship and Immigration Act*, SC 1994, c. 31, s. 4.

60. *IN THE MATTER OF an application by [Redacted] for a warrant pursuant to Sections 12 and 21 of the Canadian Security Intelligence Service Act, RSC 1985, c C-23; AND IN THE MATTER OF [Redacted]*, 2013 FC 1275. <leaksource.files.wordpress.com/2013/12/mosley-csis.pdf>.

61. Craig Forcese, "Triple Vision Accountability and the Outsourcing of CSIS Intercepts," 6 December 2013, *National Security Law* (blog), <craigforcese.squarespace.com/national-security-law-blog/2013/12/6/triple-vision-accountability-and-the-outsourcing-of-csis-int.html>.

62. *Supra* note 21 at 19.

63. Bill C-44, *An Act to amend the Canadian Security Intelligence Service Act and other Acts*, 2nd Sess., 41st Parl., 2014, (first reading 27 October 2014) [Bill C-44].

64. *Canadian Security Intelligence Service Act* s. 8(2), being part of *Bill C-44*.

65. Craig Forcese, "Foreign Spying, Information Sharing & Arar Commission Fixes to Accountability: Brief on Bill C-44," 27 November 2014, *National Security Law* (blog), <craigforcese.squarespace.com/national-security-law-blog/2014/11/27/foreign-spying-information-sharing-arar-commission-fixes-to.html>. See also Canadian Civil Liberties Association, "Submission on Proposed Changes to CSIS Act (Bill C-44)," 26 November 2014, *CCLA*, <ccla.org/2014/11/26/cclas-submissions-on-proposed-changes-to-csis-act-bill-c-44/>.

66. European Parliament, Committee on Civil Liberties, Justice and Home Affairs, *Draft Report on the US NSA surveillance programme, surveillance bodies in various Member States and their impact on EU citizens' fundamental rights and on transatlantic cooperation in Justice and Home Affairs*, European Parliament, <www.europarl.europa.eu/sides/getDoc.do?pubRef=-//EP//NONSGML%2BCOMPARL%2BPE-526.085%2B02%2BDOC%2BPDF%2BV0//EN> at 12/52.

67. *Ibid.*

68. Michael Geist, "Canada – European Union Data Sharing Agreement Sent to EU Court of Justice for Review," 3 December 2014, *Michael Geist* (blog), <www.michaelgeist.ca/2014/12/canada-european-union-data-sharing-agreement-sent-eu-court-justice-review/>.

69. *Personal Information Protection and Electronic Documents Act*, SC 2000, c. 5.

70. *Ibid.* at s. 26(2)(b).

71. *Ibid.* at s. 7(3)(c).

72. Michael Geist, "Canadian Telcos Asked to Disclose Subscriber Data Every 27 Seconds," 30 April 2014, *Michael Geist* (blog), <www.michael-geist.ca/2014/04/telco-disclosures/>.

73. Colin Freeze, "Border Agency Asked for Canadians' Telecom Info 18, 849 Times in One Year," *Globe and Mail*, 27 March 2014, <http://www.theglobeandmail.com/news/politics/telecoms-routinely-give-customer-information-to-canada-border-service-agency/article17691103/>.

74. Michael Geist, "RCMP Records Called 'Incomplete and Inaccurate' in Memo," *Toronto Star*, 27 February 2015, <http://www.thestar.com/business/2015/02/27/rcmp-records-called-incomplete-and-inaccurate-in-memo-geist.html>.

75. Government Response to the Fourth Report of the Standing Committee on Access to Information, Privacy and Ethics, <https://www.ic.gc.ca/eic/site/icgc.nsf/vwapj/ETHI-e.pdf/$file/ETHI-e.pdf> at 6.

76. *R v Spencer*, 2014 SCC 43, 375 DLR (4th) 255.

77. *Ibid.* at para. 46.

78. *Ibid.* at para. 66.

79. *Ibid.* at para. 73.

80. *Supra* note 62 at s. 7(3)(c.1).

81. Office of the Privacy Commissioner of Canada, "Bank's Notification to Customers Triggers *PATRIOT Act* Concerns," Findings under the *Personal Information Protection and Electronic Documents Act* Case Summary #2005-313, <www.privcom.gc.ca/cf-dc/2005/313_20051019_e.asp>.

82. *Ibid.*

83. *Ibid.*

84. *Ibid.*

85. US, Bill HR, *Foreign Intelligence Services Act of 1978 Amendments Act of 2008*, 110th Cong, 2008, s. 702 (enacted).

86. See Austin, Chapter IV.

CHAPTER IX

Stuck on the Agenda: Drawing Lessons from the Stagnation of "Lawful Access" Legislation in Canada

Christopher Parsons

Concerns surrounding government access to communications data are not a new social problematic. Letter mail, the telegraph, phone calls, and other technologically mediated forms of communication have routinely given rise to social privacy concerns.[1] And the politics of such surveillance have often been explosive when new technologies have been made subject to government interception requirements, and even more explosive when it is found that government has surreptitiously engaged in the surveillance of its citizens without publicly declared legal authorities. At this point, proposed legislative expansions of government agencies' surveillance capacities in Western democracies often fall under the heading of "lawful access" powers, which captures expansions of government agencies' search and seizure, communications interception, and subscriber data production powers. Governments routinely justify such expansions as needed to catch up to contemporary criminal activities, to defray or prosecute acute criminal activities, or to equalize law enforcement authorities' powers across international jurisdictions.

Governments' legislative attempts to expand state agencies' lawful access powers are not always successful. The failures of successive Canadian governments to pass such legislation is a case in point. These failures are often the result of governmental indifference and/or successful advocacy protesting expanded powers. This chapter examines the Canadian failures in order to identify some political conditions that should be met if similar legislation is to be successfully opposed in other jurisdictions.

The chapter begins by outlining how agenda setting operates and the roles of different agendas, tactics, and framings. Next, it turns to the Canadian case and identifies key actors, actions, and stages of the lawful access debates. The agenda-setting literature lets us identify and explain why opponents of the Canadian legislation have been so effective in hindering its passage and what the future holds for opposing similar legislative efforts in Canada. The final section steps away from the Canadian case to suggest that there are basic as well as additive general conditions that may precede successful political opposition to newly formulated or revealed government surveillance powers that focus on either domestic or signals intelligence operations.

Agenda Setting and Expanded Policing Powers

Before analyzing the politics that drive Canadian lawful access legislation it is helpful to turn to the agenda-setting literature to understand why certain issues are more or less successful in being placed on an agenda and then advanced to legislative action. Agendas constitute broad collections of problems, issues, solutions, and causes of problems that rise to the attention of the media, the public, and policy makers. While agendas can be as formal as lists of bills before a legislature or long-running news stories that have been planned for some time, they can also include beliefs about the significance of problems, about the need for particular solutions, or about the roles of various actors to address a problem or implement a solution.

The media agenda "mediates between policy and public agendas, constructs the public agenda and seeks to influence policy agendas."[2] This agenda is often important for amplifying, translating, or linking issues that might be on the policy or public agendas. The public agenda, in turn, refers to key issues that are in the minds of the public generally, and typically accounts for no more than five to seven items at a time.[3] In contrast, the policy agenda is composed of issues or items that the government of the day regards as its most pressing; this agenda is often made manifest through the bills that are on an Order Paper or issues being debated privately amongst influential legislators. These bills, topics, or issues may be moved to be implemented as law or withdrawn from the legislative process depending on whether the other two agendas also prioritize an issue on the policy agenda or, alternately, if these agendas are not used to stymie the passage of items on the policy agenda.

Of course, not all issues command similar degrees of importance, with importance often based on whether actors with high degrees of public, political, or media capital have prioritized a given issue. Events can arise, however, without the guidance of any particular actor or community; when a focusing event manifests even well-capitalized actors may be limited in how they can control a given issue's ascendance on the media, public, and policy agendas. A focusing event occurs suddenly and is *"relatively rare, can be reasonably defined as harmful or revealing the possibility of potentially greater future harms, inflicts harms or suggests potential harms that are or could be concentrated on a definable geographic area or community of interest, and that is known to policy makers and the public virtually simultaneously."*[4] There might, however, only be a "loose connection between the character of the happenings and their becoming a key event. The fact that an occurrence becomes a key event therefore still gives no information as to why it became one."[5] As a result, while high-capitalized actors might have their own agendas disrupted by a focusing event, all involved actors might struggle to successfully define the problem and solution within the context of the focusing event and, for parties that fear losing control of the agenda, such actors might try to use the event to suppress the issue off relevant agendas.[6]

The power of focusing events is accentuated when associated with a symbol or drawn into a pre-existing or rapidly developed narrative: in such cases, these events are "more likely to be characterized by high levels of support, high likelihood of action, and low freedom of action than those that enter through 'normal' political processes."[7] Moreover, events that are linked to symbols or narratives are more likely to rise on all agendas, simultaneously, to the point where a common consensus emerges amongst experts and non-experts alike that "something must be done."

More specifically, symbols operate as referents to deeply held social or cultural roots, and by appealing to them actors try to clarify how their framing of an issue resonates with the symbol. So, by linking a policing or security issue to protecting innocent children, for example, a set of assumptions and values (the right for children to be protected, the appropriateness of stopping harm before it occurs, the legitimacy of using force and surveillance to dilute or prevent such harms, and so on) can immediately come into play. Narratives can complement the use or cooptation of symbols insofar as they paint storylines of how to interpret a symbol, often in a reductive fashion. So, to protect children, it is important for police to have the same capabilities today as they did twenty or thirty years ago, such as the ability to passively monitor for suspicious activity and stop and ask for identification of parties who seem suspicious. Of course, in a contemporary digital policing framework, that passive monitoring might include abilities to be automatically notified by telecommunications service providers (TSPs) when the providers register a deviant activity or action, and request for identification might include the mandatory and warrantless receipt of subscriber information from a TSP. Whereas proponents for such powers may play on the reductive logic of their arguments, opponents might spin a narrative that captures the duplicity or falsity of such reductive stories or use of a culturally significant symbol.

Of course, the means by which parties are more or less successful in advancing their interests corresponds with their abilities to place issues on institutional decisional agendas that are amenable to specific actors' identifications of problems, solutions, and mechanisms of implementing solutions. Attempts to forum shop often enjoy prominent placement in the agenda-setting process. Actors routinely case their favoured forums as the most appropriate to take up a given problem and identify a suitable solution. The decision of which forum takes up an issue can be critically important when actors believe that policy debates will be settled very differently based on which adjudicator and accompanying institution comes to own the issue.[8]

As will become clear, the issue of expanding lawful access powers in Canada has followed a meandering road. Successive governments have taken up the issue, often with differing levels of interest or commitment. Aligned communities, such as TSPs and civil liberties groups, have fractured. Different narratives have been adopted to try to justify implementing the legislation, and considerations of these powers have escaped legislative institutions. And, somewhat surprisingly, one majority federal government failed to pass lawful access legislation when offered the opportunity to do so. In what follows, I argue that lawful access has been stuck on the Canadian policy agenda as a result of weak governments, strong opposition to the legislation, and damaging consequences of framing events, and that the Canadian situation provides insights for other jurisdictions where actors oppose the maintenance or expansion of novel government surveillance powers.

Canada and Lawful Access on the Agenda

Successive Canadian governments sought to pass legislation to extend domestic authorities' access to telecommunications data. These efforts began in earnest following Canada's signing of the *Convention on Cybercrime* in 23 November 2001. In brief, the convention was premised on the fact that criminal activities take place on, and through, computer equipment and that signatory nations must cooperate to detect, investigate, and prosecute criminal computer-based activities. Part of the ratification process required national governments to "create several offences, including unlawful interception, access or interference with a computer system, computer-related forgery and fraud, and offences relating to child pornography and copyright."[9]

In addition, the *Convention on Cybercrime* required the expansion of authorities' investigative powers. Several federal governments have used these requirements to justify the following: requiring TSPs to be able to intercept their subscribers' communications; enabling authorities to compel subscriber data from TSPs without a court order; mandating the creation of new preservation and production orders; potentially establishing a key escrow system for encrypted communications; and authorizing government agencies to install malware on location-aware devices such as smartphones and GPS equipment.[10] In the wake of signing the convention, government spokespersons suggested "that new communications technologies and a deregulated telecommunications environment required some serious legislative upgrading and modernization of electronic surveillance rules... The expectation was that the legislation would follow expeditiously, although there would be time for public and industry consultation before a final draft was prepared."[11] Ultimately, as a result of federal elections and successful civil liberties opposition to the legislation, along with businesses' resistance, lawful access legislation was not expeditiously made into law: it instead languished on the Canadian agenda.

There were a series of moments when lawful access legislation loomed large on public, media, and policy agendas simultaneously. At other moments, the legislation was featured more prominently on only one or two of those agendas. In each case, however, a core group of actors took part in the debates, with the actors tending to assume similar (and often self-interested) roles. Throughout, actors contested how the proposed powers would manifest as laws, as technical demands, as costs on business, and as transformative to policing practices.

The Actors

A community of governmental organizations advocated for expanded lawful access powers, whereas civil liberties groups, along with some federal opposition parties and privacy commissioners, opposed the expansions. TSPs and academics joined civil liberties groups. Together, these elite actors constituted the principal members of the Canadian policy network that took up lawful access. In the case of government actors, they were often also responsible for deciding on whether, and if so how, lawful access powers would be instantiated in policy or law. These actors also controlled the decisions as to which government policy forums took up the issue of lawful access.

Government organizations that explicitly supported the expanded powers include the federal governments that introduced the legislation and members of Canada's law enforcement community. Successive governments asserted that the powers were needed to protect Canadians from criminals and terrorists,[12] to identify and prosecute pedophiles,[13] to catch violent offenders,[14] and to deal with cyberbullying.[15] As the rationale for the legislation shifted, parties external to the government itself came onside, such as groups that regarded the legislation as useful for preventing child pornography or bullying.

Core groups that opposed the legislation included civil liberties organizations, privacy commissioners, some academics, and (at differing points) TSPs. Civil liberties organizations included the British Columbia Civil Liberties Association (BCCLA), British Columbia Freedom of Information and Privacy Association (BC FIPA), Canadian Centre for Policy Alternatives (CCPA), Samuelson-Glushko Canadian Internet Policy and Public Interest Clinic (CIPPIC), Canadian Civil Liberties Association (CCLA), and OpenMedia. Organizations with a legal focus (e.g., BCCLA, CIPPIC, BC FIPA, CCLA) emphasized legal rationales for why expansions of lawful access powers were unnecessary, unlawful, or unconstitutional, often with accompanying assertions that constitutional acceptability was the "lowest degree," rather than "highest standard," of civil liberties protection.[16] Other civil liberties groups, such as OpenMedia and CCPA, focused on mobilizing popular support and disseminating specialized knowledge produced by legally oriented groups and academics to a broader generalist and policy-oriented public. Academics, in aggregate, wrote extensively on the legal, technical, financial, and normative dimensions of expanded law enforcement capabilities, with publications linked to specific moments of the lawful access debates. Within government itself, provincial and federal information and privacy commissioners argued against the necessity and/or appropriateness of powers proposed by governments of the day;[17] the same was also true of federal opposition parties.[18]

Canada's TSPs played differing roles throughout the times that lawful access arose on the agenda. These companies raised doubts about the necessity of the powers, the reasonableness of businesses shouldering the costs for expanded surveillance practices, the technical requirements needed to implement iterations of the legislation, whether regulatory updates were to be preferred over legislative actions, and the relative value of warrantless disclosure of subscriber information.[19] The opposition to legislative measures on the basis of cost was a high-emphasis point,[20] and subtle or relatively secretive attempts to implement some lawful access powers by way of regulation (as opposed to legislation) resulted in prolific opposition.[21]

Each time lawful access arose on the agenda, journalists intermediated the discussions between the various actors. And each time lawful access arose, there was extensive media coverage in all of the flagship media organizations in Canada, as well as second- and third-tier outlets. This coverage served as a means by which proponents and opponents of the legislation evaluated the effectiveness of the framing of the issue, each time the debate (re)arose.

Early Canadian Consultations and the Drawing of Battle Lines

Lawful access has arisen recurrently on the Canadian political landscape since the *Convention on Cybercrime* was signed. Two separate consultations took place in 2002 and 2005 that brought "together a diverse group of stakeholders with sometimes competing interests" and, as the federal government stated, led to legislative proposals that "were informed by the previous consultations, and represent a balancing of the needs of law enforcement, industry and privacy groups."[22] The 2002 consultation received three hundred written

comments and submissions concerning new lawful access powers, and these entries formed the basis for in-depth consultations
in 2005. Whereas the 2002 consultations saw a diverse and largely
representative set of stakeholders (industry, privacy advocates, law
enforcement, and others), the 2005 consultations were principally
held with members of industry, vendors, and law enforcement.
Following the conclusion of the consultations, the government introduced the *Modernization of Investigative Techniques Act (MITA)* in 2005.
MITA included expanded access to subscriber number and name
information and required TSPs to make new services and products
interceptable by government agencies, in addition to new preservation and production orders. *MITA* ultimately failed to get past first
reading, with the minority government dissolved mere weeks after
introducing the legislation.[23]

In the short time it was on the Order Paper, government
attempted to frame the new powers in *MITA* as needed to "ensure
that criminals can no longer take advantage of new technologies to
hide their illegal activities from the law."[24] Moreover, the legislation
was proposed as needed to "reduce the ability of criminals, organized crime members and child pornographers to use sophisticated
technologies to carry out their activities undetected."[25] Privacy advocates maintained that it was unclear that the powers were genuinely
needed and, regardless, inadequate oversight was included in the
legislation — points that they expressed throughout their opposition
to the legislation.[26] Similarly, information and privacy commissioners
raised doubts about the need for and appropriateness of the legislation.[27] Ultimately, however, *MITA* was short-lived and subordinated
to more pressing political issues of the day. Despite appearing on the
policy (as a bill), public, and media agendas, there was insufficient
time for actors to mobilize prolonged support for or opposition to
the legislation. Even its brief period on the Order Paper, however,
provided federal public servants sufficient data to recognize that the
public had been concerned about the proposed powers, and that the
public's "underlying anxiety [was] heightened by the media and [by]
statements of privacy and civil liberties advocates."[28]

While each of the mentioned episodes merited media attention,
with various actors assuming their usual roles, it was subsequent
introductions of the lawful access powers that saw concerted aligning
of media, public, and policy agenda-setting windows, to the effect
that actors were extensively invested in framing the issues linked to

lawful access. Moreover, by this point, members of the civil liberties community and industry had largely been split from operating as an allied group; this began in 2005 with consultations where government advanced proposals to defray industry concerns (i.e., ambiguity, cost, legality). The result was to make civil liberties groups have to "work harder" to influence lawful access debates.[29]

That requirement to work harder was made clearer in 2007, when Public Safety Canada began another set of consultations that initially excluded many members of the privacy and civil liberties communities. Only after the consultation document was obtained and subsequently publicized by an academic[30] and then discussed by the media[31] did the minister of Public Safety, Stockwell Day, establish a fuller consultation. This incident was a clear example of the government attempting to quietly control an issue on the policy agenda while keeping it off the public or media agendas so as to advance negotiations. As soon as the issue exploded on the media agenda, however, the minister was forced to expand the consultation and state that any proposed powers would be protective of Canadians' privacy rights; legislation would not "grant police the power to get information from Internet companies without a warrant. That's never been a proposal... It may make some investigations more difficult, but our expectation is rights to our privacy are such that we do not plan, nor will we have in place, something that would allow the police to get that information."[32] In effect, government, law enforcement, and industry ceased being the primary actors debating the issue once it was on the media and public agendas. Participants maintained familiar roles in the expanded consultations. It was the minister's statement and not the consultations themselves that played a key rhetorical role when the government introduced subsequent iterations of the legislation.

Legislation similar to *MITA* was introduced in June 2009 and generated controversy between the actors invested in the issue. Unlike subsequent efforts, however, the government was not forced to retreat from its proposed legislation: instead, the lawful access bills (C-46 and C-47) were referred to committee but never reviewed because they died on the Order Paper when Parliament was prorogued later that year. Ultimately, the battle lines between members of the policy network had largely been drawn by the end of 2009, and it was understood that successive governments would likely repeat their attempts to pass lawful access legislation.

Aggressive Campaigning and Policy Arena Segmentation

There have been three main explicit attempts to pass lawful access laws since the battle lines were established. In 2010 a series of bills were introduced (C-50, C-51, and C-52); in 2012 Bill C-30 was placed on the Order Paper; and in 2013 the government tabled Bill C-13. C-13 received royal assent in January 2015. The first set of bills were justified by the minister of public safety on grounds that they fit within the Conservative Party's election mandate to "give law enforcement and national security agencies up-to-date tools to fight crime in today's high-tech telecommunications environment," that they were needed to "bring our laws into the 21st century and provide police with the tools they need to do their job," and that the legislation struck "an appropriate balance between the investigative powers used to protect public safety and the necessity to safeguard the privacy of Canadians."[33] While the government maintained that the legislation was balanced, it failed to frame the legislation as a solution to a problem on the public or media agendas: instead, opponents successfully framed the legislation as a problem in and of itself.

Because iterations of the powers had been introduced, and discussed, previous to the 2010 legislation, there was ample pre-existing knowledge about how they might function amongst opponents, the media, and interested members of the public. Further, opponents had been able to test lines in previous conflicts; as a result, opponents could rapidly engage in information politics, or the generation of "politically relevant information and to move it by the most effective means to the place where it will have the most impact, at the most critical time."[34] Since opponents had courted relationships with specific members of Parliament and the media, and within well-mobilized civil liberties organizations, information could be tactically dispensed as needed, often to the effect of upsetting government balancing statements or justifications for the legislation. Opponents could also rely on accountability politics, where powerful agents were held to their previously uttered public statements. Specifically, the former minister of public safety's statement that warrants would be required for information to be disclosed to state authorities was leveraged because C-50, C-51, and C-52 lacked these warranting requirements. While the lawful access legislation was introduced to Parliament, the battle over it was predominantly fought in the media, wherein opponents drew on their technical, legal, and political expertise to cast the bills in a negative light. Ultimately, the government did not forge ahead and try to pass the legislation; instead, they let it die by calling an election.

The subsequent version of the legislation, C-30, bore strong resemblance to the previously introduced lawful access bills. First given the short title, *Lawful Access Act*, it was renamed the *Protecting Children from Internet Predators Act* immediately prior to being introduced.[35] Shortly after the bill's introduction, the minister of public safety, Vic Toews, asserted that opposition parliamentarians could either "Stand with us [the government] or with the child pornographers."[36] The effect of this statement was overwhelmingly negative from the government's perspective: in his framing, the minister cast well-regarded opponents, such as Canada's privacy commissioners, and any person who had concerns over the legislation, as supportive of child abuse. While the minister and government might have believed that linking the legislation with combatting child abuse would defuse opposition, the verbal framing of the legislation had the exact opposite effect and functioned as a focusing event that activated the media and the public. Ultimately, the minister was forced to apologize for his comment in the face of public pressure just two days after introducing the legislation;[37] this apology failed to relieve the government of charges that it was smearing opponents.

A host of tactics were used to oppose C-30. Social media campaigns explained why the legislation was a problem and mocked the public safety minister.[38] Online petitions that indicated opposition to the legislation were created by activist groups[39] and political parties alike.[40] Mailings that targeted Conservative Party ridings placed pressure on members of the federal governing party.[41] And academics and privacy commissioners continued to dispute the government's statements that the legislation was "privacy protective;" this involved a range of well-reputed individuals taking complementary positions and explaining their critiques in accessible language.[42] In aggregate, this collection of techniques generated politically relevant information and disclosed it to the public at opportune times, successfully took advantage of the minister's initial comments as a focusing event to spin a narrative that the government was smearing opponents and inappropriately trying to wield the symbol of child abuse, included accountability politics in the form of pointing to past promises that warrants would be needed to access information, and finally engaged in leverage politics. This latter kind of politics involved directing action "towards those who have power in public or private organizations and who can effect change, by imposing a sanction or threat of some manner,"[43] and was manifest in the mailings to select Conservative members of Parliament. The combined result was that the media had a wide range of stories they could run about critical analyses of the legislation, across a range of media spaces.

The debates surrounding C-30 largely took place on the media and public agendas, with the issue landing on those agendas after legislation had been introduced. In reaction, C-30 ultimately was slated to go straight to committee, where it might have been modified to mollify critics. This decision showed that the government was deprioritizing the legislation on its own policy agenda. But the federal government, perhaps in light of the public opposition to the legislation, simultaneously moved to implement aspects of the lawful access powers through another policy forum. During the period of time that C-30 was on the Order Paper, Industry Canada held a consultation about bidding on newly reclaimed wireless spectrum. As part of this consultation, Industry Canada indicated that changes to the *Solicitor General's Enforcement Standards (SGES) for Lawful Interception of Telecommunications* would soon be disclosed by the Department of Public Safety. The SGES outlines how telecommunications companies must integrate interception technologies into their networks as a condition of operating a licensed wireless telecommunications service in Canada. At the same time, Industry Canada proposed making all radio-based transmissions subject to interception requirements, whereas previously only circuit-based communications were subject to such requirements.

This proposal occurred largely outside of the minds of public opponents to the C-30 legislation; the sole public advocacy group that was involved in the consultation failed to raise either of the changes as concerns. But an unexpected group arose to oppose the proposed change: the TSPs, who would have to comply with the changes, if approved. The industry group that represented most of the companies wrote that replacing "circuit switched telephony systems" with "interconnected radio-based transmission facility for compensation" "opens up several additional services to interception requirements, including Internet services, and cable and broadcasting services."[44] The association also stated that any updates to the standards should not incur a cost to the companies in its group, and that there has been no enabling legislation passed by Parliament that would require such services be intercepted, and submits that it is inappropriate for the Department to impose such requirements via a COL [Condition of License] — particularly at a time when the Government is engaged in a legislative process covering the lawful access issue at a broader level. The COL should reflect the legislative requirements that exist at the time the licences are issued, and not be crafted in anticipation of legislative requirements that may or may not be in force at some point in the future.[45]

The carriers were not alone in questioning the changes in language or proposed updates to the SGES. Documents obtained through the *Access to Information and Privacy Act* reveal confusion within the government itself: officials at Public Safety Canada, which is responsible for the SGES, believed that if wording in the SGES was modified, then it would apply "more broadly and effectively," though the changes constituted "an interim measure until full implementation of the [lawful access] legislation."[46] It was agreed by officials that the proposed changes to the SGES would not be revealed prior to the 700 MHz auction.[47] Not all of the parties that rely on the SGES were fully drawn into the private intergovernmental debate; a Canadian Security Intelligence Services analyst ended up writing, "I would like to know where this 'exercise' is going!!?? What is its overall purpose…my understanding was that we were simply trying to get the wording in the licensing regime change (& not changing the *SGES* themselves…. do you really want us to re-examine all the standards, etc; up date them to current requirements, [Redacted]?"[48]

Despite shifting lawful access to a new policy forum, and despite the absence of typical opponents of expanded state surveillance legislation (e.g., privacy commissioners or civil liberties advocates and organizations), the government was forced to backtrack: the changes would not expand the range or kinds of communications that had to be interceptable. Instead, the same kinds of communications (e.g., text messages, faxes, and voice communications) that were transmitted using radios would continue to be subject to the historical intercept requirements.[49] When the issue arose before the media a year after the initial proposed terminological changes to radio-based communications, the government asserted, "it never actually had designs on vastly expanding surveillance."[50] Further, based on documents released under *Access to Information*, it does not appear that a substantive change to the SGES took place.[51] So, the internal confusions and apparent failure to develop a common policy agenda (away from public scrutiny), combined with opposition by TSPs, undermined these backchannel attempts to expand surveillance powers.

Bill C-30 was withdrawn 11 February 2013. The justice minister stated that though efforts to modernize the *Criminal Code* would continue, such modernizations would not contain "the warrantless mandatory disclosure of basic subscriber information or the requirement for telecommunications service providers to build intercept capability within their systems...We've listened to the concerns of Canadians who have been very clear on this and responding to that."[52] Lawful access returned to the Canadian agenda shortly after the minister's statement, this time as Bill C-13. C-13 was introduced 20 November 2013 to crack down on cyberbullying. Casting about for a new symbol, the federal government latched onto the very public suicides of a pair of young women who had experienced systematic online harassment that contributed to their committing suicide. Included in the legislation were amendments to the *Criminal Code* that were identical to those in previous lawful access legislation.

Opposition was mounted in response to C-13 and included assertions that the federal government was strategically appropriating the deaths of a pair of young women for crass political purposes,[53] that authorities did not need the expanded powers to have prosecuted either of the cases,[54] and that the legislation contained clauses that would increase the sharing of information between authorities and telecommunications service providers.[55] Privacy commissioners warned that while the legislation was less problematic, it retained items of concern;[56] similar statements also came from allied academics. Surprisingly, some victims' advocates and family members of victims of cyberbullying and associated crimes also came out to question and sometimes oppose the legislation.[57]

However, having removed the elements of the previous legislation that inflamed the public (warrantless disclosure of subscriber information) and businesses (mandatory interception capabilities within telecommunications networks for new services), as well as by appealing to a powerful symbol that had captured media attention (the deaths of young girls), the government did not experience the same vociferous resistance to C-13 as it had to C-30. The public, perhaps somewhat wearied and attentive to other issues, was not popularly mobilized to resist the legislation. And the media, while covering the issue, was similarly occupied with other privacy stories: a slate of national security–related privacy issues had arisen to capture the media's and public's attention. The aggregate result was to give the government an opportunity to pass its legislation so long as the media and public agendas did not become so inflamed that the legislation was forced off the policy agenda once again.

Canadian Surveillance Legislation in 2015 and Beyond

At the time of writing, the government has successfully passed its lawful access legislation. Three events failed to disrupt this process. First, national security leaks concerning state access to telecommunications data could have placed the government on the defensive and promoted a retraction of lawful access legislation were the legislation to become associated with the activities described in the leaks. Such associations were not strongly made, however, which meant that lawful access quietly proceeded apace while civil society advocates, members of Parliament, and the media focused instead on revelations that Canada's foreign signals intelligence agency, the Communications Security Establishment (CSE), worked with its closest partners to conduct both targeted and massive surveillance operations.

Second, telecommunications companies have begun to disclose the regularity, conditions upon, and number of Canadians that are affected by state-agencies' surveillance practices in transparency reports. The reports reveal that, in aggregate, government agencies request access to telecommunications data hundreds of thousands of times per year.[58] Rather than primarily exciting attention around C-13, however, the revelations were often framed in the context of signals intelligence surveillance. Though the disclosed data could have called into question whether domestic authorities needed the powers given their existing capacities to compel, or request, data from private companies, these kinds of questions were not prominently raised on the public, policy, or media agendas. In effect, the focus on the activities of the Communications Security Establishment meant that advocates and academics alike did not use the transparency information to rhetorically combat C-13 on the media agenda as much as they might have in years before.

Third, questions put to government agencies by the federal opposition led to revelations that Canadians' personal information is already routinely accessed by these agencies.[59] The Canadian Border Services Agency, for example, made 18,729 requests for telecommunications data, though other agencies such as the Royal Canadian Mounted Police, Canadian Security Intelligence Service, and Canadian Revenue agency were all less forthcoming.[60] Though parliamentarians used the information in the House of Commons and in the media, the revelations were insufficient to force the government to deprioritize the issue on the policy agenda.

Opponents to the legislation had already prepared for its eventual passage; in 2012 a comprehensive legal analysis of proposed lawful access powers was developed to explain why elements of the lawful access bills were on questionable constitutional footing.[61] And courts, including the Supreme Court of Canada, have asserted that government agencies need a judicially authorized order to access subscriber data;[62] companies likely cannot disclose such data without running afoul of the law, nor can authorities request it absent exigent circumstances. A constitutional challenge was also launched to overturn parts of Canadian federal privacy legislation that prevents TSPs from informing their customers when specific customers' information is disclosed to government institutions.[63] The result is that next steps that are largely outside of the legislative agenda-setting process can be, and are being, taken up by critics of the lawful access powers.

Drawing Lessons

After examining how lawful access became stuck on the Canada policy agenda, we can identify some basic and additive conditions that might precede successful political oppositions to expansions or solidifications of government surveillance powers, be they targeted toward domestic surveillance operations or signals intelligence operations. We can also identify how opposition to one form of government surveillance, such as domestic lawful access legislation, can establish a common network of actors who are well-coordinated to oppose to other state surveillance activities.

Basic requirements begin with governments being responsive and reactive to the public and media agendas. If the government can unilaterally pass highly controversial legislation and is willing to spend its political capital in doing so, then even if opponents are successful in negatively framing surveillance issues on the public or media agendas, the framing might not affect the passage of the legislation. The likelihood of a government being responsive to changes on the media and public agendas will correspond with the importance the government places on the surveillance powers and the extent to which the government's proposals can be taken up in political forums. If the proposed legislative action is at the bottom or towards the middle of the government's policy agenda and can be effectively challenged in legislative arenas, then opponents are more likely to be able to force the issue down or off the agenda, as compared to highly important issues that the government is willing to invest with large sums of its political capital or that operate in opaque or secretive corners of government.

When it comes to deeply secretive practices, such as the CSE's signals intelligence activities, there is heightened difficulty in opposing government policy because ministerial directives and other kinds of policy guidance that authorize and direct the CSE's activities are largely inaccessible to the public. As a result, there are evidentiary and policy difficulties in negatively framing the signals intelligence activities because the precise nature of the CSE's activities and rationales for them are off the public record. Absent whistle-blowers, it is almost impossible to develop enough understanding of the intelligence agencies and their practices to identify what should even be negatively framed in the first place.

Whereas controversial surveillance legislation such as lawful access will open up space to debate the legislation's merits or flaws in the legislative assemblies, committees, and so forth, there is not an equivalent space that is necessarily opened when debating signals intelligence-related directives, which are developed within, and authorized by, the executive branch of government. The result is that finding a legislative space to even frame signals intelligence activities on an ongoing basis can be difficult without a permanent legislative-based intelligence committee. Compounding the difficulties is the secrecy concerning how signals intelligence organizations interpret their authorizing legislation and the classification of their internal policy guidance documents. Even when privacy and civil liberties groups force discussions of signals intelligence activities onto the political agenda, the effectiveness of subsequent framing may be unclear insofar as the actual consequence of the government's proposed amendments, or those accepted by the opposition parties, may not be understood by anyone other than members of the intelligence community who already enjoy privileged interpretations of existing legislative and policy frameworks. In effect, there is no clear way for opponents of government surveillance practices to be certain their efforts to restrain or modify signals intelligence agencies' practices will be successful. In fact, experience in the United States, where attempts to restrict access to business records actually led the National Security Agency to expand its domestic surveillance operations, make it clear that passing laws meant to delimit such surveillance may be interpreted around by the executive branch and members of the intelligence community.[64]

Two other basic requirements must be met for opponents to successfully set the agenda: there must be sufficiently empty (and interested) media and public agendas. In the case of the former agenda, the media is restricted in how many items are important enough to be covered in any depth at a given time. For an issue to be successfully framed, opponents must be able to either place a handful of stories that are sufficiently explosive to capture the media's and public's attention (and lead to shaping the policy agenda) or else enjoy ongoing access to the media in order to provide negative framings for weeks or months. In effect, the media must not be so entranced with other issues that opponents cannot successfully capture the attention of the press. With regards to the public agenda, it is typically capable of handling no more than nine items at a time. As a result, opponents of expanded surveillance legislation must enjoy either a suitably empty public agenda that is receptive to paying attention to lawful access or, alternately, opponents must reveal information that captures the public's attention away from other issues it is already attentive to. The media, effective appropriation of culturally resonant symbols, or narratives that capture the public imagination can all enhance the chances of opponents successfully placing their framing of surveillance issues on the public's agenda.

Signals intelligence-related surveillance issues can quickly rise on a media agenda when and if a clear and explosive scandal is revealed, and so long as the scandals do not routinely appear. Since Edward Snowden's revelations began to appear, some media organizations have become weary of reporting on the stories, to the point where even leading national security journalists may not read or report on revelations that are part of their normal coverage area. Similarly, the public can pay an incredible amount of attention to signals intelligence-related agenda items but are more likely to prioritize the general issue of signals intelligence when what is revealed is new and shocking. The constant outpouring of Five Eyes documents, and the technical and legal and policy knowledge required to fully understand them, can make it challenging to explain the significance of each document, which, in turn, reduces the likelihood that revelations will surface on the public agenda. Moreover, a weariness takes hold as stories are constantly written by the media and civil society, such that they blend together. While each Snowden document may reveal a new program, for the public the issue becomes less about any one program and instead about broader kinds of questions: Are the intelligence services accountable? Are the services overreaching? Are they behaving inappropriately? After one to three months, the public will have largely reached its conclusion about any given issue on the agenda. As a result, while the ongoing revelations may influence a minority of people who are attentive or sensitive to intelligence-related issues, the public agenda writ large will likely only shift following major new revelations with explosive discoveries that would challenge the public's conclusions concerning the intelligence services.

Beyond these basic conditions, at least two separate conditions can enhance the likelihood of successfully opposing proposed surveillance expansions. First, by revealing information or being prepared to exploit an explosive event, opponents can either create or (try to) control a focusing event. Governments often enjoy routine opportunities to introduce, debate, and pass legislation. Focusing events, either in the form of a minister's poor choice of words (i.e., breaking news) or reports and findings prepared by opponents, but not revealed, in advance of the introduction of legislation (i.e., *Access to Information* documents that are kept in reserve, or legal findings that are not disclosed until media attention is high) can provide opponents with a way of reframing surveillance-authorizing legislation as a problem in itself, instead of as a solution to a problem. Similarly, planning to release op-eds or engage in public action following the release of an explosive signals intelligence revelation can be an attempt to create, and use, a focusing event to the framers' own ends. Second, a diversified set of experts can enhance the likelihood that proposed surveillance power is opposed. A blend of activists, advocates, lawyers, scholars, and interested journalists are helpful in registering repeated critiques of lawful access powers, mustering public support, and ensuring that editors or others media owners can publish a wide range of critical articles about the powers. This blend is especially important when analyzing highly technical or nuanced documents, such as those released by Edward Snowden, as few individuals will have a total understanding or awareness of public information pertaining to signals intelligence practices, law, or policy.

The presence of a diversified group of activists, advocates, lawyers, scholars, and journalists is also essential for continually highlighting and opposing the legitimization of surveillance activities as they (re)arise over the course of successive legislative sessions. In Canada, a group formed organically out of opposition to lawful access. Though its attention was swayed from lawful access through the course of C-13 as national security revelations linked to Edward Snowden's disclosures become public, the group as a whole was swayed; its membership did not fragment and attend to unrelated issues. And many of the actors of the group have played normal roles and assumed typical positions in their advocacy, which is the result of having worked together throughout the contests over lawful access. Some of this collaboration has been demonstrated in public coverage of Canada-related Snowden disclosures, with lawyers providing legal analysis of documents, technologists providing analyses of how the surveillance practices are designed and operated, policy analysts noting how the CSE's activities either fit into or seemingly run counter to the *National Defence Act* or *Charter* rights, and civil liberties groups launching challenges to the government's domestic surveillance practices.

Whereas opposition to lawful access revolved around demystifying and critiquing the legislation — to prevent the law from coming into being — opposition to signals intelligence practices involved ascertaining what activities were being conducted, how they were carried out, who they affected, and how the activities fit with publicly available legislation and policy documents. The opposition to signals intelligence activities had at least two goals: to understand the state of practices and to subsequently push back against practices that were seen as inappropriately intruding upon the rights of those affected. As of early 2015, there were few legislative victories beyond a handful of members of the Canadian Parliament and Senate critiquing existing practices, and it remained to be seen whether the courts or the legislature would (or could) operate as a way to effectively challenge the CSE's practices. Nevertheless, the opposition that was mustered depended on previously established close working relationships born of critiquing domestic lawful access legislation and the experiences of how to work in concert with one another. The actual effectiveness of that opposition, however, remained to be seen.

Ultimately, for opponents of surveillance powers to successfully frame the issue according to their interests, a government must be responsive to competing agendas, not highly prioritize the surveillance authorizations amongst its broader legislative agenda, and public and media agendas must be receptive to, and capable of receiving, negative framings of surveillance. If these basic conditions are not met, then focusing events or effective uses of symbols or narratives on the parts of diversified expert opponents might be insufficient to dissuade strong governments from legislating expanded lawful access powers. And all of these efforts are even more challenging when opposing signals intelligence-related issues given the secrecy of the practices, the secret interpretations of law, and the challenge in maintaining media and public interest in the kind of technically and politically complicated processes that signals intelligence agencies are involved in.

The diversity of groups opposing state surveillance practices is perhaps most important when the groups are unsuccessful in framing a proposed surveillance authorization as inappropriate or unneeded. Efforts to prevent the passage of legislation or inhibit newly revealed signals intelligence operations can represent just the first step of a much longer campaign, as legal challenges against the newly authorized surveillance powers are mounted, as new political parties with different priorities enter office, or as new technologies that operate outside the expanded powers are created and deployed to counter government-authorized surveillance capabilities. Policy problems, solutions, and framings will continue to circulate even as court proceedings are ongoing, thus giving perpetual hope to opponents of government surveillance activities that their interpretations of these activities will eventually be taken up by either the courts or in one policy forum or another.

Notes

1. Andreas Busch, "Privacy, Technology, and Regulation: Why One Size is Unlikely to Fit All," in *The Social Dimensions of Privacy: Interdisciplinary*

Perspectives, eds. Beate Roessler & Dorota Mokrosinksa (Cambridge: Cambridge University Press, June 2015).

2. Chas Critcher, "Media, Government and Moral Panic: The Politics of Paedophilia in Britain 2000–1," (2002) 3:4 *Journalism Studies* 521 at 530.

3. Maxwell E. McCombs, *Setting the Agenda: The Mass Media and Public Opinion* (Cambridge: Polity Press, 2004) at 38.

4. Thomas A. Birkland, *After Disaster: Agenda Setting, Public Policy, and Focusing Events* (Washington, DC: Georgetown University Press, 2007) at 22.

5. Hans Mathias Kepplinger & Johanna Habermeier, "The Impact of Key Events on the Presentation of Reality," (1995) 10:3 *European Journal of Communication* 371 at 373 [emphasis in original].

6. Thomas A. Birkland, "The World Changed Today: Agenda-Setting and Policy Changes in the Wake of the September 11 Terrorist Attacks," (2004) 21:2 *Review of Policy Research* 179 at 180.

7. Jarol B. Manheim, "A Model of Agenda Dynamics," in *Communication Yearbook,* ed. Margaret L. McLaughlin (London: Sage, 1987) 499 at 510.

8. Hannah Murphy & Aynsley Kellow, "Forum Shopping Global Governance: Understanding States, Business and NGOs in Multiple Areas," (2013) 4:3 *Global Policy* 139–49; Mary Garvey Algero, "In Defence of Forum Shopping: A Realistic Look at Selecting a Venue," (1999) 78 *Nebraska Law Review* 79; Christopher Parsons, "The Politics of Deep Packet Inspection: What Drives Surveillance By Internet Service Providers?" PhD dissertation, University of Victoria, Victoria, 2013, 192–228.

9. Daphne Gilbert, Ian Kerr & Jena McGill, "The Medium and the Message: Personal Privacy and the Forced Marriage of Police and Telecommunications Providers," (2006) 51:4 *Criminal Law Quarterly* 569 at 480.

10. Canada, Department of Justice, "Lawful Access – Consultation Document," (Ottawa: DOJ, 25 January 2002). For historical overview of successive legislative efforts, see also Philippa Lawson, *Moving towards a Surveillance Society: Proposals to Expand "Lawful Access" in Canada* (Vancouver: British Columbia, Civil Liberties Association, 2012); Kevin McArthur & Christopher Parsons, "Understanding the Lawful Access Decryption Requirement," *Social Sciences Research Network* (2012) (unpublished paper), <http://papers.ssrn.com/sol3/papers.cfm?abstract_id=2148060>; Christopher Parsons, "Canadian Cyberbullying Legislation Threatens to Further Legitimize Malware Sales," *Technology, Thoughts, and Trinkets* (blog), 4 June 2014, <http://www.christopher-parsons.com/canadian-cyberbullying-legislation-threatens-to-further-legitimize-malware-sales/>.

11. Reg Whitaker, "The Curious Tale of the Dog That Hasn't Barked (Yet)," (2012) 10:3/4 *Surveillance & Society* 103 at 340.

12. Canada, Department of Justice, "Summary of Submissions to the Lawful Access Consultation," (Ottawa: DOJ, last modified 7 January 2015, <http://www.justice.gc.ca/eng/cons/la-al/sum-res/faq.html>.

13. Jesse Kline, "Vic Toews Draws Line on Lawful Access: You're with Us, or the Child Pornographers," National Post, 14 February 2012, <fullcomment.nationalpost.com/2012/02/14/vic-toews-draws-line-on-lawful-access-youre-with-us-or-the-child-pornographers/>.

14. Daniel Proussalidis, "Magnotta to Be Charged with Criminal Harassment of PM," *Toronto Sun*, 1 June 2012, <www.torontosun.com/2012/06/01/internet-snooping-bill-would-be-helpful-in-lin-case-toews>.

15. Tabatha Southey, "Bill C-13 Is about a Lot More than Cyberbullying," *Globe and Mail*, 6 December 2013, <www.theglobeandmail.com/globe-debate/columnists/maybe-one-day-revenge-porn-will-be-have-no-power/article15804000/>.

16. Michael Vonn, "How Will the Reduction in EU Privacy Affect Canadians' Right to Access Information?" (Lecture delivered at the Sunshine Summit, Victoria, BC, 27 September 2013) [unpublished]; see also Lisa Austin, "Getting Past Privacy? Surveillance, the Charter, and the Rule of Law" (2012) 27:3 *Canadian Journal of Law and Society* 381.

17. Canada, "Response to the Government of Canada's 'Lawful Access' Consultations," Office of the Privacy Commissioner of Canada, May 2005, <http://www.priv.gc.ca/information/research-recherche/sub/sub_la_050505_e.asp>; Jennifer Stoddart et al., "Letter to Public Safety Canada from Canada's Privacy Commissioners and Ombudspersons on the Current 'Lawful Access' proposals," Office of the Privacy Commissioner of Canada, 9 March 2011, <http://www.priv.gc.ca/media/nr-c/2011/let_110309_e.asp>; Privacy Commissioner of Canada, "Statement from the Privacy Commissioner of Canada regarding Bill C-13," Office of the Privacy Commissioner of Canada, 28 November 2013, <http://www.priv.gc.ca/media/nr-c/2013/s-d_131128_e.asp>.

18. Lindsey Pinto, "NDP Leader Responds to StopSpying.ca Campaign," 25 May 2012, *OpenMedia*, <openmedia.ca/blog/ndp-leader-responds-stopspyingca-campaign>.

19. Dominique Valiquet, "Telecommunications and Lawful Access: I. The Legislative Situation in Canada," (Canada: Library of Parliament, 21 February 2006), <http://www.parl.gc.ca/Content/LOP/ResearchPublications/prb0565-e.html>.

20. Nestor Arellano, "Small ISPs Foresee Cost Burden In 'Lawful Access' Bills," 27 June 2011, *ITBusiness*, <www.itbusiness.ca/news/small-isps-foresee-cost-burden-in-lawful-access-bills/16419>; Christopher Parsons, "Unpacking the Potential Costs of Bill C-30" (2012) 9:6 *Canadian Privacy Law Review* 57.

21. Nicholas Kyonka, "Telcos Object to Industry Department's 'Lawful Intercept' Proposal for 700 MHz Band," *Wire Report*, 9 July 2012, <www.thewirereport.ca/news/2012/07/09/telcos-object-to-industry-department's-'lawful-intercept'-proposal-for-700-mhz/25496>; Christopher Parsons, "Lawful Access is Dead; Long Live Lawful Intercept," *Technology, Thoughts, and Trinkets* (blog), 11 February 2013, <www.christopher-parsons.com/lawful-access-is-dead-long-live-lawful-intercept/>; Colin Freeze & Rita Trichur, "Wireless Firms Rejected Ottawa's Changes to Surveillance Rules over Cost Concerns," *Globe and Mail*, 16 September 2013, <www.theglobeandmail.com/technology/mobile/wireless-firms-reject-ottawas-changes-to-surveillance-rules-over-cost-concerns/article14363379/>.

22. Public Safety Canada, "Memorandum for the Minister: Proposed Consultation Strategy on Access to Customer Name and Address Information (For Decision)," (Canada: PSC, 11 July 2007) at 4.

23. *MITA* could be read as an attempt by the government of the day to appear "tough on crime" instead of constituting a genuine legislative attempt. For more, see "Liberals Try to Resuscitate Big Brother Plan for the Internet," *Ottawa Citizen*, 27 March 2007, <www.canada.com/ottawacitizen/news/business/story.html?id=b987660e-cf6d-432c-aafb-c39075caa972>.

24. "Harper Government Should Adopt Liberal Bill on Surveillance: MP," *CBC News*, March 29, 2007, <http://www.cbc.ca/m/touch/canada/story/1.635923>.

25. Public Safety and Emergency Preparedness Canada, "Legislation to Modernize Investigative Techniques Introduced Today," Government of Canada, 15 November 2005.

26. Lawson, *supra* note 10; David Christopher, "OpenMedia.ca Concerned 'Cyberbullying' Legislation Will Unnecessarily Erode the Privacy of Law-Abiding Canadians," 20 November 2013, *OpenMedia*, <openmedia.ca/news/openmediaca-concerned-%E2%80%9Ccyberbullying%E2%80%9D-legislation-will-unnecessarily-erode-privacy-law-abiding-canad>.

27. See Access To Information And Privacy document A-2012-00010, Public Safety Canada, pp.105–127/421.

28. Michael Geist, "Liberal MP Reintroduces Lawful Access as Private Members Bill," *Michael Geist* (blog), 2 February 2014, <www.michaelgeist.ca/content/view/1827/>.

29. Michael Geist, "Public Safety to Release Lawful Access Consultation," *Michael Geist* (blog), 13 September 2007, <www.michaelgeist.ca/content/view/2233/125/>.

30. Michael Geist, "Public Safety Canada Quietly Launches Lawful Access Consultation," *Michael Geist* (blog), 11 September 2007, <www.michaelgeist.ca/content/view/2228/99999/>.

31. Civil Liberties Groups Fear Erosion of Privacy Rights," *CanWest News Service*, 13 September 2007, <www.canada.com/nationalpost/news/story.html?id=378b169e-036d-4ea8-9aba-8f10d7a570d6&k=77186>; "Government Moving to Access Personal Info, Sparking Privacy Fears," *CBC News*, 12 September 2007, <www.cbc.ca/news/technology/government-moving-to-access-personal-info-sparking-privacy-fears-1.631075>.

32. "Warrant Needed to Pull Data on Internet Users: Day," *Ottawa Citizen*, 14 September 2007, <www.canada.com/ottawacitizen/news/story.html?id=af578ca9-0d7e-4785-b939-58364e4f5845>.

33. "Privacy Watchdog Reiterates Lawful Access Concerns," *CBC News*, 27 October 2011, <www.cbc.ca/news/technology/privacy-watchdog-reiterates-lawful-access-concerns-1.996304>.

34. Colin Bennett, *The Privacy Advocates: Resisting the Spread of Surveillance* (Cambridge, MA: MIT Press, 2008) at 96.

35. Sarah Schmidt, "Can You Spot the Difference on 'Lawful Access' Bill?," *Canada.com*, 15 February 2012, <http://o.canada.com/news/politics-and-the-nation/can-you-spot-the-difference-on-lawful-access-bill>.

36. "Online Surveillance Bill 'Will Put an Electronic Prisoner's Bracelet on Every Canadian'," *National Post*, 4 February 2012, <news.nationalpost.com/2012/02/14/online-surveillance-bill-will-put-electronic-prisoners-bracelet-on-every-canadian/>.

37. Laura Payton, "Toews Steps Back from Child Pornographers Comment," *CBC News*, 16 February 2012, <www.cbc.ca/news/politics/toews-steps-back-from-child-pornographers-comment-1.1127817>.

38. Laura Payton, "'Tell Vic Everything' Tweets Protest Online Surveillance," *CBC News*, 16 February 2012, <www.cbc.ca/news/politics/tell-vic-everything-tweets-protest-online-surveillance-1.1187721>.

39. "Stop Online Spying," *Open Media*, 2013, <https://openmedia.ca/StopSpying>.

40. "Don't let Harper read your e-mails," Liberal Party of Canada, 2013, <http://petition.liberal.ca/online-privacy-surveillance-lawful-access-bill-c30-liberal-amendment/>.

41. Steve Anderson, interview with the author, 2013.

42. Privacy Commissioners of Ontario, Alberta, British Columbia, "RE: Police Chiefs Speak out," *Information and Privacy Commissioner of Ontario* (first appeared in *Windsor Star*), 7 November 2012, <http://www.ipc.on.ca/english/About-Us/Whats-New/Whats-New-Summary/?id=263>.

43. Bennett, *supra* note 34 at 96.

44. Canadian Wireless Telecommunications Association (CWTA), "Re: Consultation on a Licensing Framework for Mobile Broadband Services (MBS) — 700 MHz Band," *Canadian Radio-television Telecommunications Commissioner*, 22 June 2012, <https://www.ic.gc.ca/eic/site/smt-gst.nsf/

vwapj/DGSO-002-12-comments-CWTA-submission.pdf/$FILE/DGSO-002-12-comments-CWTA-submission.pdf>; see also Parsons, *supra* note 21.

45. (CWTA), *supra* note 44.
46. See Access to Information and Privacy document A-2012-00457 released by Public Safety Canada, at 83–84.
47. *Ibid.*, at 324
48. *Ibid.*, at 30–31.
49. Colin Freeze & Rita Trichur, "Ottawa Sought Broader Access To Smartphone User Data, Records Show," *Globe and Mail*, 16 September 2013, <www.theglobeandmail.com/technology/mobile/ottawa-sought-broader-access-to-smartphone-user-data-records-show/article14343991/>.
50. Freeze & Trichur, *supra* note 21.
51. By this I mean that, while the 2012 *SGES* lacks the annotations found in previous iterations of the *Standards*, the wording of the *Standards* themselves has not changed. It remains possible that the annotations, which themselves explain how the *Standards* are to be implemented, may have changed.
52. Laura Payton, "Government Killing Online Surveillance Bill," *CBC News*, 11 February 2013, <www.cbc.ca/news/politics/government-killing-online-surveillance-bill-1.1336384>.
53. Southey, *supra* note 15.
54. Michael Geist, "Is C-13 Needed?: How Canadian Law Already Features Extensive Rules to Combat Cyberbullying," *Michael Geist* (blog), 13 January 2014, <www.michaelgeist.ca/content/view/7046/125/>.
55. Michael Geist, "The Privacy Threats in Bill C-13, Part One: Immunity for Personal Info Disclosures without a Warrant," *Michael Geist* (blog), 25 November 2013, <www.michaelgeist.ca/content/view/7006/125/>.
56. Canada, "Statement from the Privacy Commissioner of Canada regarding Bill C-13," Office of the Privacy Commissioner of Canada, 28 November 2013, <http://www.priv.gc.ca/media/nr-c/2013/s-d_131128_e.asp>.
57. Kathryn Blaze Carlson, "Bullying Victims' Families Split over Crime Bill," *Globe and Mail*, 13 May 2014, <http://www.theglobeandmail.com/news/politics/bullying-victims-families-split-over-crime-bill/article18653112/>; Evan Dyer, "Cyberbullying Bill Draws Fire from Diverse Mix of Critics," *CBC News*, 20 October 2014, <http://www.cbc.ca/news/politics/cyberbullying-bill-draws-fire-from-diverse-mix-of-critics-1.2803637>.
58. Colin Freeze, Christine Dobby & Josh Wingrove, "TekSavvy, Rogers Break Silence over Government Requests For Data," *Globe and Mail*, 5 June 2014, <http://www.theglobeandmail.com/technology/tech-news/

teksavvy-opens-books-on-government-data-requests/article18999107/>; David Paddon, "Telus Issues First 'Transparency' Report on Requests for Customer Information," *Canadian Press*, 18 September 2014, <http:// www.thestar.com/business/2014/09/18/telus_issues_first_transparency_report_on_requests_for_customer_information.html>.

59. Ms. Borg (Terrebonne-Blainville), "Q-233," Notice Paper No. 36, Tuesday, 28 January 2014, <http://www.parl.gc.ca/HousePublications/Publication. aspx?Language=E&Mode=1&Parl=41&Ses=2&DocId=6391359&File=11>.

60. Christopher Parsons, "Mapping the Canadian Government's Telecommunications Surveillance," *The Citizen Lab*, 27 March 2014, <https://citizenlab.org/2014/03/mapping-canadian-governments-telecommunications-surveillance/>.

61. Lawson, *supra* note 10.

62. *R. v. Spencer*, 2014, SCC 43.

63. *Corporation of the Canadian Civil Liberties Association et al. v. Canada (Attorney General)*, Court File No. CV-04-504139, Notice of Application, 13 May 2014, <http://ccla.org/wordpress/wp-content/uploads/2014/05/Notice-of-Application-re-PIPEDA-Issued.pdf>.

64. Jim Sensenbrenner, "How Obama Has Abused the Patriot Act," *LA Times*, 19 August 2013, <http://articles.latimes.com/2013/aug/19/opinion/la-oe-sensenbrenner-data-patriot-act-obama-20130819>.

Contributors

Lisa Austin is Associate Professor in the Faculty of Law at the University of Toronto. She holds both a law degree and a doctoral degree in philosophy from the University of Toronto. Prior to joining the faculty, she served as law clerk to Mr. Justice Frank Iacobucci of the Supreme Court of Canada. Professor Austin's research and teaching interests include privacy law, property law, and legal theory. She is the co-editor (with Dennis Klimchuk) of *Private Law and the Rule of Law* (Oxford, 2014). Her work has appeared in a number of leading journals, including *Legal Theory* and *Law and Philosophy*, and has been cited by the Ontario Court of Appeal and the Supreme Court of Canada. Professor Austin has worked as a consultant for the Canadian Judicial Council, helping to draft their *Model Policy for Access to Court Records in Canada*.

Andrew Clement is Professor in the Faculty of Information at the University of Toronto, where he coordinates the Information Policy Research Program and co-founded the Identity Privacy and Security Institute (IPSI). Among his recent privacy/surveillance research projects are: the Snowden Surveillance Archive, a complete, indexed, searchable collection of all published documents that whistle-blower Edward Snowden released to journalists; IXmaps.ca, an Internet mapping tool that helps to make more visible the secret NSA Internet interception sites and the routing of personal data through them; and

SurveillanceRights.ca, which documents (non)compliance of video surveillance installations with privacy regulations and helps citizens understand their related privacy rights.

Craig Forcese is Associate Professor in the Faculty of Law (Common Law Section) at the University of Ottawa. He teaches public international law, national security law, administrative law, and public law/legislation. Much of his present research and writing relates to national security and democratic accountability. He is the author of *National Security Law: Canadian Practice in International Perspective* (Irwin Law, 2008) and co-editor of *Human Rights and Anti-terrorism* (Irwin Law, 2008). He is also co-author of *International Law: Doctrine, Theory and Practice* (Irwin Law, 2nd ed. 2014) and *Laws of Government: The Legal Foundations of Canadian Democracy* (Irwin Law, 2nd ed. 2011) and co-editor of *Public Law: Cases, Commentary and Materials* (Emond Montgomery, 3rd ed. 2015).

Michael Geist is Professor of Law at the University of Ottawa, where he holds the Canada Research Chair in Internet and E-commerce Law. He has obtained a Bachelor of Laws (LL.B.) degree from Osgoode Hall Law School in Toronto, Master of Laws (LL.M.) degrees from Cambridge University in the UK and Columbia Law School in New York, and a Doctorate in Law (J.S.D.) from Columbia Law School. Dr. Geist is a syndicated columnist on technology law issues, with his regular column appearing in the *Toronto Star* and the *Hill Times*. Dr. Geist serves on many boards, including the CANARIE Board of Directors, the Canadian Legal Information Institute Board of Directors, the Canadian Internet Registration Authority Board of Directors, and the Electronic Frontier Foundation Advisory Board. He has received numerous awards for his work, including the Kroeger Award for Policy Leadership and the Public Knowledge IP3 Award in 2010, the Les Fowlie Award for Intellectual Freedom from the Ontario Library Association in 2009, the Electronic Frontier Foundation's Pioneer Award in 2008, CANARIE's IWAY Public Leadership Award for his contribution to the development of the Internet in Canada, and he was named one of Canada's Top 40 Under 40 in 2003.

Steve Hewitt is Senior Lecturer in the Department of History at the University of Birmingham in the United Kingdom. He has written extensively on topics related to security and intelligence in a

Canadian, British, and American context. Past books include *Spying 101: The RCMP's Secret Activities at Canadian Universities, 1917–1997* (University of Toronto, 2002), *The British War on Terror: Terrorism and Counterterrorism on the Home Front since 9-11* (Bloomsbury, 2008), and *Snitch: A History of the Modern Intelligence Informer* (Bloomsbury, 2010). Currently, he is working on a history of terrorism and counter-terrorism in Canada.

Tamir Israel is staff lawyer with the Samuelson-Glushko Canadian Internet Policy & Public Interest Clinic (CIPPIC) at the University of Ottawa's Centre for Law, Technology & Society, where he leads CIPPIC's privacy, net neutrality, electronic surveillance, and telecommunications regulation activities. He has participated in a range of technology-law policy making activities. This has included provision of expert testimony before parliamentary committees on various digital issues; participation in regulatory proceedings at the Canadian Radio-television and Telecommunications Commission and the Office of the Privacy Commissioner of Canada; interventions in various appellate courts, including the Supreme Court of Canada; active participation in a range of Internet governance processes, including at the Organization of Economic Co-operation and Development; and assisting in the development of the International Principles on the Application of Human Rights to Communications Surveillance. Tamir is also a member of the Advisory Board of Privacy International and lectures on Internet regulation at the University of Ottawa, Faculty of Graduate & Post-doctoral Studies. He has a B.A. from the University of British Columbia and a J.D. from the University of Toronto.

Jonathan A. Obar is Assistant Professor in the Faculty of Social Science and Humanities at the University of Ontario Institute of Technology. He also serves as a Research Associate at the Quello Center for Telecommunication Management and Law at Michigan State University. He received his PhD from Pennsylvania State University. Dr. Obar has published research in a variety of academic journals about the relationship between digital media technologies, ICT policy, and the protection of civil liberties.

Christopher Parsons received his Bachelor's and Master's degrees from the University of Guelph, and his PhD from the University of Victoria. He is currently the Managing Director of the Telecom

Transparency Project and a Postdoctoral Fellow at the Citizen Lab, in the Munk School of Global Affairs with the University of Toronto. His research focuses on the rationales, processes, practices, and politics of third-party access to telecommunications data. In addition to publishing in academic journals and presses, he routinely presents findings to members of government and the media. He is also a Privacy by Design Ambassador and a Principal at Block G Privacy and Security Consulting.

Kent Roach (FRSC) is Professor of Law at the University of Toronto and a 2013 Fellow of the Pierre Trudeau Foundation. He served on the research advisory committee of the Arar Commission, as director of research (legal studies) for the Air India Commission, and as the General Reporter on Counter-Terrorism Law for XIX International Congress on Comparative Law. His books include *The Security of Freedom* (University of Toronto, 2001), *September 11: Consequences for Canada* (McGill, 2003), *Global Anti-Terrorism Law and Police* (Cambridge, 2nd ed. 2012), *The 9/11 Effect: Comparative Counter-Terrorism* (Cambridge, 2011; co-winner of the 2012 Mundell Medal), and *Comparative Counter-Terrorism* (Cambridge, 2015). With Craig Forcese, he has produced extensive commentary on Bill C-51 at www.antiterrorlaw.ca. They are working on a book on the subject, to be published by Irwin Law.

Reg Whitaker is Distinguished Research Professor Emeritus at York University, and Adjunct Professor of Political Science at the University of Victoria. He is the author of many books on Canadian politics, security and intelligence, and the surveillance state, including *Cold War Canada: the Making of a National Insecurity State* (University of Toronto, 1996; with Gary Marcuse); *The End of Privacy: How Total Surveillance is Becoming a Reality* (New Press, 2000); and most recently co-author of the prize-winning *Secret Service: Political Policing in Canada from the Fenians to Fortress America* (University of Toronto, 2012). He is a member of the Board of the British Columbia Civil Liberties Association.

Law, Technology and Media

Edited by Michael Geist

The *Law, Technology and Media* series explores emerging technology law issues with an emphasis on a Canadian perspective. It is the first University of Ottawa Press series to be fully published under an open access licence.

Previous titles in this collection

Jane Bailey and Valerie Steeves (eds.), *eGirls, eCitizens*, 2015

Michael Geist (ed.), *The Copyright Pentalogy: How the Supreme Court of Canada Shook the Foundations of Canadian Copyright Law*, 2013

Printed in May 2015
at Imprimerie Gauvin,
Gatineau (Quebec), Canada.